DAN GOOKIN'S

WEB WAMBOOLI

~ DOES IT TASTE GOOD?

DAN GOOKIN'S WEB WAMBOOLI

CAN YOU TEACH IT TRICKS?

Peachpit Press

DAN GOOKIN'S WEB WAMBOOLI

Dan Gookin

Peachpit Press
2414 Sixth Street
Berkeley, CA 94710
510/548-4393
800/283-9444
510/548-5991 (fax)

Find us on the World Wide Web at:
http://www.peachpit.com

Peachpit Press is a division of Addison Wesley Longman

Editor: Nancy Davis
Copyeditor: Michael Katz
Indexer: Steve Rath
Cover illustration: John Grimes
Cover and interior design: Mimi Heft
Production: Jimmie Young, ProImage
Inhouse production: Kate Reber

Colophon
This book was created with QuarkXPress 3.32 on a PowerMac 7500/100. The fonts used were Stone Informal and Formata, both from Adobe, and Fajita, from Image Club. Final output and printing were done by R.R. Donnelley & Sons in Indiana, and it was printed on 50# Athens Cavalier Opaque English.

ISBN 0-201-88597-2

9 8 7 6 5 4 3 2 1

Printed and bound in the United States of America

CONTENTS

INTRODUCTION

In 1994 I was chatting with some colleagues in the Computer Book Biz about the hot computer topics of the day. Eventually the subject drifted to the Internet and it dawned on me how Internet-illiterate I was. Trying to keep up appearances, I added something I thought would sound technical and would let everyone know I wasn't out of touch. I said, "The PPP hook-up relies too much on the Wambooli protocol."

Everyone nodded in silent agreement with my deep wisdom, even though the word Wambooli is one of my favorite make-up words. It means nothing. Yet, in the high-tech, fast-paced, cutting-edge world of the Internet, it seemed like an appropriate term. In fact, I imagine others in the group sneaking off later to consult their various computer dictionaries for what a Wambooli was—in addition to all the other terms no one knew anything about.

Two years later, I'd like to introduce the world to *Web Wambooli.* This is my personal attempt to make the Internet tame and understandable. The idea here is not to become an Internet nerd. Instead, this is a friendly, entertaining introduction to one of the hottest topics of the day: the World Wide Web and the Internet. And it's all done in a purely Wambooli style.

Assumptions

This book assumes as little as possible:

- You have a computer and a modem.
- You would like to hook up to the Internet to find out what it's all about.
- You know how to use a mouse in Microsoft Windows.

That's the basics. This book will not teach you how to use your computer, how to click a mouse or how to do Windows. It will, however, help you connect with the Internet. To that end, you'll need a few other items you may not already have:

- You'll need Internet software, specifically the latest version of Netscape.
- You'll need an Internet provider.

I highly recommend Netscape as the most versatile and complete Internet software package available. You'll manage here with other software, but with Netscape you'll be doing very Wambooli.

It's not important that your software be installed already. It's also not important that you have an Internet provider; Chapter 1 tells you how to find a good Internet provider, so read up on the subject there before you go out and do something unwise.

How This Book Works

This book is a tutorial for people who want to know about the Web and Internet but don't want a lot of technical background blather. I wrote most of it while under the influence of double-espresso, so there really was no time to jabber away at trivialities! Cut to the chase. Get to the meat. Leave the vegetables for kids and cows!

Each chapter in the book progresses logically, from hooking up and configuring software, to touring the Web, mail, news, all that stuff. You can easily read this book from front to back. Even so, I've modularized it so that you can refer to any one section to brush up on specific information. This allows the overly impatient to immediately go to the information they need. No dallying.

Commands are given in the tutorials using the following format:

▶ **Read the next paragraph**

If you're in a real hurry, all you need to do is read the text you find in the above format. That will tell you exactly what to do. The extra text sandwiched in-between explains things in further detail—adding zest to the process, like garlic croutons in a salad.

Text you may see on your computer screen, or stuff you're supposed to type in, looks like this:

```
Boring. Dull. Tedious. Weary.
```

When you're asked to type something in, type it in *exactly* as listed above, with the periods, slashes and other whatnot.

What's Covered Here

This book covers installation and setup of Internet software on a PC or Windows computer. It then takes you on a tour of the World Wide Web ("the Web"), e-mail, mailing lists, newsgroups and a smattering of other Web Wambooli topics.

What's Not Covered Here

This book does not cover IRC or "chat," FTP, Archie, Wais, Telnet or other esoteric Internet stuff. A lot of those topics are really nichey. Most of what they can do is already being handled by the World Wide Web, so they're actually fading away as specific topics in Internet books.

Oh, and this book does not use the word "cool," an over-exploited term when it comes to the Web. In fact, the single mention of the tired old idiom above is the only time you'll find it in this book.

Hey! This Book Has Its Own Web Page

In a new trend, this book has a companion page on the World Wide Web. And it's not just a promotional or sales gimmick. The Wambooli Web page lists information about this book, updates, fun places to go, important references and other information that actually supplements the text you have in your hands.

Even though the sight of a Web page address will probably jar you at this early stage, here is the Wambooli home page address:

```
http://www.wambooli.com
```

No need to fret over that now. When the time comes, you'll learn how to visit the home page. Those instructions, and that home page address above, are given later in this book.

Icons and Stuff Used in This Book

TIP: Some nifty shortcut or elegant way to solve a particular problem.

FYI: This is a trivia note, tossed in just because I like trivia.

THIS "SHOUTING TEXT" IS A REMINDER OR COMMENT THAT HELPS YOU UNDERSTAND SOME CONCEPT.

Some Final, Soothing Words of Advice

I'm not going to lie to you. The Internet is a daunting place. And learning how to use the Web, e-mail and newsgroups can be frustrating and intimidating. This book helps more than any other on the subject, but that cannot change the basic nature of the Internet. I can dress you up nice and warm, but it's still going to be cold outside.

Part of the problem is your modem. It may randomly hang up on you. Or your software may disconnect you while you're reading through a tutorial, forcing you to start all over again. Or your Internet software may suddenly die on you. It can be truly agonizing.

Don't take any of those stumbling blocks personally—and please don't blame them on me! Random crashes and modem mishaps happen to everyone, and there's really nothing anyone can do about it. Even the experts have to put up with this nonsense (though they rarely admit it). But don't let this dampen your experience. For the most part, the Internet and the Web offer a fun, entertaining, engaging and educational place for everyone to enjoy.

Visit the world. Discover something new. Have fun.

PART ONE

DULL, BORING SETUP INFORMATION

1

THE "I'M JUST GETTING STARTED" CHAPTER

http://www.cocacola.com

They're popping up everywhere, even on the most recognized logos in the world. It's that WWW thing. Looks like gibberish, like baby Vern playing on the typewriter. HTTP-something. It's frustrating, yet enticing. It's the Internet. The Web. And the hype will consume you.

Welcome to the Wambooli orientation chapter. This is the necessary stuff. The stuff "they" never tell you. A lot of questions and answers here. All-important background info. Skip it if you dare, read it if you care.

This chapter covers the following subjects:

- **What you need to connect to the Internet**
- **Descriptions of various Internet software (which they call softwares in foreign countries)**
- **Descriptions of the hardware you'll need**
- **How to find an Internet Provider**
- **Proper instructions on installing your Internet software.**

Some Quick Questions to Get Out of the Way

Q: What is the World Wide Web?

A: The World Wide Web, or just *Web*, is merely one part of the Internet. In a way, the Internet is every highway, road, street, and driveway in the world. The Web is merely the fun parts, the scenic drives, the 4-lane expressways, the whoopty-whee hills.

Q: What's that `http://` thing I see more and more on the TV and in magazine ads?

A: That's just a small sample of the cryptic part of the Web. For now, think of it as part of an address or phone number—which is all it really is, anyway.

Q: Will this Web stuff run up my phone bill?

A: Not unless your phone company is charging you by the minute. Whether you or your computer makes the phone call the charge is the same. If calling the Web is long-distance for you, those charges apply. If all your local calls are charged at a flat rate, then that's what the Web's phone calls will cost you. Of course, there are other fees involved, which you can cry about later in this book.

Q: Are you going to tell me all about the history of the Internet?

A: No.

Q: I'm already hooked up to the Internet.

A: Why are you here? Go immediately to Chapter 2 unless you want to risk certain redundancy in your life.

Q: How long can I expect my goldfish to live?

A: The oldest known goldfish lived to the ripe old age of 41. Its name was Fred.

Just Tell Me What I Need to Get on the Internet Without Boring Me to Death

You need four things to connect up to the Internet and surf the Web:

1. Internet software
2. Hardware, a computer and a modem
3. An Internet provider
4. Money.

Nothing here is that difficult to accomplish. The only hard part is trying to get everything to work together. The easy part is that you only need to do that once (except for number 4, the money, which flows in a constant outward direction).

Ten Things That Are Harder to Do Than Setting Up the Internet

1. Build a copy of the Mona Lisa entirely out of toast.
2. Throw a surprise party for a psychic.
3. Configure your VCR to record HBO while you watch something else on cable.
4. Construct an outdoor play set.
5. Arrange a date for your 31-year-old cousin Milford.
6. Install Disney Interactive software.
7. Set the clock in your car radio.
8. Make a left turn anywhere in Boston.
9. Convince the IRS that *they* are in the wrong.
10. Voluntarily go to the dentist.

What Kind of Software Do I Need?

Just about any of the fine Internet software packages available will suit you well. Yup, they're all pretty good. Yes, sirree bob.

- Honestly, most of the Internet software you get will be junk; you don't need half the stuff. The only program you truly need is a *Web browser.*
- A Web browser is the software you need to see stuff on the World Wide Web. It allows you to view the various Web "pages" as well as do other interesting Internetty things.
- Internet software is a general term for a hodgepodge of different programs that help you do various wonderful and interesting things on the Net.
- Internet programs typically come bundled together in some uniform product like Netscape Internet in a Box, or many of the book-disk combinations that litter the shelves at your favorite computer bookstore.
- Above all, I recommend a good Web browser.

So what is a good browser?

If you have Netscape, you may have the only software you'll ever need to work the Internet and the Web. That's it. Simple purchase. No problems. Other browsers do the job, but Netscape is hands-down the best. I use it. It's shown in all the examples in this book. And, no, I don't even own any Netscape stock.

NETSCAPE BE THE HIGH-BROWSER.

- A browser is a piece of software you use to see Web pages.
- Netscape is the name of a program that contains a highly useful Web browser.

- Many people confuse Netscape with "browser." The Netscape Web browser is merely one of several Internet programs you get with Netscape.
- This book uses the term "browser" to refer to the Netscape Web browser, or whichever Web browser you happen to be using (Mosaic, Cello, etc.).

Other options while you're waiting for Netscape to come mail-order

If you don't have Netscape, you're not stuck. You can also access the Web through one of the national online networks: America Online (AOL), CompuServe or Prodigy.

- Honestly, I don't recommend using those services for the Internet. Get Netscape and connect with an Internet provider, as described later in this chapter.
- An advantage to using a national online network is that you don't have to learn any new software.
- The big disadvantages are speed and cost: Those systems are generally slower than a true Internet provider, and they charge by the hour—something few Internet providers do.
- Refer to the section "This 'Internet Provider' Nonsense" later in this chapter for information on Internet providers.

What about the Microsoft Internet Explorer program that comes free with Windows 95?

Does it come free? Heck. I didn't know that.

In Microsoft's desperate attempt to get all of us to use only their software, they've come up with a not-so-bad Web browser called the Internet Explorer (not to be confused with the Explorer, which is a disk file-management program). You can even get it free from Microsoft (which is why I call them desperate). Even so, Netscape is a more inclusive package, containing a decent e-mail program and news reader that I find far superior to anything Microsoft currently offers.

You Need Hardware (But Probably Already Have Most of It)

To run your Internet software you need hardware. Specifically, you need a computer and a modem.

I'll bet you already have a computer

For the computer, the Internet isn't picky. Unlike a four-year-old at a smorgasbord, who only bothers with the crusty macaroni and cheese and the pudding bins, the Internet can swallow any type of computer.

- The Internet doesn't care how fast your computer is. Heck, my first foray into the Internet was on an old TRS-80 in 1983. Dinosaur days!
- It helps if your computer has a nice color monitor attached. That way you can see all the wonderful colors and graphics on the Web.
- Another helpful recommendation: Windows. Since the Windows operating system is just so blasted friendly, it helps to have a computer that can run Windows, specifically one that can run Windows 3.1 or later—which means Windows 95.
- Windows 95 comes with its own Internet access and its own Web browser, the Internet Explorer (and I'm not talking about the Microsoft Network [MSN] here). Even so, get Netscape.
- If you have Windows 95, make sure your Web browser specifically supports Windows 95. It should say so on the box. And it will say "designed for Windows 95" not "runs on Windows 95" or "runs on Windows 3.1 and later."

Modem advice for the Web Wambooli serious

BUY THE FASTEST MODEM. SPEED! SPEED! SPEED!

My modem advice is simple: Buy the *fastest* darn modem you find.

Don't worry about saving a few dollars by getting a slower modem. You want speed!

- The modem is what lets your computer talk to the Internet using the phone lines.
- A slow modem is 9600 BPS (bits per second).
- Anything less than 9600 BPS (meaning 2400 BPS) isn't slow. It's *dead.*
- A 14,400 BPS modem is okay.
- You really want a 28,800 or 28.8K BPS modem.
- Faster? How about 57.6 ISDN modems? Ho-baby! Hummina, hummina.
- It doesn't matter if the modem is internal or external, or if it's a fax/modem, or how many blinkin' lights it has.
- I would also recommend staying away from extremely cheap or discounted modems. While most modems sold today are fairly standard, there is an off-chance you could pick up a "bargain" at a swap meet only to find out it's a piece of junk when you get it home.
- Why all the speed? *Graphics.* It takes time for that graphical image of Vern next to his 40-pound tomato to show up on the screen. Without a fast modem you would be on the Net for *centuries.*
- Some Internet providers may not even let you connect at slower speeds.

This "Internet Provider" Nonsense

An Internet provider is the outfit that gives you access to the Internet. It's like the cable company, but without the tardy individual who (eventually) comes to your home to hook you up. There is no Internet cable guy! It's up to you to hook yourself up. But unlike the cable company, there are many Internet providers out there. Picking the right one is important.

Internet provider? Why bother?

> If there was a big Internet computer, it would have to be in Texas.

On the surface, it seems rather stupid that an Internet provider should be necessary. After all, can't you just dial up the big Internet computer in Texas?

Well, there is no big Internet computer. Not in Texas, not anywhere. Instead there are hundreds of places that offer Internet access. This book refers to them all as Internet providers. You need to do business with one of them to get the whole ball rolling.

- If you already have an Internet provider, you can skip merrily up to Chapter 2.
- The Internet is not a single entity, but rather a bunch of computers all over the world linked together with telephone lines. They chatter back and forth, receiving information, storing information, sending information.
- To join the Internet, your computer has to be connected to one of the computers already linked into the Net. That's what your provider offers: a link into the Net.

How can I find an Internet provider right here in town?

There probably isn't a Yellow Pages entry for Internet providers yet (but I haven't looked so I really wouldn't know). Therefore, the best places to ask are: computer stores, software stores, stores that sell computer books, and maybe even a Radio Shack. Maybe.

- The next section tells you what to look for in an Internet provider. For now, just try to get names and numbers.
- You may not even need an Internet provider. The place where you work may have access—especially if you work at a university or an institution that deals with the government or computers.

- There is no need to visit the office of a potential Internet provider. Most of them operate out of back rooms (which are full of phone cables). You really only need to talk to them on the phone to set everything up.
- I found my Internet provider on a bulletin board in a supermarket. (I mean I found their *number*. The provider is actually in another building.)

Things to ask a potential Internet provider

There are some items your Internet provider should have available for your Net consumption. Of course, you probably don't know what most of this stuff is. Even so, recite from this list the following questions. The more "yes" answers you get, the better. A lot of "no" answers means you should look for another Internet provider. The most important questions are listed first.

You say: Do I get a Net mailbox?

They should answer: Yes.

- Your Internet provider should give you an electronic mailbox.
- Your mailbox is the place that stores electronic mail (e-mail) and files that are sent to you.
- The provider will give you a mailbox ID or network name.
- See Chapters 15 and 16 for more information on getting and sending e-mail.

You say: Do I get to choose my mailbox name?

They should answer: Yes.

- The mailbox name will probably have to be of a certain length. For example, `J` won't be okay, but `jeremiah` probably will be.
- Not only can mailbox names be too short, but some can be too long. If your real name is Walamalakabalazingzangdoodleoni, you might consider using something about six to 12 letters long as your mailbox name instead.
- The name you choose cannot be used by someone else. For me, there was already some guy named `dan` on the system I use, so I had to either A) kill him or B) pick another name. After some thought, I opted for another name.

You say: Do you have newsgroup access?

They should answer: Yes.

- A provider who offers no newsgroups should never be considered.
- *Newsgroups* are available to all the Internet providers, though they must *subscribe* to those groups and then store the news messages on their computers.
- Newsgroups are also referred to as *USENET*. They may use that term when they respond. Please, please, forgive them.
- See Chapter 22 for more information on what newsgroups are, and why they are neither news nor groups.

You say: How many newsgroups do you carry?

They should answer: All of them.

- Newsgroups are like cable channels; not every cable company carries them all.
- There are currently about 15,000 newsgroups.
- Newsgroups take up a lot of storage space, so some Internet providers don't offer all the newsgroups, but rather a selection. That's okay. But make sure the selection is somewhere close to that 15,000 number.

You say: Do you have file storage space?

They should answer: Yes.

- About five megabytes (5 MB) of storage space is great. This allows you to store fairly large files on the Internet provider's computer.
- You can usually lease more space for a fee. Ask.

You say: Can I have my own Web page?

They should answer: Yes.

- A Web page is a place anyone on the World Wide Web can visit. Very trendy.
- Though you may not use it until later, it's nice to have the option of keeping your own, private Web page on the Internet provider's computer.

You say: Do you have a setup disk or booklet?

They should answer: Yes.

- If you're lucky, then your Internet provider may have a custom disk with all your Internet software already set up for you.
- Keep this in mind when you choose an Internet provider: Any provider who offers their own disks, or even provides products like Netscape, is definitely worthy.

You say: So what's this all gonna cost me?

They should answer: Yes.

- Most Internet providers charge you a sign-up fee, typically somewhere around the $20 to $35 range. Expect to pay more if you're getting software and freebie classes—something you might need anyway.
- Beyond the sign-up fee, you'll need to pay monthly access charges. Some Internet providers offer their services for a flat rate. Some charge you by the hour. Some offer a mixture of both: say 100 hours a month for $25 and then extra for each hour over that. You shouldn't pay more than $40 a month for this service. Around $20 is typical.
- Extra things will cost you extra. Some Internet providers will charge you extra for a Web page. You may be able to add a family member to your account for a small fee. And I'm sure there are plenty of other things they can charge you for. Ask for a charge sheet when you sign up.

Don't forget your service and support!

Support is that after-the-sale thing that most companies would sooner forget. However, with something as obnoxious and intimidating as the Internet, it's an important part of your Internet provider selection.

The key issue here is, will they help you after you sign up? Will they accept your phone calls? Do they offer classes? These are all key elements of service and support.

- Don't feel bad asking about service and support. After all, you're buying a *service* from your Internet provider and they need to help you with it. You should insist on getting something back for that sign-up fee.
- The better providers will give you a booklet that describes how to configure your PC for the Internet and how to sign on or "log in."
- Consider it a bonus if your Internet provider offers classes and phone support in case you get stuck.

- If a potential provider seems annoyed when you question them about any of this, go elsewhere. It's not worth the hassle or your time to use them as your Internet provider.
- You'll usually find more than one choice of provider—even in the sticks.
- There are four providers in my wee home town of Coeur d'Alene, Idaho.
- On the planet Triskellion there are three providers.

What should I tell my Internet provider?

WRITE DOWN THAT SETUP INFORMATION IN APPENDIX A!

Your Internet provider will generally ask you a few questions, primarily about what type of Internet software you have. In response, they'll give you various bits of information to help you with your setup.

Internet setup information—even from the best Internet providers—can be massively confusing. Therefore, I've created fill-in-the-blanks tables for you to use, which you'll find in this book's Appendix A.

Quiz your Internet provider to help you fill in the blanks in Appendix A. You don't need to know what each item represents, only which values to fill in. This will be of great help later, when you actually install your Internet software.

2 Installing the Internet Software

Setting up Internet software is truly vague and cryptic. Keep in mind that the Internet's guts hang on the backbone of a primitive computer operating system called UNIX, which is probably the most cryptic thing man ever invented (next to the U.S. Tax Code). Sure, it could be easier. But most of the people creating this stuff wore pocket protectors and verified their lunch bills using slide rules. If you go through the setup process with the fact that "they're working against me" in your mind, it makes it easier.

This chapter covers specific problems not everyone will have. You need only visit the sections here that apply to you. If you don't see anything in the following list that applies to you, move on up to Chapter 3:

- General setup overview
- Setting up Netscape for Windows
- Setting up Netscape for Windows 95
- Setting up Windows 95 for the Internet.

Setup Overview for Everybody

REMEMBER; YOU ONLY NEED TO SET THIS UP ONCE.

You, human, take disks. Feed disks into computer. Computer churns and churns. You answer questions. Puzzle over questions. Answer more questions. Click Finish button. You're done. Simple enough.

- Your Internet software is usually set up using some type of configuration program. If your Internet provider gave you the software, then they should tell you how to set things up, either in a booklet or on a sheet of paper.
- If you bought an Internet connection kit as a software package, instructions in the box will help you (maybe) to get started.
- This book concentrates on Netscape, so its setup instructions are discussed in the next few sections. Refer to the proper section in this chapter for the details.
- If you have another software package, you'll do okay—providing you had your Internet provider help you properly fill in the tables in Appendix A.
- Yes, don't forget Appendix A.

My Best Advice for Getting This Job Done

Seriously: Hire someone else to do all this for you. It's *worth* it.

- If you work in a business, have the office computer guru set things up for you. I'm serious. No one should bother with this mess. It's egregious what they've done, especially with Windows 95.
- **e-gre-gious** (ĭ-grē´jəs) *adj.* Ultimately offensive. Very bad. Naughty. Sinful. Typically overused by those who know what it means.

Setting up Netscape for Windows 3.*x*

Netscape has one of the best setup programs witnessed by human eyes. If you've ever installed a terror like Microsoft Office or WordPerfect on your computer, then installing Netscape will be a piece of cake. Chocolate cake. With brown things.

- This information here is for overview purposes only. Your Netscape manual has more detailed and specific information—should you dare need it.
- The information may be subtly different, depending on which version of Netscape you have.
- Criminy, I've seen versions of Netscape for accounting packages. I kid you not.

▶ Quit any important programs you're running

The Netscape manual says to "quit everything." That's a half-truth. You should quit any application you're using to create something: your word processor, spreadsheet, database, graphics program, and so on. Save your stuff to disk. Other programs, such as the File Manager or other handy things, don't have to be shut down.

▶ Open the Netscape box

You've probably already opened the box. If not, open it, already! There's only a couple of manuals, a quick reference, lots of propaganda and a CD-ROM disk or satchel of floppy disks.

▶ Locate the CD-ROM disk or disk 1 of the stack of floppy disks

Hold it firmly in your quivering hand.

▶ Insert the disk into the proper disk drive

The CD-ROM goes into the CD-ROM drive. Floppy disks go into your PC's A drive—or the only drive if you have one floppy drive.

- I don't need to break into any popular disk etiquette here; this book assumes you know how to stick a disk into a computer. If you find yourself sticking the disk into the toaster, you'll need to buy one of those "Dummy" books.
- Yes, you might have some disks left over after you're done. The Setup program may even ask you to insert the disks out of sequence. Follow the instructions on the screen and remember: Computers are not logical.

▶ In the Program Manager, choose File→Run from the menu

Locate the Program Manager's window. Choose the Run command from the File menu. The Run dialog box appears, as shown in Figure 2-1.

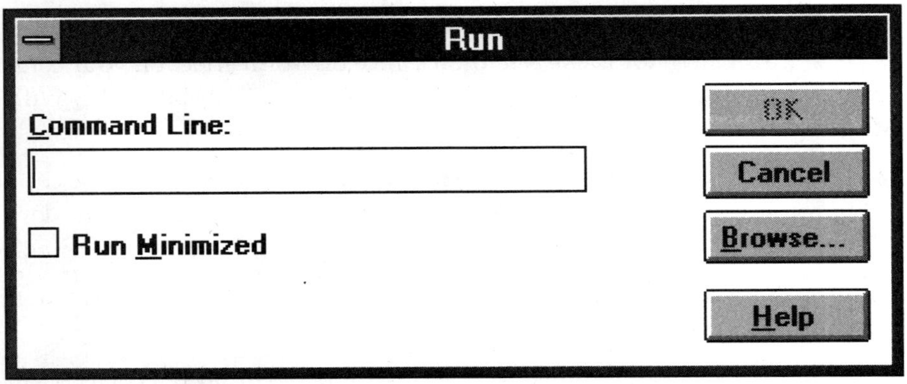

Figure 2-1. *The Run dialog box.*

▶ Type the proper SETUP command into the Run dialog box

If you're using a CD-ROM disk, you'll need to know your CD-ROM drive letter. For most PCs, it's drive D. So you would type the following into the box:

```
D:SETUP
```

That's `D`, a colon, then the word `SETUP`.

If you're using a floppy disk, type the following:

```
A:SETUP
```

That's `A`, a colon, then the word `SETUP`.

- Type the proper command into the text box right there inside the Run dialog box.

▶ Press the Enter key

Windows goes out and finds the Netscape Setup program.

▶ Watch as Setup runs

What the Setup program does now may vary from PC to PC. Basically, heed these instructions as you follow through the setup process:

- Always choose whichever option the Setup program suggests. For example, choose a "Typical" installation as opposed to "Custom."
- Click the Next button to advance through the various Setup screens.

KEEP APPENDIX A HANDY FOR THE TOUGH STUFF.

- If you're installing from floppy disks, you'll be asked to exchange them: remove the disk in the drive and replace it with the next disk in sequence.
- Remember that penguins can jump as high as 6 feet in the air. Don't let it freak you out.

▶ Installation finishes

The installation part merely copies Netscape's files to your PC's hard drive. The next part of the adventure actually configures your PC to contact your Internet provider.

▶ Watch as the Account Setup Wizard runs.

"Wizard" is the new term for any program that's supposed to be smart and friendly, Wizard having the same root as the word *wise*. But then, after you run the Wizard, you'll realize it's merely a silly old installation program; install coming from the root word *stall*, which means to sputter to a frustrating halt.

- If the Account Setup Wizard program doesn't start automatically, you'll need to start it yourself. Locate the Netscape window in the Program Manager, find the Account Setup Wizard icon, and double-click on it to start the operation.

▶ Follow the instructions on the screen

- Use the information in Appendix A to help you fill in the blanks.
- Click the Next button as appropriate.

TIP: Your internal modem is probably on COM2. External modems are either COM1 or COM2. Flip a coin.

▶ Installation is complete

Yeah, I'm leaving a lot of steps out. It would be tedious to copy them all down here.

▶ When asked, let the Wizard program reset your computer

Netscape will prompt you to reset your PC. Go ahead and choose the option that lets you reset.

- Don't fret: Windows will remind you to save any unsaved stuff in any of your programs.
- Of course, you should have already quit those programs, per earlier instructions.
- DOS programs can't be quit automatically in Windows. If you're running any DOS programs, quit them yourself. Then exit Windows and restart your computer.

HEY! THERE MAY STILL BE A DISK IN YOUR DRIVE. BE SURE TO REMOVE IT AND PUT IT BACK IN THE BOX FOR SAFE KEEPING.

▶ After resetting, Netscape will try to register you online

Ack! No! Don't, don't! There is no need to register right now. It's okay if you want to, but you should refer to Chapter 3 for information on how to quit your Web browser and disconnect from the Internet first. Just a friendly warning.

FYI: The study that concluded "Breakfast is the most important meal of the day" was sponsored by a group of cereal companies.

Setting up Netscape for Windows 95

Installing Netscape on your Windows 95 computer is like slipping on the ice: it may be easy to do, but it's still a pain in the rump.

- These instructions may change slightly, depending on which version of Netscape you install. Consider this a general overview.
- If you really need specific instructions, your Netscape manual has them.
- Yech.
- You might have to set up your computer to access the Internet before you install Netscape. This is a question you should pose to your Internet provider: "Will Netscape configure my Windows 95 computer or do I have to do it manually?" If you have to do it manually, refer to the instructions in the section "Setting up Windows 95 to Behave on the Internet" later in this chapter.

▶ Quit any important programs you're running

This is assuming you have important programs in the first place. Actually, if you heed the Netscape manual, it says to "quit everything." Obviously this is a blunder, since that would mean you'd have to quit Windows as well.

- What they're really telling you is to save all your work and quit any major programs you're running.
- Saving your stuff now is important: Netscape may have your computer reset before it's done and you don't want to lose anything.
- Definitely quit any DOS programs you're running.

▶ Open the Netscape box

Hmmm. Smell that shrink-wrap. Enjoy that out-of-box experience.

▶ Ignore all the junk in the box, locate and remove the CD-ROM disk or the stack of floppy disks

- If you're unfortunate enough to be installing from floppy disks, find disk 1 of the stack.
- Sure is a lot of air in that big box.

▶ Insert the disk into the proper disk drive

- Put the CD-ROM into your computer's CD-ROM drive.
- Or put the floppy disk into your PC's A drive.
- If you don't know which drive is A, then you've been sitting at the computer for too long. Go out and absorb yourself in a good William F. Buckley book. Bring a thesaurus.

▶ Open the Control Panel

There is no Wambooli way to install Netscape; you must use Windows 95's cheesy conventions here. From the Start menu, choose Settings→Control Panel. The Control Panel's window appears.

▶ Open the Add/Remove Programs icon

Double-click on that icon using your mouse.

▶ In the Install/Uninstall panel, click on the Install button

Another dialog box appears.

▶ Click the Next button.

Windows should go out and find Netscape's Setup program presently.

- If Windows can't find the Setup program, then the disk is in the drive incorrectly. Put the disk in the drive the proper way, or consult with a disk drive expert, such as any nine-year-old.

▶ Windows finds Netscape's Setup program

▶ Click the Finish button

At this point, Windows passes the baton of installation over to Netscape, which then starts its own Setup program.

▶ Watch as Setup runs

What the Setup program does now may vary from PC to PC. Here are the general instructions for the entire operation:

- Click the Next button to advance through the various Setup screens.
- Always choose whichever option the Setup program suggests. For example, choose a "Typical" installation as opposed to "Custom."

- If you're installing from floppy disks, you'll be asked to exchange them. When you see the dialog box begging for a new disk, remove the disk currently in the drive and replace it with the next disk in sequence.
- Don't be alarmed if you're asked to insert disks out of sequence. The moral of the story is to read the information on the screen. Never assume anything—especially with a computer.

▶ Installation finishes

The installation part merely copies Netscape's files to your PC's hard drive. The next part of the adventure actually configures your PC to contact your Internet provider.

- Be sure to remove any floppy disks that you still have lurking in drive A.
- You can also remove your CD-ROM disk now, if you installed from one. This isn't as crucial as removing the floppy disks.
- Store your original diskettes in a safe place. I usually keep the disks in the software box, and then I put the box on my software shelf I bought at Costco.

KEEP APPENDIX A HANDY FOR FILLING IN THE DETAILS.

▶ Locate the Account Setup Wizard program

Its window should be open on your screen. (Odd that Netscape doesn't start this program instantly.)

▶ Open the Account Setup Wizard

Double-click on the Account Setup Wizard using your mouse.

▶ Follow the instructions on the screen

- Use the information in Appendix A to help you fill in the blanks.
- Click the Next button as appropriate.

TIP: Your internal modem is probably on COM2. External modems live on either COM2 or COM1. (The modem is probably on the one you don't choose first.)

► Installation is complete

► Reset your computer

Netscape might prompt you to reset your PC. Go ahead and choose the option that lets you reset.

► Netscape may try to register you online

Stop! Stop! There is no need to register right now. It's okay if you want to, but you should refer to Chapter 3 for information on how to quit your Web browser and disconnect from the Internet before you venture off.

FYI: The Russian city of Grozny translates as "Terrible."

Setting up Windows 95 to Behave on the Internet

There is an off-chance that your Internet software won't behave with Windows 95. The installation program will work, but you just won't be able to dial out or connect. And it will frustrate the Wambooli out of you.

In several rare instances, it's up to you—not your Internet software—to set the whole dang doodle up for Windows 95. The only way Microsoft could make this more difficult would be to have you insert needles under your fingernails after completing each step.

MICROSOFT MADE WINDOWS 95 MUCH, MUCH EASIER THAN PLAIN OLD WINDOWS.

I'll try to make these steps as painless as possible. Remember the mantra: You only have to do this once. You only have to do this once . . .

- You might, just might, need your original Windows 95 CD-ROM or floppy disks for this operation. Better go out and hunt for them now—or be a realist and just keep them right by your computer.
- Seriously: *Do not* go through these steps if you've already installed your Internet software and everything appears to be running normally.

Install the Dial-up Networking thing

The following steps will show you if you already have all the things necessary to use your modem and the Internet.

▶ Open the My Computer icon on your desktop

Double-click on the My Computer icon to open 'er up. This displays a window full of disk drives and stuff.

▶ Look for the Dial-Up Networking folder

- If you see the Dial-Up Networking folder, sing the Hallelujah Chorus and then move up to the next section, "Installing the TCP/IP Dial-Up Adapter thing."
- If you don't see the Dial-Up Networking folder, you'll have to install it on your PC. Sing the Volga Boatman's dirge and keep reading.

▶ From the main Start button, choose Settings→Control Panel

The Control Panel window opens.

▶ Open the Add/Remove Programs icon

Double-click the mouse on that icon to open it. The Add/Remove Programs Properties dialog box appears.

▶ Click on the Windows Setup tab to bring that panel forward

Figure 2-2 shows what you should see on your screen.

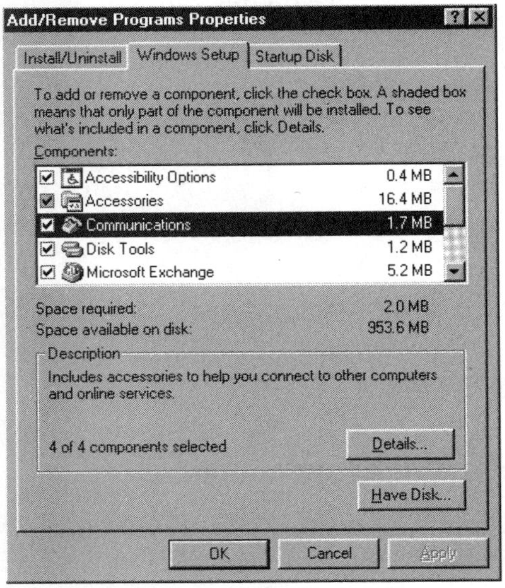

Figure 2-2. *The Add/Remove Programs Properties dialog box, Windows Setup tab.*

▶ Click the mouse on the Communications item in the center of the panel

Click on the little phone icon to highlight it, just like in Figure 2-2.

▶ Then click on the Details button

Details, details. A Communications dialog box appears (see Figure 2-3).

▶ Say to yourself, "Wow this is so much better than that boring, breezy old Windows 3.1 installation routine."

Better still, say it out loud.

Meanwhile, back in the Communications dialog box…

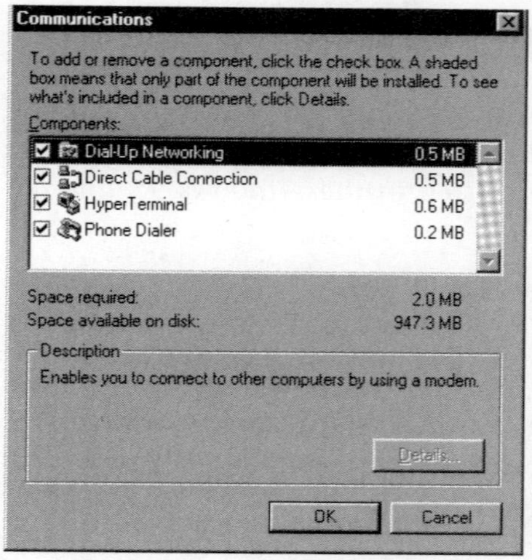

Figure 2-3. *The Communications dialog box.*

▶ **Locate the item Dial-Up Networking in the Communications dialog box**

- If there is a check mark by that item on your screen just as there is in Figure 2-3, you're okay: Click OK to close the various dialog boxes (OK, OK, OK), but don't close the Control Panel. Move on to the next step, "Installing the TCP/IP Dial-Up Adapter thing," in the next section.
- If there isn't a check mark by Dial-Up Networking, you must continue your painful journey:

▶ **Click the mouse in the little box by Dial-Up Networking**

This puts a check mark by that item.

▶ **Click OK to close the various dialog boxes**

OK, OK, OK.

▶ **At some point Windows will ask you for the installation CD or diskettes**

Go get that CD disk or the huge stack of floppy disks that come with Windows 95.

▶ **Stick the disk(s) into the proper drives so that Windows can update your system with Dial-Up Networking**

The instructions on the screen will give you more information here.

▶ **Your computer may or may not want to reset itself, depending on the number of sun spots**

- Sun spots are most prominent in August.
- Keep reading and doing.

Installing the TCP/IP Dial-Up Adapter thing

The next step in this joyous process is to set up TCP/IP on your computer. We just called it "TP" when I was a kid. In this techno age, it must be called TCP/IP. Whatever; here's how to get this next fun step in the Windows 95 Internet Sweepstakes accomplished:

▶ Open the Control Panel (if you have to)

From the Start button, choose Settings➔Control Panel to see the Control Panel's window.

▶ Open the Network icon by double-clicking on it with the mouse

The Networking dialog box appears.

▶ Click the Configuration tab in the Networking dialog box

What you see now should look like Figure 2-4.

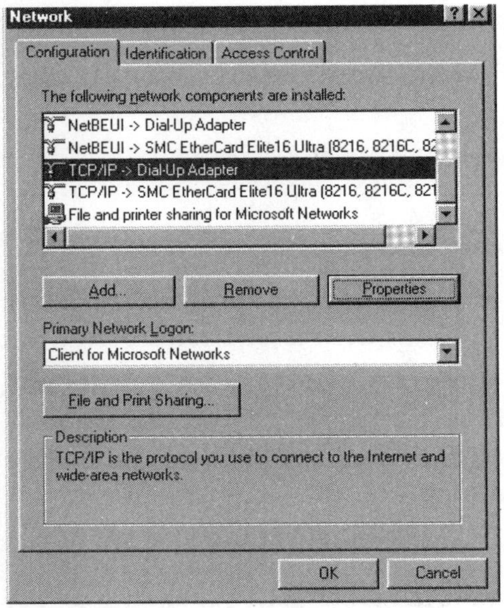

Figure 2-4. *The Configuration part of the Network controller doojobbie.*

▶ Look for the TCP/IP➔Dial-up Adapter thing in the list

Scroll down through the list in the center of the dialog box and look for TCP/IP➔Dial-Up Adapter (as shown in Figure 2-4).

- If you find TCP/IP➔Dial-Up Adapter, you're doing just dandy. Skip up to the section "Configuring the TCP/IP thing."
- No TCP/IP➔Dial-Up Adapter thing? Unfortunately, you'll need to install it. More fun.
- The British refer to "TP" as "loo rolls." Please don't confuse this with Lou Rawls, the singer.

▶ Click the Add button in the Network dialog box

The Select Network Component Type dialog box appears. There should be four items listed: Client, Adapter, Protocol and Service—like a nerdy law firm.

▶ Double-click on Adapter

The Select Network adapters dialog box appears (see Figure 2-5).

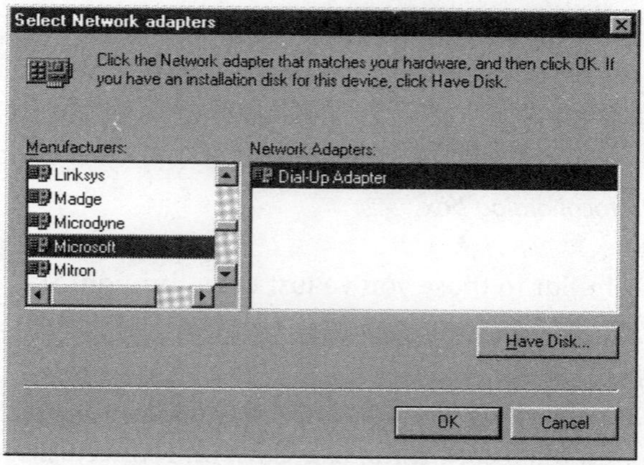

Figure 2-5. *The Select Network adapters dialog box.*

▶ From the list of Manufacturers (on the left), choose Microsoft

Scroll down until you find Microsoft in the list on the left side of the dialog box. Click on Microsoft once using your mouse. The list on the right side of the dialog box will change, showing one item, Dial-Up Adapter (just like in Figure 2-5).

▶ Click on Dial-Up Adapter once with your mouse.

► **Click the OK button.**

The Select Network adapters dialog box goes away.

The Select Network Component Type dialog box reappears.

Don't think you're done yet, because you're not.

► **Double-click on the Protocol item**

In the Select Network Component Type dialog box, locate the Protocol item and double-click on it. The Select Network Protocol dialog box appears (see Figure 2-6).

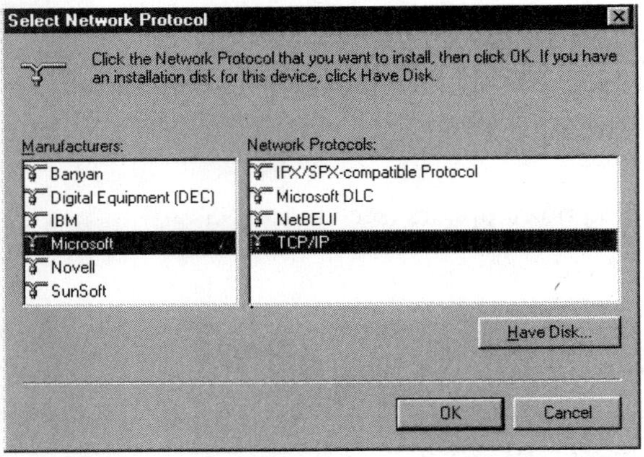

Figure 2-6. *The Select Network Protocol dialog box.*

The next few steps are boringly similar to those you've just been through. Still, follow carefully:

► **From the list of Manufacturers on the left side of the dialog box, choose Microsoft**

Scroll down (if you have to) to find Microsoft in the list. Click on it once using your mouse.

► **From the list of Network Protocols on the right side of the dialog box, choose TCP/IP**

Click on it once using your mouse.

► **Click the OK button**

► **Close the Select Network Component Type dialog box (if you have to)**

Location check! Campers, you should now be back at the Network dialog box, Configuration panel. (Refer back to Figure 2-4.) If not, blow your whistle three times and Ranger Rusty will come to rescue you.

(If you're really lost, close all the dialog boxes by clicking OK and start over again. Be more careful next time!)

▶ **Scroll through the list of networking doodads and locate the line that says TCP/IP→ Dial-up Adapter**

Your screen should now look similar to Figure 2-4.

- Yes, all these steps were required merely to add TCP/IP → Dial-up Adapter to the list. After that you need to configure the TP-thing.
- Funny, but you would think that since these steps are identical for every Windows 95 human who has to use the Internet, they could somehow be automated? Aren't computers supposed to *save* us all time?

Configuring the TCP/IP thing

This step requires information from your Internet provider. Pray that you've filled in all the information in Appendix A so you can complete this task.

▶ **In the Network dialog box, click on the line that says TCP/IP→ Dial-up Adapter**

This highlights that line, as in Figure 2-4.

▶ **Click the Properties button.**

The TCP/IP Properties dialog box appears, complete with six tabs of do-it-yourself Internet horror. Unless your Internet provider has specific instructions here (and they probably won't), you'll only need to mess with three of the tabs in this dialog box.

> **BETTER PUT A THUMB IN APPENDIX A NOW. YOU'RE GOING TO NEED THAT INFORMATION.**

▶ Click on the IP Address tab

- If your provider is using dynamic addressing, then choose the Obtain an IP address automatically item.
- If your provider requires you to use the same address every time (called "static" addressing), then click on the Specify an IP address button and then enter your static IP Address and Subnet Mask numbers per your provider's instructions (see Appendix A).
- If your provider requires you to use salad addressing, click on the Blue Cheese crouton.

▶ Click on the Gateway tab

▶ Type in your Gateway number as listed in Appendix A

Click the mouse on the text box beneath New gateway. Type the numbers into the box. Each three-digit number goes into its own place, separated by a period. Such as:

```
123.123.123.5
```

Double-check your typing.

▶ Click the Add button when you're done

After clicking the Add button, the numbers you entered will appear in the Installed gateways list.

▶ Click on the DNS Configuration tab

Choose the Enable DNS option; click in the radio button by that text to put a dot inside the hole. This opens up the rest of the dialog box for all sorts of strange things to fill in.

Constantly refer to Appendix A here.

▶ Into the Host box, type the first part of your e-mail name

Type the part or your e-mail name *before* the @ sign. For example, my e-mail name is `dgookin@wambooli.com`. I would type `dgookin` into the box. You do something similar on your screen (but don't use `dgookin` unless it just happens to be your e-mail name as well).

▶ Into the Domain box, type your Internet provider's domain name

In Appendix A there is a separate entry for your Internet provider's domain name. Type that name. For example, this book's domain name is `wambooli.com`.

▶ Locate the text box below DNS Server Search Order

Click the mouse in that text box.

▶ Type the number for your provider's DNS Server 1 (from Appendix A)

- This could also be called the Name Server.
- You must type in a number here. If your provider gave you a name and a number, type in the number only.
- Type in all four numbers, each set separated by a period. For example:

  `123.123.123.9`

- Double-check what you typed.

▶ Click the Add button

▶ Locate the text box below Domain Suffix Search Order

Click the mouse in that box.

▶ Type in your Internet provider's domain name again

Yes, you've already typed this name in at the top of the dialog box. Do it again here.

▶ Click the OK button to close the TCP/IP Properties dialog box

This has the same psychological effect as mailing away your tax forms.

▶ Then click the OK button to close the Network dialog box

Windows invariably wants to reset at this point. You do need to reset, so go ahead and heed the instructions on your screen.

▶ Reset as instructed

- This is a nice spot for a break. Heck, this would be a nice spot for a coma.
- Go drink a tall, cool glass of water since, you know, people don't drink as much water as they should.

Setting up the Connection (dialer) thing

And you thought you were done? No way! Windows is *really* going to make things easy for you now. The task at hand is to configure the TP-thing to dial into your Internet provider.

- Doesn't this entire operation seem like you're cleaning up a mess of Jello using a toothpick?

▶ Double-click on the My Computer icon to open its window

▶ Open the Dial-Up Networking icon.

You'll see a window similar to the one shown in Figure 2-7.

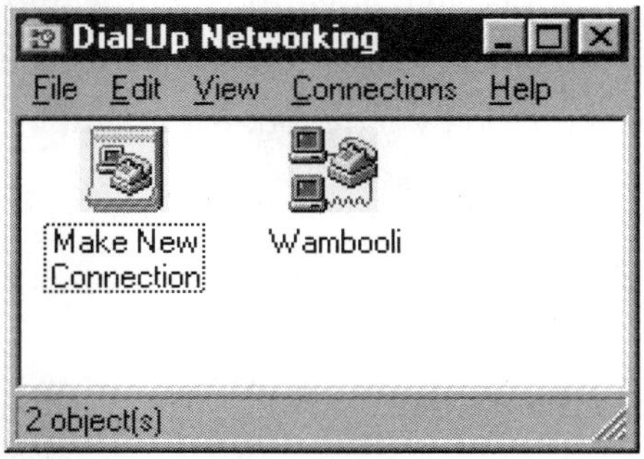

Figure 2-7. The Dial-Up Networking window.

▶ Open the Make New Connection icon by double-clicking it

The Make New Connection wizard appears (see Figure 2-8).

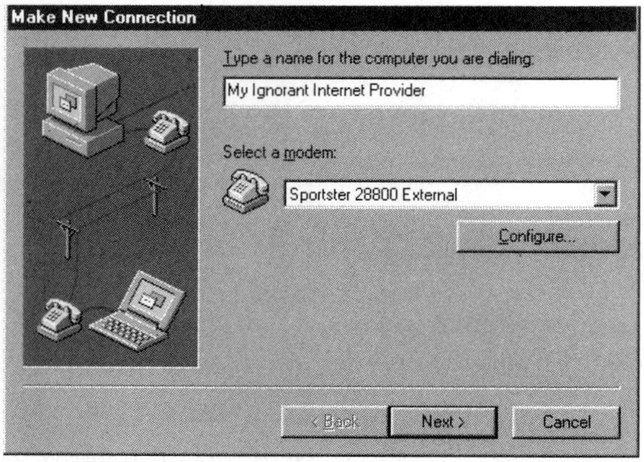

Figure 2-8. The Make New Connection wizard.

▶ **Type your Internet provider's name into the top text box**

- Or type in a name that will remind you of them. (This doesn't need to be accurate; it's just a name.)
- There's no need to mess with the modem part of the Make New Connection dialog box. Your modem was installed when Windows 95 was first set up or when you plugged in your modem.

▶ **Click the Next button**

▶ **Type in your provider's phone number**

Refer to Appendix A, since unlike the phone number for Domino's Pizza, you'll probably never have this one memorized.

▶ **Click the Next button**

▶ **Click the Finish button**

Q: Am I really done?
A: No way!

- Your Dial-Up Networking window now contains an icon with your Internet provider's name on it. You'll use that icon to dial your Internet provider and connect to the Internet.
- Dialing into your Internet provider is covered in Chapter 3.
- You *still* need to configure some more stuff, as described in the next section.

Configuring even more stuff

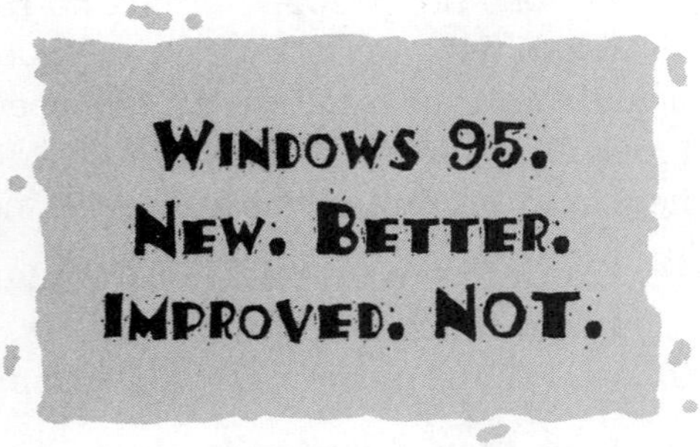

▶ **In the Dial-Up Networking window, locate your Internet provider's icon**

Refer to the previous section ("Setting up the Connection (dialer) thing") for information on opening the Dial-Up Networking window. I'm just too tired to retype those instructions here.

▶ **Click on your provider's icon once to select it**

▶ **Choose File→Properties from the menu**

A special Properties dialog box appears for your Internet provider.

▶ In the Internet provider's Properties dialog box, click the Server Type button

The Server Types dialog box appears, as shown in Figure 2-9. Try not to faint or pull out your hair upon the site of it.

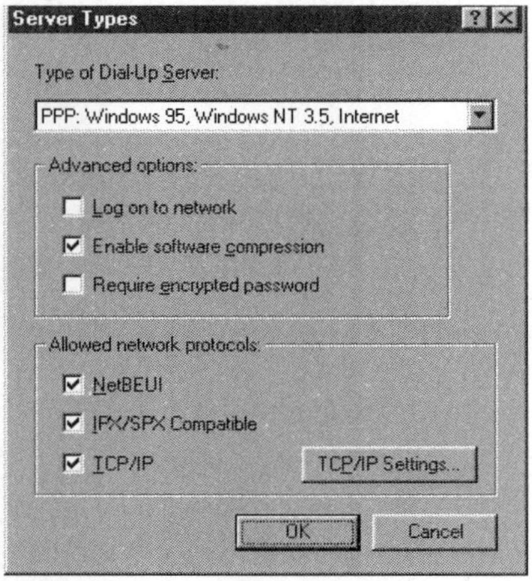

Figure 2-9. *Yet another dialog box to wrestle with.*

▶ Refer to the Connection trivia in Appendix A

This tidbit of knowledge is the first item in Table A-1.

▶ Choose the proper connection from the Type of Dial-Up Server drop-down list.

It could be CSLIP, SLIP or PPP, all depending on what type of connection your provider requires. Again, check the table in Appendix A. Choose the proper item from the drop-down list by clicking on it with your mouse.

▶ Check to see that the last item in the Server Types dialog box, TCP/IP, has a check mark in its box.

If not, click the mouse in that box to put a little check mark there.

▶ Click the OK button to close the dialog box.

▶ Click OK to close the other dialog box as well.

Am I done yet?

Yes, you're actually done.

- Providing you didn't goof up any of the numbers, everything is done.
- You'll never have to do this again. Never.
- If there's ever a computer geek version of *American Gladiators*, this entire task is bound to be one of the "games" they play. "Megabyte Melvin is about to enter his TCP/IP address—oh, and he makes it. Sorry and condolences to our challenger, Terrie from Thurston, Texas."

Bonus: How to have Windows automatically redial a busy number

If you live in a city with limited Internet access (like any place in Hawaii), you'll often encounter the annoying bzzz-bzzz-bzzz of a busy number when you try to connect with the Internet. That may happen every darn doodle time you dial. Nothing you can do about that. However, you do have it in your power to direct Windows to automatically redial a busy number, which can save a lot of mouse-work.

Personally, I recommend a two-week vacation in someplace nice—like outside—before you attempt the following steps. Piling this upon the previous task is something even Hercules would blanch at.

▶ Locate your Internet provider's icon in the Dial-Up Servers folder

If you've been following along through this chapter, this step should be second nature by now.

▶ Choose Connections→Settings from the menu

The Dial-Up Networking dialog box appears (Figure 2-10).

▶ Click the mouse to put a check in the box by Redial if there isn't one there already.

There, Windows will now redial the number.

Other items in the box you can fill in on your own if you care, if you're still awake, if your limbs can still function.

- There is no "infinity" value for the Before giving up retry box.
- I should add that the phone company doesn't like it when you redial your phone rapidly as if you're calling in for a radio station give-away.

- Another reason not to rapidly redial: anything shorter than 15 seconds is wasting your time; it takes the Internet provider's modem about that long to reset after hanging up from a previous call.
- Poor Vern couldn't swim, so when he fell into the cesspool he merely went through the movements.

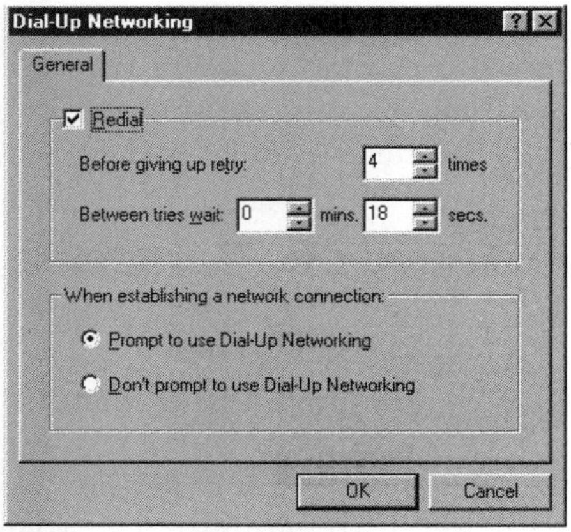

Figure 2-10. *The redial-until-you're-dead dialog box.*

The old "manual log-in" ploy

If your Internet provider requires you to manually "log in," boy, are you in for more Wambooli fun.

ONLY DO THIS LOGIN WINDOW STUFF IF YOUR PROVIDER REQUIRES IT. OTHERWISE, YOU'RE NEARLY ALMOST DONE.

You need to configure your connection so that a little "log in" window is displayed. That allows you to type information at your Internet provider—the login stuff.

► **Locate your Internet provider's icon in the Dial-Up Networking folder**

► **Right-click the mouse on the Internet provider's icon**

This displays a pop-up shortcut menu.

► **Choose the Properties command**

A dialog box appears for your Internet provider.

► **Click the Configure button**

Your modem's Properties dialog box appears.

► **Click on the Oedipus tab**

Wait. There is no Oedipus tab.

► **Click on the Options tab**

The Options panel in your modem's Properties dialog box jumps forth.

► **Click in the box by Bring up terminal window after dialing**

This puts a check mark in the box, which will present you with a tiny login window, which is what your Internet provider desires.

► **Click OK twice**

This closes all relevant dialog boxes.

Everything is Okey-dokey.

FYI: Proving that there is still enough government money to fund such studies, scientists have determined that every person has a unique tongue print.

3 Connecting to the Internet

http://www.totalny.com

Each day you connect to the Internet you'll be following the same steps over and over. They are required before you can use your Internet software. It's like wearing a special hat for word processing. But unlike donning a word processing tarboosh, you must induce your modem to phone up the Internet *before* you can use your Internet software. You must be on the Net before you can do the Net.

This chapter covers the topic of making that all-important Internet connection:

- **Connecting to the Internet**
- **Running Internet software and your Web browser**
- **Recognizing Web browser pieces parts**
- **Reading a Web page**
- **Doing the Net thing**
- **Quitting the Internet software**
- **Signing off from the Internet.**

Dialing Up the Net

You start your Web Wambooli day by dialing up the Internet. Unlike the cable company, which is always connected to your house providing 24-hour service with 56 channels and nothing to watch, you must manually make the connection to your Internet provider. This has to be done each and every time you want to use the Web—or anything Internetty.

- Your Internet software must already be installed before you can do any of this. Refer to Chapter 2 for more information.
- The way you connect depends on what kind of setup you have on your PC.
- If you're using Windows 3.11 or earlier (pre-Windows 95), then you should read the section "Connecting with a dialer."
- If you're using Windows 95, skip ahead and refer to the section "Connecting to the Internet in Windows 95."
- Ever wonder why Alexander Graham Bell said "Mr. Watson, come here, I want you" instead of "Mr. Watson, come here, I *need* you"?

Connecting with a dialer (Windows 3.11 and its ilk)

To connect with the Internet you need to use a special dialer program. This is a step that will take maybe 5 nanoseconds and 3 brain molecules for you to accomplish in the future. For now, read over the following steps *before* you try them. Then whisk through here later at an accelerated pace.

▶ If you have an external modem, make sure it's on

External modems must be turned on before you can dial out. If you have an internal modem, then it's on all the time.

▶ Locate your dialer program's icon

EVERYTHING STARTS WITH THE DIALER PROGRAM

- The dialer program's icon can be found in the Windows Program Manager.
- For Netscape, locate the Netscape Personal Edition window or icon. If you see the icon (at the bottom of the Program Manager's window), double-click it to make it big.
- Three typical dialer program icons appear on the previous page.

▶ Open the dialer icon

Double-click on the program's icon to open it up and see the dialer program's window appear on the screen. Figure 3-1 shows you the Netscape dialer program.

Figure 3-1. *Dialing in with Netscape.*

- You might have to type in some information at this point. In Figure 3-1, Netscape has already filled in all the proper blanks for you. In some instances, however, you may be required to manually type in your login name and password.
- In some instances you may be quizzed as to what type of modem you have and other annoying information. Just use Appendix A and fill in the information as best you can. This stuff needs only to be done once.

▶ Dial in!

How you dial in depends on which program you're using:

- For the Netscape dialer, click the mouse on the Dial button
- For the Trumpet Winsock program, you have to choose Dialer➜Login from the menu. (Hopefully this has been set up by your Internet provider.)
- Other programs may use other techniques to dial in. Most of the time it is a Dial button.

▶ Sit back and watch

- The dialog box tries to explain what your dialer program is doing. Don't expect any of it to make sense.
- Hopefully everything will work smoothly. If not, refer to Chapter 11, the section "O! Those Random Modem Things" for some troubleshooting tips.

▶ The Connection dialog box appears

Eventually, when everything goes right, you'll see the Connection dialog box appear, such as the one shown in Figure 3-2. Ta-da, you've made it.

Figure 3-2. *The Connection dialog box.*

- Some dialer programs may simply shrink themselves down to an icon on the bottom of the screen. In this case there is no Connection dialog box! Even so, you're connected and ready to go.
- If you're using the Trumpet Winsock program, wait until after you see the login and password messages. You might see a message such as PPP session starting or My IP Address is displayed. That means you're connected and ready to go.

TIP: If you see a Connection dialog box such as the one shown in Figure 3-2, then click on its wee li'l Minimize button to shove it out of the way. This shrinks the window down to an icon at the bottom of the screen. Otherwise the window would "float" above everything else on your screen and annoy you.

► Skip ahead to the section titled "Running Your Internet Software (the Web Browser)"

You're now connected to the Internet and ready to do something.

- Skip up to the section "Running Your Internet Software (the Web Browser)" for more instructions.
- You might want to check out the section "An almost quicker way to connect to the Internet" before that.
- Oh, heck, just read the whole book.

Connecting to the Internet in Windows 95

In Windows 95, everybody uses the same dialer program to connect. This is part of the "new" aspect of Windows 95. (The part that makes everything "easy-to-use" is still being worked on up at Microsoft.)

TIP: These steps will take no time to accomplish when you get them down. For now, read over the following information to lodge it in your brain. Then, once you've read through this stuff, you can dial in for reals.

In Windows 95, take these steps to connect to the Internet:

► If you have an external modem, turn it on

Unlike internal modems, which are on all the time, you must make sure your external modem is on before it can dial out.

► Open the Dial-Up Networking folder

The Dial-Up Networking window appears.

- The Dial-Up Networking folder lives in the main My Computer window. Open the My Computer icon by double-clicking on it with your mouse. Then look for the Dial-Up Networking folder. Double-click on it to open.

▶ Locate your Internet provider's icon

- You should have created an icon for your Internet provider when you initially set up Windows 95 for the Internet. If not, refer to Chapter 2.

TIP: If you're adept with Windows 95, or can bribe someone who is, have them make a shortcut to your Internet provider's icon and place it on your Windows desktop. That makes accessing it a lot easier.

▶ Open the Internet provider's icon

Open the icon by double-clicking with the mouse. This opens a Connect To dialog box, similar to the one shown in Figure 3-3.

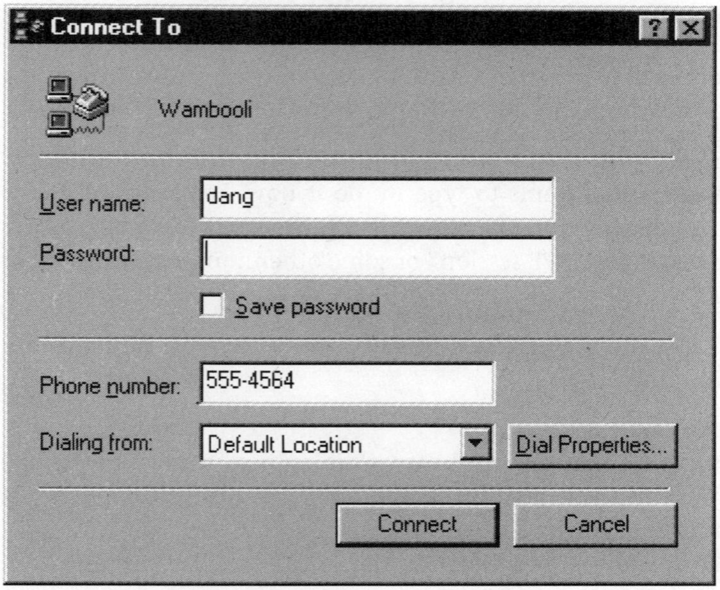

Figure 3-3. *The Windows 95 Connect To program.*

▶ Type in your login name if it doesn't appear

Your login name should already appear in the User name box. If not, type it in.

▶ Type in your password

Type your password into the Password box.

- Your password won't display on the screen; you'll see asterisks—****—instead.

- Because of the asterisks, no one looking over your shoulder will see your password.
- That also means that *you* won't see your password. If you screw up, just erase the whole thing with the Backspace key and start typing your password all over again.

▶ Click the Connect button

Windows will dial up your provider and attempt to connect.

- If the connection isn't made you'll see a whiny "I can't connect" dialog box. Try again.
- Refer to "Bonus: How to have Windows automatically redial a busy number" in Chapter 2 for information on forcing your modem to automatically redial your Internet provider if the number is busy.

▶ If you see a logon screen, manually type in your login name and password

- After the connection is made, you might see a login screen where you have to type in your login name and password. If not, keep on reading with the next step.
- If there are any other items to type in, do it now. For example, some providers may display a menu after you log in—something like, "Press the 3 key to begin your PPP session" or some other nonsense. Heed those instructions.
- Press the F7 key when you're done typing. Windows will continue connecting you to the Internet.

▶ The Ta-Da dialog box appears

Eventually you'll see a Connected to Whatever dialog box, similar to the one shown in Figure 3-4. Once you see that dialog box, and it says Connected at 28800 bps (or whatever), you're logged into the Internet and you can start using your Internet software. Jump ahead to the section titled, "Running Your Internet Software (the Web Browser)."

- If you end up waiting and waiting, then you'll probably need to use the login screen—as described in the previous step. Refer to the Windows 95 setup information in Chapter 2: the section "The old 'manual log-in' ploy" contains information on configuring the login screen.

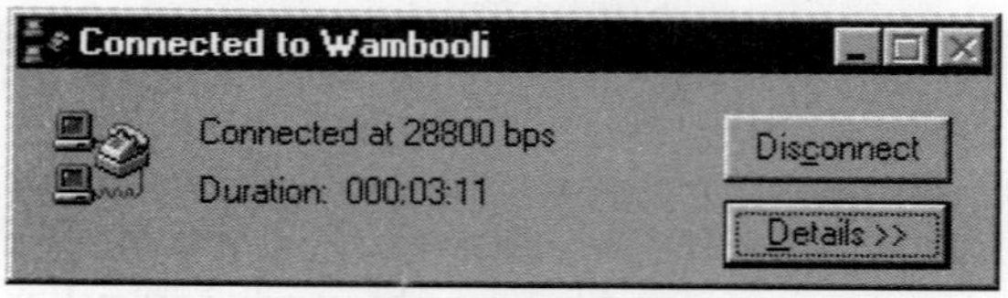

Figure 3-4. *The "ta-da" dialog box you've been waiting for.*

An almost quicker way to connect to the Internet

Here's a shortcut way into the Internet for any version of Windows:

▶ **Start any of your Internet programs**
For example, open Netscape by double-clicking on it. This generally starts your dialer program, which connects you to the Internet and gets things rolling.

- There is a rare circumstance where this technique won't work. If you see an error message announcing that the Winsock can't be found, then you'll have to connect to the Internet in the old fashioned way: use your dialer program as described earlier in this chapter.

Yet another way to connect to the Internet

This is the cheating, but effective, way to access the Net: You dial up CompuServe, AOL or Prodigy. There is no worry about starting this program first or that; you just dial up your network and use whichever commands take you to the Internet part.

- I don't particularly find this a *satisfying* way to connect to the Internet. A direct connection through an Internet provider is best.
- Information on using the major online services to connect to the Internet is provided in Appendix B.

Running Your Internet Software (the Web Browser)

After making the connection, you can use Netscape or any of the Internet programs that came with your Internet software.

- If you're using Netscape in Windows 3.1, the Netscape dialer will have automatically started your Netscape browser.
- If no program starts, locate the window in your Program Manager that contains all your Internet goodies (Figure 3-5 shows an example). You can now start any of those programs as you would start any other program in Windows; since you're connected to the Internet, they'll all run properly.

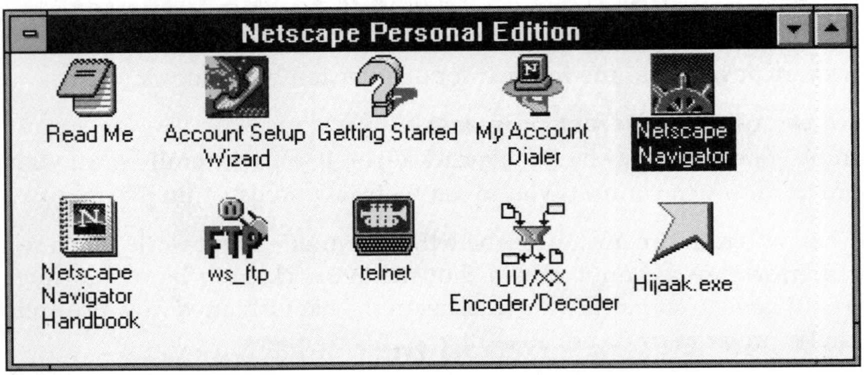

Figure 3-5. *A medley of Internet programs.*

- In Windows 95, locate your Internet programs from the Start menu.

TIP: If you're handy with Windows 95, you can create shortcuts to your Internet programs and place them on the Windows desktop. This is about the handiest way to access your Internet programs.

- The first program you'll probably want to start is your Web browser.

Start up your browser

The Web browser is the program you use to see various pages on the Web. This is also Netscape's main program (remember that Netscape is several programs in one, the first of which is the Web browser).

▶ If your browser hasn't started yet, fire it up on the screen

- Locate your browser's icon and double-click on it to start if it hasn't started already.
- Your browser's icon is *not* the same icon as your dialer (the program you used to connect to the Internet).

- Figure 3-6 shows Netscape's browser. If you see that on your screen already, you're doing just fine.

► **Maximize your browser's window**

No, maximizing your browser doesn't mean you feed it that Hi-Carb mix they sell to muscleheads at the gym. No, click on the Web browser window's Maximize button, the one that zooms the window out to fill the entire screen the way God intended.

- The browser is the most powerful Internet software you have. Even though your Internet connection kit may have come with an assortment of programs, the browser is the one you'll be using most often.
- With Netscape's browser, just about anything you'd want to do on the Internet is possible. It's a heck of a program.

The Web browser whirlwind tour

You don't have to do anything as your Web browser starts. Just sit back and watch as the text and graphical images explode on your screen. But as your browser awakens, take time to notice its four major parts:

- The control gizmos
- The Busy thing
- The command box
- The main screen.

Figure 3-6 shows what's where on a typical Netscape screen. The most important of those items is the main screen, the biggest part of the Web browser, where you actually see the various Web pages.

- **Gizmos.** The most popular Web commands typically appear as buttons along the top of the Web browser's window. These are the gizmos; the buttons and menus that control how you surf the Web.
- **Busy thing.** When the Busy thing is twitching, you wait. It means that the Web is thinking or busy; whatever request you made is being processed and it's not quite done. Basically the Busy thing tells you the computer is still alive when everything else would seem to indicate otherwise.

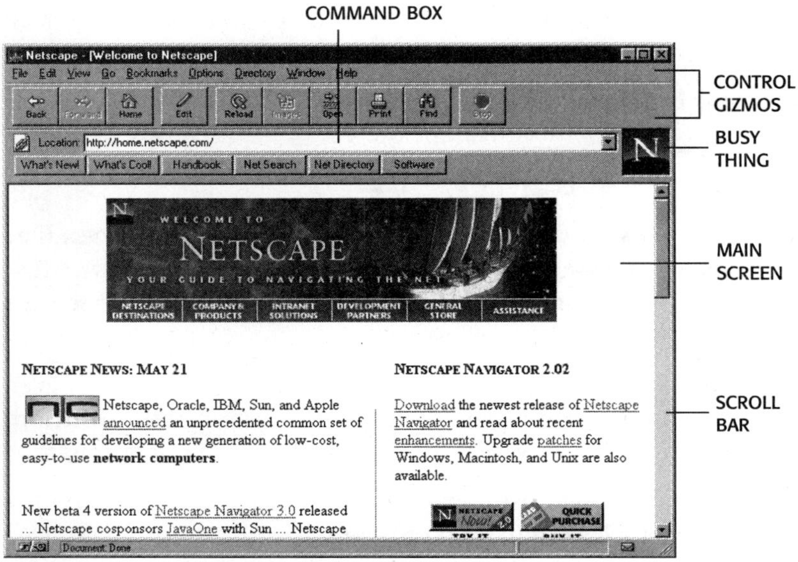

***Figure 3-6.** Pieces parts of the Netscape browser.*

- **Command box.** Into this box you'll type various *addresses* of Web pages you want to visit. In Netscape, the command box has the word Location by it. Other browsers may have the ugly acronym URL by the command box. Whatever, it's still the command box.
- **Main screen.** The big picture comes in on the main screen, which is where you see the information the Web sends you.
- The Busy thing will be busy a lot.
- The true purpose of the Busy thing is to tell you that, yes, the computer is still alive and everything is okay.
- When the Busy thing stops its dance, it means the Web page is fully in view. You're still connected to the Internet. You're still browsing the Web. It just means all the information that needed to be sent has been sent to your computer; all the text and graphics are now ready for your mind to absorb.

- Of course, you don't have to wait for the Busy thing to stop being busy. You're always free to go anywhere on the Web, even if it's busy. This subject will be covered in depth in the next few chapters.
- Keep in mind that Web pages can be quite long; several screen "pages" in fact. That's what the scroll bar on the right side of the main screen is for. And if the page is kind of wide, a scroll bar appears on the bottom of the main screen as well. The point: Never assume that you see the entire page at first glance.

TIP: Netscape has a third row of optional gizmo junk in its window, called Directory Buttons. These are pretty useless (though I'm sure Netscape would argue the point). To make them go away, choose Options→Show Directory Buttons from the menu.

- It's tempting to want to click the mouse in Netscape's Busy thing. Don't! Doing so takes you to Netscape's Web page, which is probably not what

you intended. No, you just got lazy and thought, "Hey! Here's something I can click with the mouse." How do I know this? Allow me to impart some wisdom: Good judgment comes from experience and experience comes from bad judgment.

Read that Web page!

Welcome to the Web. Now read! Look at the pretty graphics. Read the amazing text.

The thing you're looking at presently is what's called a *home page*. This is the first page of information you'll see when your browser starts. It may contain pictures, text or a mixture of both. If it's text, it will come up quickly. Graphics take longer.

- The home page you're looking at will be Netscape's home page if you just bought Netscape, though it could also be your Internet provider's home page.

- More information on what a home page is can be found in Chapter 5. You'll also learn how to choose a different home page for yourself, if you're so inclined.
- The home page you're looking at may be taller than your screen. If so, use the up-and-down scroll bar to see the rest (bottom) of the home page.
- If the home page is wider than your screen, a right-and-left scroll bar appears at the bottom of the browser's window. Use it to see those wide pages.
- Fortunately, only a handful of Web pages are wider than your screen.
- If the home page is deeper than your monitor, then you're reading this book in the future when we all have 3-D monitors.
- Basic scroll-bar navigation is assumed here. If you don't know how scroll bars work, pick up a good book on Windows—preferably something you can use in real life.
- Personally, I think scroll bar should be one word, like toothpaste is one word. "Scroll bar" sounds like a place where Plato and Aristotle would go for drinks.

Don't dawdle

TIP: Some Web browsers may impose a limit on your online reading. If you've been enjoying a Web page, you may be startled by your computer beeping and your connection dialog box warning you that you only have 15 seconds left before the computer self-destructs.

Figure 3-7 shows a typical disconnect dialog box. When that ugly sucker appears, click the Don't Hang Up button quickly! That should keep you connected.

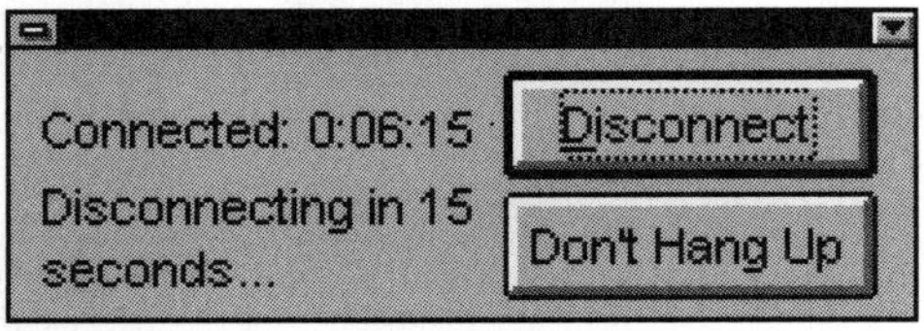

Figure 3-7. *Uh-oh! Better do something quick.*

- If you don't catch the Don't Hang Up button fast enough, then click on your browser's Reload button. That should reconnect you to the Internet and keep things going as they were before.
- See Chapter 4 for more information on the Reload button.
- Chapter 8 has information on how to copy a Web page to your hard drive. You can do that for extra-long Web pages, where idle reading may cause the "you're dawdling" warning to appear. If you save the Web page to disk, you can then read it later when you're not under the disconnect death threat.

To avoid seeing the ugly disconnect dialog box, follow these steps *before* you connect to the Internet the next time. (Alas, you can't do this now; you have to hang up first.)

▶ Bring up Netscape's dialer program

Do this just as you would dial into the Internet on any day (see the section "Connecting with a dialer (Windows 3.11 and its ilk)" earlier in this chapter if you need to.

▶ Locate the Properties button in the Dialer's window

See Figure 3-1. It's the middle button.

▶ Click the Properties button

The Properties dialog box appears.

▶ Click on the General tab

What you see on your screen will look similar to Figure 3-8.

▶ Remove the X by the Disconnect item.

Click your mouse in the box beside Disconnect after 5 minutes of inactivity. Removing that X tells Netscape to personally care less about how much time you dawdle on the Internet.

▶ Click the OK button to close the Properties dialog box

Now you can dial into the Internet as you would normally, without the threat of being disconnected hanging over your head.

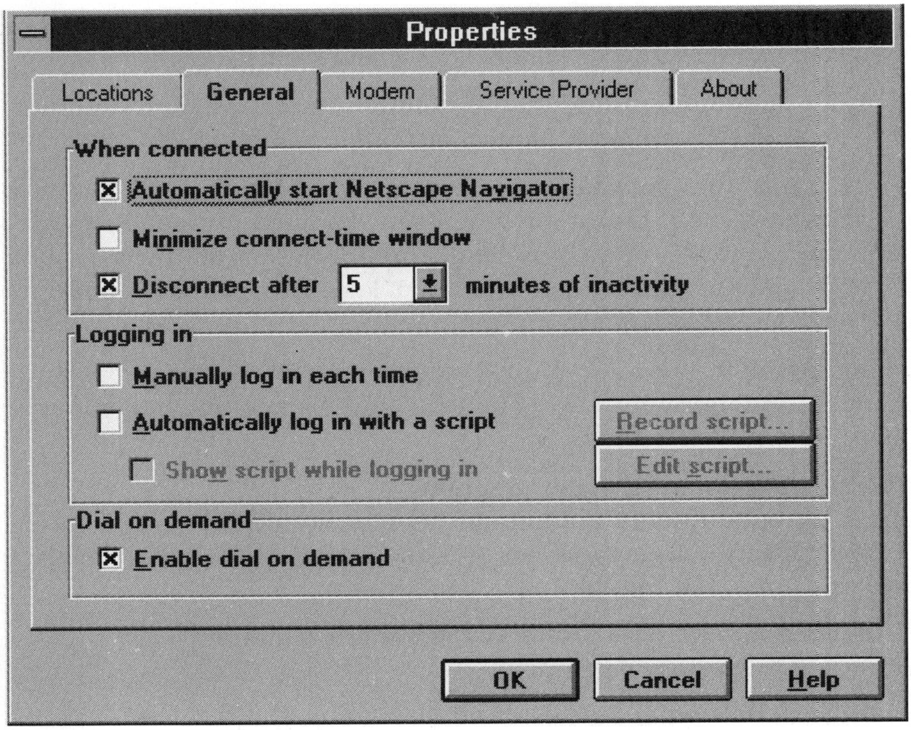

Figure 3-8. *Netscape's Dialer Properties dialog box.*

What to do on the Net

> O! THE NET CAN BE SO MUCH WAMBOOLI FUN.

This entire subject of Web-this-and-that, plus various Internet this-and-thats, is covered in the remaining parts of this book. No need repeating them here or this chapter would be unduly long.

- If you're really starting a full Internet day now, go ahead and continue reading Chapter 4. However, you'll need to return here for information on quitting your Internet software and disconnecting with your dialer program.

- One thing that may interest you, especially when you're just starting out, is Chapter 11, "Has This Ever Happened to You?" This covers some of the, er, unexpected things you may encounter while using the Internet or browsing the Web.

Quitting your Internet Software

This one is cinchy: Internet programs are just like any other program you run in Windows. The only big deal is that you need to be connected to the Internet for any of them to work. When you're done with some Internet program, simply close its window.

▶ **Choose File → Exit from the menu**

This closes your browser window, quitting that Internet program.

> YOU'RE ONLY QUITTING YOUR INTERNET SOFTWARE HERE. YOU'RE NOT DISCONNECTING FROM THE INTERNET.

There. That's it. That's how you quit your Internet programs.

- In Windows 3.1, you can also close a window by double-clicking on the Close button in the window's upper left corner.
- In Windows 95 you click on the X button in the upper right corner to close a window.

- To quit a Netscape program, choose File→Close from the menu

TIP: If you choose File→Exit from Netscape's windows it closes all your Netscape programs (mail, browser, news). Therefore, to close any one of those windows, choose the File→Close command instead.

- Windows is just so darn easy there must be a zillion ways to do anything. Too bad cooking isn't like that.

Hanging Up

When you're done using the Net—which will typically be a larger chunk of time than you originally thought—and have quit all your Net programs, it's time to say *buh-bye* to your Internet provider and tell the modem to hang up the phone.

Hanging up should be done properly, first because it's right and second because if you don't, your Internet provider may charge you for time you're connected but not using the Internet.

► Restore your dialer program's window

- In Windows, locate your dialer program's icon on the bottom of the screen. Double-click on that icon to restore it.
- If you're using Windows 95, locate your dialer's button on the Taskbar. Click that button once to restore the dialer window.

► Disconnect

Your dialer program hangs up.

- Click the Disconnect button.
- In some instances the Disconnect button may be labeled Hang-up (or Hangup). If so, click that button instead.
- With the Trumpet Winsock, choose Dialer→ Bye from the menu. Then close your dialer or connection program (if it doesn't close itself automatically).

- After you disconnect in some versions of Netscape, the connection window (titled Netscape Personal Edition) reappears. I suppose Netscape is eager for you to reconnect *right away*! Oh, well. Close that window by double-clicking its Close box. Bye, Netscape!

FYI: Thomas Edison was afraid of the dark, and they say that Sigmund Freud had a morbid fear of ferns. Me? I fear only plumbing.

HOW MUCH WILL I BE CHARGED IF I FORGET TO HANG UP?

Actually, most Internet providers may hang up the phone for you. For example, if you don't do anything for a period of 10 or maybe even 20 minutes while using the Internet, your provider may hang up on you just because. This is good for when you rush out of the room because the drapes are on fire, and other times similar to that.

The reason most providers (and nearly all the online services) have this time limit isn't because people walk away from their modems (or the drapes). No, it's because they usually have a limited number of phone lines. If you're just deadweight on a line, they'll hang up on you to make room for someone else. This problem is really pronounced in Hawaii, where some people go through enormous efforts to stay online since there are so few lines connected to the Internet. (I was just in Hawaii so I know these things.)

PART TWO

WILD WILD WEB

Chapter 8: General Web Page Use, Abuse and Theft

Printing, copying, saving and borrowing stuff from a Web page

Chapter 9: Having Fun Mit Sound

Hear the Web

Chapter 10: Strange Things on the Web

Forms, Frames, Animation and Java

Chapter 11: Has This Ever Happened to You

Dealing with the weird of the Web

Chapter 12: The Fine Are of W-W-Waiting

Waiting made easy on the Web

Chapter 13: Off Into the Wild, Web Yonder

Some final, consoling words of advice

4

Going Places, Hither, Thither and Yon

http://www.vatican.va

Impatience is a vice. Yes, it's temptation at its worst. It may not be one of the seven deadly sins, but it's certainly one of the 14 dozen gravely wounding sins. You must restrain yourself, especially when it comes to the Web. There are a kazillion Web pages out there waiting for you to come and visit. You can't do it all at once. Remember what Lao Tsu said, "A journey of 1,000 miles would take only 400 miles if Dad would stop and ask for directions every so often."

This chapter shows you how to visit various Web pages on the Internet. This involves some typing and some mouse clicking, so do your finger exercises before you begin; no sense in getting a cramp at an awkward moment—like when you're "just visiting" the Cindy Crawford (or Mel Gibson) Web page and your spouse pops into the room.

This chapter shows you how to zoom around the Web in the following sections:

- **Visiting a certain Web page by typing in its address**
- **Visiting a Web page by clicking on a link**
- **Going back with the Back button**
- **Going forward with the Forward button**
- **Reloading a Web page (and why)**
- **Stopping the Web page.**

Going Someplace, Any Place, Else on the Web

The Web is full of pages, but don't wear out your thumb or the upper corner of your monitor trying to turn them. The Web is not a book. To visit another page on the Web you have two choices:

1. Type in a Web page address
2. Click a link.

- You type a Web page address into the browser's command box. How this works is discussed in the next section.
- The easy way to visit another Web page is to find a *link*.
- A link is either text or a graphic image you click on using your mouse.
- Clicking on the link takes you to another Web page, one that somehow relates to the text or graphic you just clicked on.
- Lancelot Link, Secret Chimp.
- Unfortunately, links don't exist for everything on the Web. At some point in time, you do have to type in a Web page address into your browser's command box.
- In practice, you'll be using both typing-in-the-command-box and clicking-on-a-link techniques to surf the Web. So don't prep yourself to be a link-only person. On the Web, everyone surfs with both the keyboard and the mouse.

Typing a Web page address into the command box

To see any Web page in the known universe you only need to know that Web page's address—just as you need to know someone's address to mail them a bill or eviction notice. The Web page address is typed into your browser's *command box*.

▶ Click your mouse in your browser's command box

- The command box is located near the top of your browser (see Chapter 3, Figure 3-6).
- The command box might already contain some other http-colon-slash-slash-something. Delete it; press the Backspace key to back up over whatever text you see there and erase it.

▶ Type in the Wambooli Internetty Stuff address

`http://www.wambooli.com/internetty.htm`

Above you see the Wambooli Internetty Stuff Web page address. Here's a breakdown of what to type:

`http://`	Type `http,` a colon and two forward slashes
`www`	Three little `w`'s for World Wide Web
`.`	A period
`wambooli.com`	Type `wambooli,` a period, then `com`
`/`	A forward slash
`internetty.htm`	Type `internetty,` a period, then `htm`

- All the little symbols—the colon, slashes and periods—are important. Like ugly DOS commands of yore, a Web address must be typed in exactly.

TIP: Double-check your typing. No spaces. Use a colon, not a semicolon. Use the forward slash, found on the same key as the question mark (?) on every PC keyboard. Use periods, not commas. Double-check your work before you press the Enter key.

▶ Press the Enter key

Pressing the Enter key tells your Web browser to find the address you typed in. You've done your part; now it's up to the Internet to find that Web page.

- What *really* happens after you press the Enter key? You wait. Some Web pages seemingly take an eternity to appear.
- If you mess up typing in a Web page address, Netscape typically displays an error message explaining that it can't find the Web page address you typed in. This isn't as horrid as the old Bad command or File Name error message DOS spewed out. It's just a casual "Huh?" from Netscape. If that happens, click the OK button and start over again typing in the proper Web page address.

Soon the information will be displayed on your screen. Figure 4-1 shows what the Wambooli Internetty Stuff web page will probably look like. (I might change it from time to time, so what you see on your screen may be different.)

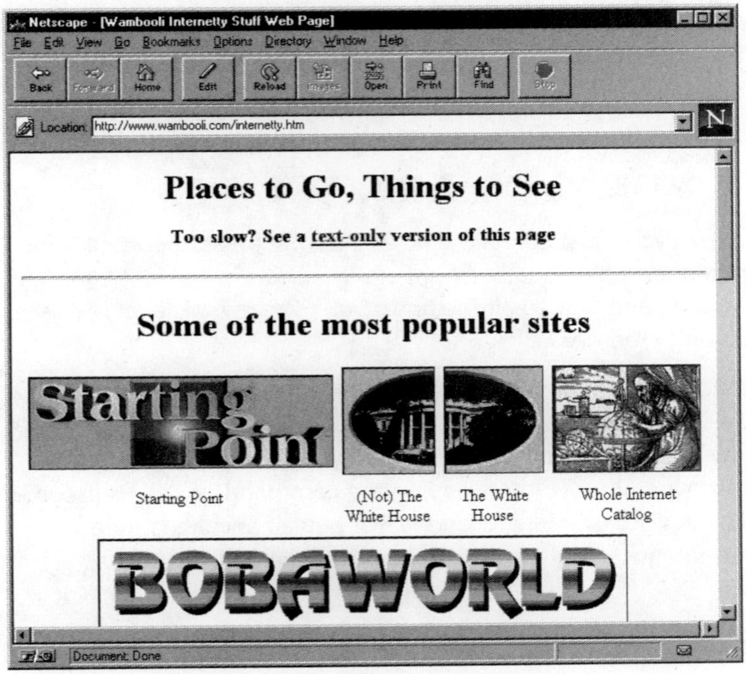

Figure 4-1. *The Wambooli Internetty Stuff Web page.*

Go ahead and wait here at the Wambooli Internetty Stuff page for a moment. Continue reading here and in a few paragraphs you'll be doing something exciting. Promise.

- What you're typing into the command box is a Web page address. The technical term is URL, which is discussed in the sidebar "You. You Are. URL."
- You don't have to read the sidebar if you don't want to.

TIP: You don't have to click the mouse and erase the text in the command box in Netscape. Instead, use the Ctrl + L key combination, where the L stands for Location. Then type the Web address into the box that appears. Click the Open button to visit that site.

- A Web page address is just like a street address, though it's for the Internet and not the Post Office. So instead of *1600 Pennsylvania Ave.*, you would type in:

  `http://www.whitehouse.gov`

That's the Web page address for the White House. Hey—no zip codes on the Web!

YOU. YOU ARE. URL.

A truly awful Web term you must contend with is *URL*. The most important thing here is how to pronounce it. Personally, I want to say *earl* as in Duke of Earl. Alas, I'm woefully wrong and told so all the time. Don't live my mistake! URL is pronounced letters-only: *You Are El*.

A URL is a command you type into your Web browser's command box. Most of the time the URL will be a Web page address. That's officially known as the HTTP URL; HTTP is the Web browser's command to go out and fetch a Web page address. But you can type other commands into the command box as well, some of which this book will discuss in later chapters. For now, if anyone is rude enough to use the term, just think of a URL as a Web page address.

A few things to remember when manually typing in a Web address

None of this Web page typing stuff is hard but, like hearing Italian for the first time, a lot of it will be strange to you. Try to keep the following points in mind as your fingers dance on the keyboard to enter a Web page address.

- All Web page addresses start with the `http://` thing. That's `http`, colon, and two forward slashes.
- In Netscape, typing the `http://` thing is optional. Netscape is smart enough to recognize a Web address. This is probably why their stock went up so high.

- Some Web pages have www in their address, some do not. You should type in the www part whenever it's listed that way. If the www part is missing, you don't need to type it in.
- Do not use backslashes in a Web page address, as you would in a DOS command.
- Web addresses do not contain spaces.
- Instead of spaces, some Web addresses use underlines. Don't let this throw you.

  `beware_of_underlines_instead_of_spaces`

- Some Web pages use the ~ or tilde character. This is the little squiggly line you can find in the upper left corner of your keyboard (by the number 1 key).
- The first part of any Web address is pronounced: H-T-T-P, colon, slash, slash. The rest of the address is W-W-W (for World Wide Web), dot—which is a period but pronounced "dot"—a name, such as wambooli, then dot and finally com (which means company or sometimes communist).
- You pronounce *Eau Claire* as in "Oh Claire." *Coeur d'Alene* is pronounced "Core-duh-lane."

Visiting someplace by clicking a link

A link is merely a way to see another Web page. It appears as underlined text on your screen, or it can be a graphical image. You point the mouse at the link, click, and by the magic of the Web, you instantly see another Web page.

Typically the link lets you know where you're going to go. For example, the text may say `Bubba's Favorite Hang-Outs`, in which case clicking on that text takes you to the Bubba's Favorite Hang-Outs page. Or you may see a graphic of Larry "Bud" Melman, in which case clicking your mouse on the graphic takes you to Larry "Bud" Melman's home page.

Return to your Web browser and mind the following instructions.

▶ **On the Wambooli Internetty Stuff Web page look for the following text**

`Too slow? See a` *`text-only`* `version of this page.`

► Hover your mouse over the text-only part of that sentence

- Notice how the mouse pointer turns into a pointing hand? That's your clue you've found a link.
- Underlined text, or text that appears in a different color, is another clue that a link lurks in the text. Even so, that pointy hand is your best clue.
- A tiny gray box at the bottom of the screen will show you the address of where the link takes you. This isn't important, but you'll probably see that stuff down there and it would bug you if you didn't know what it was.

► Click the mouse

Your browser takes you to another Web page. No typing!

- Don't worry about losing your place; you'll be returning to the first Wambooli Internetty Stuff Web page in just a few paragraphs.
- The Web page you see is an alternative version of the Wambooli Internetty Stuff Web page, but without the graphics. Many Web pages offer this alternative method of viewing information, specifically because some graphics take an eternity to load.
- On the text-only Wambooli Internetty Stuff Web page, you'll see a lot of text links. Basically, this page is a collection of links to various Web pages that contain even more links—like a quick road map to lots of more detailed road maps.
- Yes, in case you haven't figured it out yet, they call it the "Web" because nearly all the information you see is linked together, like strands of silk in a spider's web.

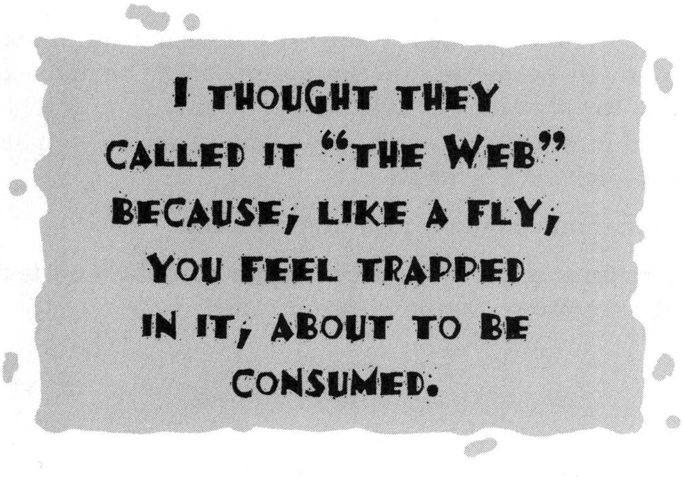

Returning to the graphical Wambooli Internetty Stuff page

If the speed seems okay, you can return to the graphical version of the Wambooli Internetty Stuff page. Locate the link at the top of the text-only page that says:

`Too fast? See a` *`graphical`* `version of this page.`

► **Click the word *graphical***

Your browser takes you right back.

- A better way to go back is to use the Back button. See the section "Go back, go back!" later in this chapter.
- Generally speaking, it's very hard to get "lost" on the Web. Chapter 6 goes into detail on various tricks you can use to re-find places you once were.
- Used links change color. Do you see any darker-colored links on the Wambooli Internetty Stuff page? Every time you visit a page and click on a link, your browser remembers that. When you visit the same page again, those links you've already selected appear as another color, typically a darker blue in Netscape. That's a good way to know where you've already been and to help you quickly locate links you haven't yet explored.

Clicking on a graphical link

There are two types of links displayed on your screen (if you've returned to the graphical Wambooli Internetty Stuff page) and in Figure 4-1. At the top of the page you'll see some graphic images that are really links.

► **Hover your mouse pointer over the (Not) The White House graphic**

Notice how the mouse pointer turns into a pointing hand? That's a clue you've found a link. For graphic images that are links, this is your best clue. (Some graphic images have a colored outline, though it's not that easy to see.)

- It doesn't matter whether a link is text or graphics. Either way, clicking the mouse takes you to wherever the link goes.
- Click the mouse if you want to visit the (Not) the White House Web page.
- Be prepared: Some World Wide Web pages take eons to load.

There are no links!

Some Web pages have no links. That's fine. It typically means the page is information only. That happens a lot. I just read a movie review on a Web page that had no links. When I was done, I just clicked the Web browser's Back button to get back to where I was.

WAITING IS THE "FOURTH W."

- Also, be on the lookout for Web pages that are all graphics and have no underlined words. In that case, the graphics may be the links you need. The links are there, they are just hidden in the graphics.
- In all cases, the mouse pointer changes to a pointing hand when you've found a link.
- Oh, and that movie review Web page address is:

  `http://numedia.tddc.net/joebob`

Gizmos to Get You Here, There and Everywhere

Rearview mirrors were invented in World War One. Before then, no one ever backed up.

Seriously, biplane pilots used the mirrors to help them dogfight. You could be flying along without a care when some Fokker would sneak up behind you and you wouldn't even know he was there. The importance of this wasn't lost on automobile designers: it always helps to know what's behind you. This can be good news, especially when you see something horrible like, say, Fresno in your rearview mirror.

The subject here isn't mirrors at all. In your browser, you use links to go to other Web pages. But those links never quite remember how to get back again. Instead, that job is up to one of the handy browser gizmos, the Back gizmo.

- Refer to Chapter 3, Figure 3-6, for the location of the gizmos on your browser's window.
- Personally, I have nothing against Fresno. I even did a report on it in the 4th grade. They grow raisins there.

Go back, go back!

To return to the previous Web page—the one you were visiting before you clicked on a link—click on your browser's Back button.

- Clicking on the Back button is like flipping back pages in a book. It takes you back to the previously viewed Web page.

TIP: You don't have to wait for the entire Web page to appear before you click the Back button. As soon as you see, say, Fresno, you can click the Back button and get the heck out of there.

- You can keep clicking the Back button as often as you like. Your browser remembers the past several Web pages you've visited and returns you to wherever you were with each click of the Back button.
- If you really plan on clicking the Back button more than a couple of times, what you really should use is your browser's Recently Visited list. See Chapter 6.

FYI: Prego is Italian for "please," though in parts of Oklahoma it means "with child."

Go forward

Flipping back a page is common, either on the Web or in a book or magazine. But when you do that, you typically leave your thumb in to mark your place so you can flip forward again. Your browser has the same feature, the Forward button.

If your browser is up and running, follow these steps:

▶ Find a link and click on it

If you need to, return to the Wambooli Internetty Stuff page, as described near the start of this chapter. Then locate a link and click on it.

- An interesting link to click is `This Day in History`.

▶ Read the new Web page

La-di-da.

▶ Click the Back button

Lo, you're returned to the previous Web page.

▶ Click the Forward button

Hey! You're where you once were.

- The Forward button only works after you've used the Back button. So if you lurch ahead, you can look back with the Back button and then lurch ahead with the Forward button. Something like that.
- Honestly, no one uses the Forward button much. Maybe the French do. I wouldn't know.
- No, you won't wear out your browser's "clutch" if you repeatedly click the Back and Forward buttons.

Reload!

The Reload (or Re-load) button is used to visit the current Web page all over again—just as if you were first visiting the page. At first, this sounds kind of stupid. Even so, there are two good instances for using this button:

- Some Web pages update themselves every time they're visited, so clicking the Reload button shows you a new "version" of the Web page.

- Sometimes your browser may load an "old" version of a Web page, in which case clicking the Reload button forces your browser to get off its lazy rear and load the most current version of the page.

▶ Visit the Wambooli Internetty Stuff Web page

Instructions for doing this are covered in the first part of this chapter.

- Yes, you can click on the Back button to return to the Wambooli Internetty Stuff page if you've ventured off.
- You may have to click the Back button several times.

TIP: A quicker way to return to any Web page is to use the Recently Visited list, which is covered in Chapter 6. See the section "Using the Recently Visited List."

▶ Locate the section that reads Some Sites Updated Daily

This heading is near the bottom of the Wambooli Internetty Stuff Web page. You may have to scroll down a bit to find it.

▶ Click on `The Current Time` link

The `Current Time` link takes you to a page (sponsored by the US government, no less) that displays the current time. This could be construed as silly, but it could be useful I suppose. Note that the time is only current when the page is first displayed, as shown in Figure 4-2.

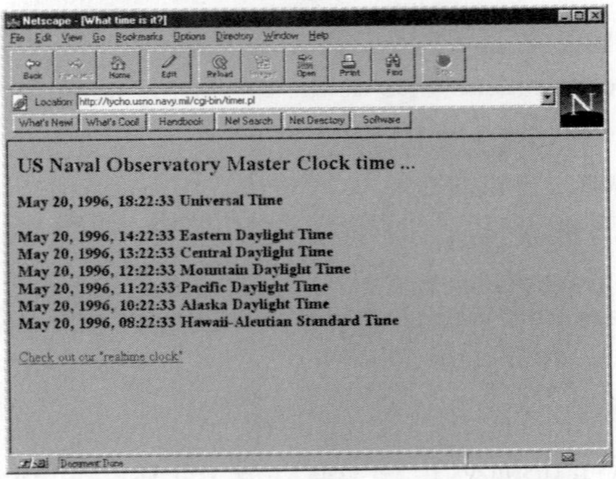

Figure 4-2. *The current time (at least when this screen shot was taken).*

Now get your watch ready.

▶ Click the Reload button

The Reload button tells the Web browser to revisit the current Web page as if it's never been there before. On the Current Time page you'll see a new time as the page is reloaded.

- Another fun place to Reload is the (Not) White House Web page. That link can be found at the top of the Wambooli Internetty Stuff Web page.
- The USA Today Web page is another one you might want to use the Reload button on. Apparently, they update the news stories there quite often. Again, you can find a link to this site on the Wambooli Internetty Stuff Web page.

Stop!

All Web browsers have a Stop button shoulder-to-shoulder with the other gizmos. Basically, it tells the browser to stop whatever it's doing.

The most common instance when you'll use the Stop button is when you click on the wrong link and—whoops!—want to stop the browser before it takes you off somewhere you don't want to go. Try this:

▶ Return to the Wambooli Internetty Stuff page

Use the Back button or just type in the address as you did earlier in this tutorial.

▶ Click on the Starting Point link

The Starting Point is one of those graphical links at the top of the page. Go ahead and click on it. Do it. Now.

▶ Quickly, click the Stop button

Whoops! You really didn't want to go there. Click the Stop button before the browser gets too serious.

- Sometimes, if you're still reading a Web page you've stopped, you'll see a message displayed, something like the following:

```
Transfer interrupted!
```

That's just the message your browser displays to let you know the Stop button was clicked.

- If you change your mind about stopping, you can click the Reload button to start over again with the current Web page.
- If the Starting Point page started to display, then just click the Back button to return to the Wambooli Internetty Stuff page.
- Another time the Stop button seems necessary is when the Web is taking an inordinate (meaning *l-o-n-g*) amount of time to display some long page. You may find the information you want right up top, in which case you can click on the Stop button and do *whatever* with the information that's already displayed.
- Chapter 8 discusses how to do *whatever* with information on a Web page.
- You know, the Starting Point page isn't that bad. You might want to reconsider and visit it.
- Is the Stop sign gizmo flashing? That usually means the Web page is performing some type of animation or some other fancy stuff. Don't let the blinking Stop bug you.

FYI: At 5'0", Queen Victoria may have been one of the world's shortest rulers, but she was still a foot too tall to play in the McDonaldland ball pit.

5 Hello, Home Page

http://www.wambooli.com/salad.htm

When you first fire up your Web browser you'll see what's known as your *home page*. This is nothing more than the first page you see when you start your Web browser—a circular definition, but they had to call it something. Consider it like the blank page that appears when you fire up a word processor, only it's not blank. It's home!

Home pages are important because they start your Web day for you. And since they're called *home* pages and not intro pages or starting pages or even rampages, there must be something *personal* about them.

This chapter covers home pages and the following homey topics:

- Understanding the home page concept
- Choosing a new home page
- Returning to your home page.

There's No Place Like Home Page

Not everyone has the same home page. You can customize your browser to show you any old Web page when it starts. Heck, you have the whole universe to choose from. And whatever you select, that Web page becomes your home page.

- Any page on the Web can be your home page.
- When you first install your browser, your home page will probably be that of your Web browser's developer, such as Netscape.
- Your home page might also be that of your Internet provider.
- If you're using America Online, CompuServe or Prodigy you'll see that organization's home page.
- If you've created your own custom Web page, you can make it your browser's home page.

Setting Up a Specific Home Page

Whose home is this anyway?

Until you create your own home page, or discover some Web page you want to keep as your home page, you can reset your browser's home page to this book's home page. Doing so is a snap.

The following instructions are for setting up a specific home page in Netscape.

▶ Choose Options→General Preferences from Netscape's menu

The Preferences dialog box appears.

- If the Appearance panel isn't forward, click on the Appearance tab.
- What you see on your screen will look something like Figure 5-1.

▶ Make sure the Home Page Location item is selected

In the middle of the dialog box, across from the text Start With, is a radio button captioned Home Page Location. Click the button next to it if there isn't a dot there already.

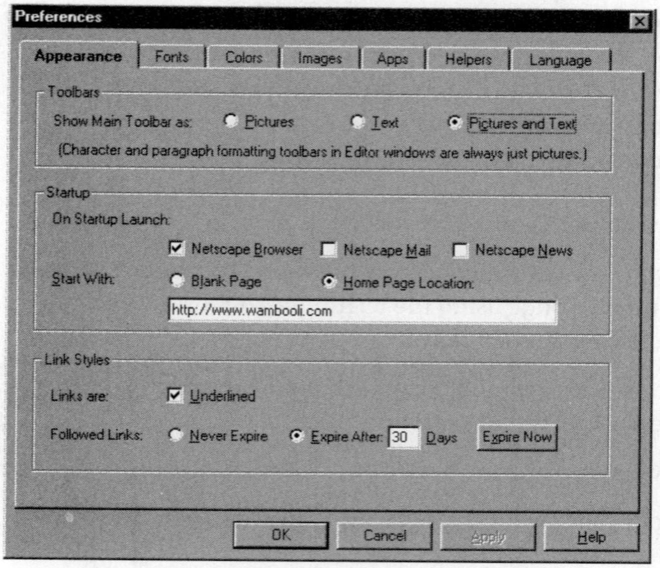

Figure 5-1. *The Preferences dialog box, home page portion.*

▶ Into the text box just below Home Page Location, type your new home page address

- For example, this book's home page is:

  `http://www.wambooli.com`

- Type that gobbledygook in carefully; it's `http`, colon, slash-slash, `www`, period, `wambooli`, period, `com` with no period at the end.
- You can type in any Web page address you like (or not change anything). You'll be using the Wambooli home page often as you read through the next few chapters, so it might not be a bad choice for now.

▶ Click OK

This closes the Preferences dialog box. Your home page has been reset. Ta-da.

- Granted, you don't have to use this book's home page as your own.
- If you're resetting your home page to something else, type its address instead of the Wambooli home page above.
- You can change your home page at any time. Just repeat these instructions and type in the new home page address.

TIP: The best home pages are those that are updated daily, including the news, stock prices, pictures of coffee pots or what-have-you. The Wambooli Internetty Stuff page lists a lot of these Web pages. Refer to it at the following address:

```
http://www.wambooli.com/internetty.htm
```

- Chapter 7 tells you how to find stuff on the Web. You might want to search for a unique Web page using the techniques discussed there, then return here to reset your home page.
- If these instructions don't seem to work with your browser, visit the following Web page for any updated information:

  ```
  http://www.wambooli.com/updates.htm
  ```

- Average home price in America: $98,000. Average Web page price: $20/month.

Going Home

Going home is easy in your Web browser. Just click your mouse on your browser's home gizmo. That takes you instantly to your home page from wherever else you are on the Web.

- The Home button usually has a tiny house on it, assuming that no one lives in apartments, high-rises or geodesic domes.
- If you just changed home page locations as described in the previous section, you'll see your new home page displayed on the screen. As always, have patience. It may take some time to display.
- If you see a "DNS Server" type of error message, refer to Chapter 11.

FYI: Adult humans have 206 bones. Children have 300 bones. Boneless chickens have no bones.

6 Keeping Track of Where You've Been

A big part of Web browsing is wandering and getting lost. But unlike being stuck in the automotive section of a 10,000-square-mile members-only warehouse, wandering aimlessly about the Web can be quite enjoyable, almost mesmerizing...

Sooner or later, however, you'll leave the Internet Hypnosis Zone and want to return to where you once were a long time ago. "Hey? Wasn't that a fun Web page I was at a few hours (or days) ago? I wonder how I get back?"

Getting back is what this chapter is all about. It's more than just clicking the Back button (covered in Chapter 4). After all, you could click the Back button for weeks and never return to some places you've been to. Happily, your browser does come with not one but two solutions.

These time-saving, never-get-lost devices are covered in the following sections:

- **How to get un-lost**
- **Using your browser's Recently Visited list**
- **A Recently Visited list tutorial**
- **Dropping bookmarks to remember favorite Web places**
- **Visiting your bookmarked sites**
- **Organizing your bookmark list**
- **Deleting a bookmark**
- **Renaming a bookmark.**

The Art of Getting Un-Lost

Unlike Dad driving the car on a summer vacation, your Web browser always remembers where it's been. You can easily jump back to any Web page you've visited, providing you use two handy tools, the Recently Visited list and the Bookmark feature.

- The list of the Web pages you've been to are stored in what I call the Recently Visited list. Revisiting any of your previously-stomped-on Web pages is as easy as plucking the proper address from that list.
- The Recently Visited list only keeps track of Web pages you've been to during your current Internet session. When you hang up, all those pages are forgotten. That's why there's the Bookmark feature.
- The Bookmark feature allows you to store favorite sites long-term. If you like a place and want to revisit it often, then tell your Web browser to bookmark it. That way you can easily revisit that site later by plucking its bookmark from a handy list.

Using the Recently Visited List

Unless you remember to leave small rocks or bread crumbs along the path you've taken through the Web, you'll never get back. Pretty soon, you're hopelessly lost and some old hag in a high-cholesterol house is fattening you up for dinner. Wait. That's *Hansel and Gretel.* I digress.

Whenever you want back to where you once were, you need to use the Recently Visited list. Unlike the Back button, you can pluck any Web page from that list and revisit it instantly.

- Netscape keeps the Recently Visited list in the Go menu.
- Some browsers keep the Recently Visited list in a drop-down list on the command box. Click the mouse on the down-pointing arrow on the right side of the command box to see the Recently Visited list.

- The only problem with Netscape's Recently Visited list is that it doesn't seem to remember every place you were. There is only room on the menu for a handful of items, and those items change as you bounce back and forth between sites. For that reason, I recommend making liberal use of Netscape's Bookmark feature, as described in the latter half of this chapter.
- Refer to Chapter 4 for more information on the Back button.

A Recently Visited List Tutorial

It's time to go to Hollywood. Grab your sunglasses, hop in your Corvette (well, a *virtual* Corvette) and take an electronic journey to the land of glitz and glitter.

▶ **Visit the following site:**

```
http://www.disney.com/DisneyPictures
```

Don't spend too much time here. Just wait for the graphics to appear and then you can move on.

▶ **Now visit this site:**

```
http://www.mca.com/universal_pictures/
```

Be patient with these sites. Movie people like graphics and graphics take a while to load. (At least they don't show them on the closed curtains before the movie starts.)

▶ **Quickly go here:**

```
http://www.paramount.com/
```

You know, if it wasn't for Norma Desmond, there wouldn't be any Paramount studios. But they didn't like your audition, so keep moving on:

▶ **Don't forget to stop here:**

```
http://www.fox.com/
```

The 20th Century Fox studios claim they won't change their name after the turn of the century. Sounds like a bad idea to me. Better stop by one more spot.

▶ **Finally, visit this place:**

http://www.warnerbros.com

Thebbidi, Ebbity, Da, That's all folks!

That concludes your whirlwind Hollywood tour. Now you need to sit and wait for the phone to ring. But in the mean time:

► In Netscape, click on the Go menu

The last several places you've been to are all stuffed into the bottom half of the Go menu. You should see your Hollywood tour listed there (see Figure 6-1).

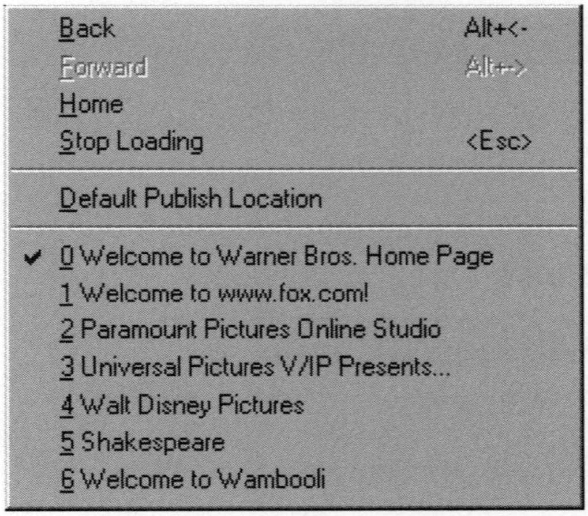

Figure 6-1. *Netscape's Recently Visited list.*

To revisit some place, simply choose the proper item from the menu.

► Choose Walt Disney Pictures from the list

Locate the menu item that reads Walt Disney Pictures and click on it with your mouse. This takes you instantly back to that Web page.

- You can select any item from the list and your browser will take you immediately there. It doesn't matter where the Web page is listed in the Go menu.
- Hey! Those Web pages sure load faster the second time around. This is something Netscape (and most browsers) do for you: they keep a memory of previously-loaded graphical images. It's called a *cache*, something I'd rather not go into right now.

Creating, Using and Abusing Bookmarks

The Recently Visited list is a fine tool you'll use every time you fire up the Web browser. But for long-term storage of favorite places, you need something more memorable. All browsers offer this feature, which I call the Bookmark feature.

- Using a bookmark to remember the location of a Web page is much easier than dog-earing your monitor—which could be an electrical hazard.
- Netscape, and most of the other nifty Web browsers, call this feature Bookmark. Other browsers may call it a Hotlist or Favorite Places or something equally silly but meaning the same thing.

> **YOU CANNOT USE THE BOOKMARK FEATURE ENOUGH! BOOKMARK YOUR WEB PAGES LIKE A CRAZED LIBRARIAN!**

Dropping a bookmark

Say you stumble across some highly useful Web page, a place you can see yourself returning to time and time again. Create a bookmark so that you'll always have a way to get back there.

▶ **In your browser, type in the following Web address**

```
http://www.usatoday.com
```

Press the Enter key when you're certain you have everything spelled right.

- In Netscape you can enter the address by pressing the Ctrl+L key combination. Type in the Web address, then press the Enter key to visit that page.
- In a few moments, the USA Today Web page appears, chock full of stuff some people might refer to as "news."

To immortalize this Web page as a bookmark, do the following:

▶ **Choose Bookmarks→Add Bookmark**

USA Today's Web page is now stored in your browser's Bookmark list.

- *Do this a lot!* Drop bookmarks each day! *Do this a lot!* Drop bookmarks, I say!

TIP: The Netscape shortcut for dropping down a bookmark is the handy Ctrl+D key combination.

- Don't be afraid to add a bookmark; you can always edit out the boring or trivial bookmarks later. See the section "Deleting a bookmark entry" later in this chapter.

THINK: CTRL+D FOR DROP BOOKMARK

Revisiting a bookmarked Web page

To visit any site you've bookmarked, simply choose it from Netscape's Bookmarks menu. Just look for the name of the Web page you want to visit, then click that menu item.

▶ In Netscape, choose the Bookmarks menu

Or you can press the Ctrl+B key combination.

▶ Choose a Web page from the list

- If you only have one item—the USA Today Web page—then you can choose it. However, since you may already be visiting that site, choosing its bookmark doesn't do much for you.
- The USA Today bookmark is named *Top of the news,* which is the title of the Web page. (On the USA Today Web page it says *Top of the news,* which is also how your bookmark was saved.)
- Keep this in mind: not all Web pages save themselves as bookmarks by the names you remember them as. That's okay because you can change the name of your bookmarks. This is covered in the section "Changing a bookmark's name" later in this chapter.

TIP: If you're looking for a Web page you just bookmarked, look at the end of the list. That's where Netscape adds new items.

- You can't understand how useful a bookmark is until you need one. New Web surfers seldom set bookmarks. Then, one day, you realize, "That *was* a handy site I was at the other day. But how did I get there?" That's the day you start over-using your bookmarks.
- Most browsers let you store a nearly infinite number of bookmarks. The better ones also let you organize them into groups for better access. This is covered in the next section.

"I can't find my bookmark site on the menu!"

Netscape's Bookmarks menu can only hold a coupla dozen bookmarks. When it gets full, the last item on the menu will be *More Bookmarks*. Choose that item to see your complete list of bookmarks in Netscape's fancy Bookmarks window (see Figure 6-2).

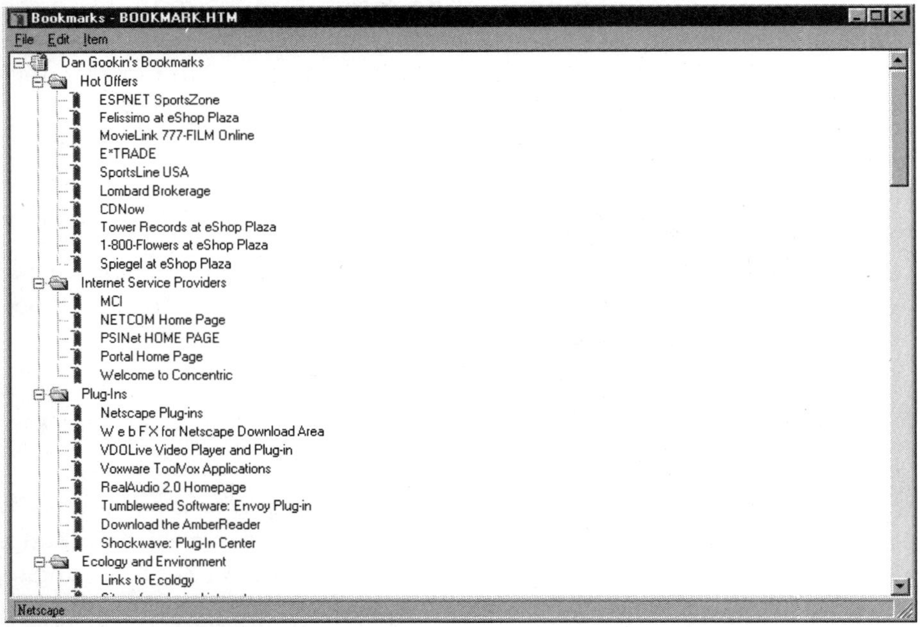

Figure 6-2. *The Bookmarks window.*

Use the scroll bar to scroll through the list of bookmarks, scanning for the one you need. When you find it, double-click on that bookmark using your mouse. The Bookmarks window telepathically connects to your browser, which then scurries off to visit that Web page.

- The bookmark you're looking for will probably be toward the end of the list.
- You can use the Edit➜Find command in the Bookmarks window to locate a bookmark when the list gets horrendously long. Type in the bookmark's name and click the Find Next button. Click the Cancel button when your bookmark has been found.
- The shortcut for the Edit➜Find command is the Ctrl+F keyboard combination.
- You can also open the Bookmarks window by pressing the Ctrl+B keyboard combination.
- There's more madness that takes place in the Bookmarks window. The next few sections give you a tour of the Asylum.

All done with the Bookmarks window

Netscape's Bookmarks window is really a separate program, like any other program in Windows. When you're done with it, you should close the Bookmarks program window: Choose the File➜Close command from the menu.

- There's no need to save the information in the Bookmarks window. Heck, there isn't even a Save command. When you close the window, Netscape saves your bookmarks automatically.
- Gotta love that Netscape.

Messing with the Bookmarks

Bookmarks are really the key to hopping around the Web. I can't stress enough how you should wantonly drop bookmarks all over the place. You can even afford to be sloppy since Netscape lets you go back and edit your bookmark list by using the handy Bookmarks window.

▶ In Netscape, choose Bookmarks➜Go to Bookmarks from the menu

This displays the Bookmarks window where you can organize, edit and delete your bookmarks. The next few sections detail a few of the things you can do.

- The shortcut key for getting at the Bookmarks window is Ctrl+B.

- Netscape comes out of the box with a beehive of places to go, all stored in a pre-arranged Bookmarks list. Feel free to use this list and add to it.
- If all those Web pages in Netscape's preset Bookmarks list excite you, go visit them! But don't overwhelm yourself. The Web has *even more* places to visit. Chapter 7 tells you how to get there.
- I went ahead and deleted all the bookmarks Netscape came with. You can do this too: Refer to the instructions in the section "Deleting a bookmark entry."

Moving a bookmark around in the list

> **YEAH, THERE'S A LOT OF MESSIN' YOU CAN DO WITH YOUR BOOKMARKS.**

Whenever you drop a bookmark, Netscape places it at the end of the bookmark list. However, if that's a place you want to go often, you might consider moving it up to the top of the list. This is cinchy.

► In Netscape, open the Bookmarks window if it isn't opened already
Press the Ctrl+B key combination.

► Locate the bookmark you want to move
For example, locate the *Top of the news* bookmark entry in the list. This is the entry you might have created when you visited the USA Today Web page earlier in this chapter.

- If you just added the bookmark, it will be the last entry.
- You can use the Edit→Find command to locate a stray bookmark in a list hundreds of entries long.

If your Bookmarks list is small, you can drag the bookmark to a new spot on the list. For example, point your mouse at the *Top of the news* bookmark entry, press the mouse button down and drag up. Keep dragging the mouse until *Top of the news* is at the top of your bookmark list.

If your bookmark list is huge, you'll need to cut and paste. Follow these steps:

► Locate the bookmark and click on it once
This highlights the bookmark.

▶ **Press Ctrl+X to cut the bookmark**

Scroll up to the top of the list, or to wherever you want to place the bookmark.

▶ **Click the mouse on a bookmark in the list**

The bookmark you're moving will be pasted immediately *below* the bookmark you've just highlighted.

▶ **Press Ctrl+V to paste the bookmark**

The bookmark has been moved.

TIP: You'll want to put your most favorite links at the top of the list.

- To paste a bookmark as the very first item in the list, click the mouse on the top item in the list—the one that says "_____'s Bookmarks," where the blank part is your name. (Or it might be just blank.) Then paste the bookmark.
- If you're dragging the bookmark instead of pasting, then drag it to the very top item in the list to make that bookmark your first.

Creating a new sub-menu (folder) to organize your bookmarks

A good way to organize a bursting list of bookmarks is to use sub-menus, which appear as folders in the Bookmarks window. This is a way to not only organize your bookmark list but to keep the Bookmarks menu from becoming too long on the screen.

To create a sub-menu, follow these steps:

▶ **Click the mouse at the spot in the list where you want a new folder (sub-menu)**

The new folder will be created immediately below the item you highlight.

▶ **Choose Item → Insert Folder from the menu**

The Bookmark Properties dialog box appears. (See Figure 6-3, which isn't exactly what you'll see but kinda sorta.)

▶ **Type in a name for the folder**

- The name should reflect the folder's contents. For example, "Joke Pages" or "Government stuff" or "Nasty pictures."

- I have a folder for the various Babylon 5 Web pages I frequent. Another folder holds various news sites I visit. These folders are named *Babylon 5* and *News*, respectively.
- You might consider a folder for your friends' Web pages. Call it *Friends Web Pages*.

▶ **Click the OK button**

- The folder is placed in the list—but it's empty. You'll need to drag bookmarks to the folder to place them there. Refer to the previous section.

TIP: You can only add bookmarks to the folder by dragging or pasting them. Do this by dragging (or pasting) the bookmark right on top of the folder name. This places that bookmark inside the folder.

- The folders appear only in the Bookmarks window. In Netscape, they'll look like sub-menus.
- Close the Bookmarks window when you're done (press the Ctrl+W key combination). Back in Netscape you can peek at the Bookmarks menu to see your changes.

Deleting a bookmark entry

Six months ago your friend Tom had a hot Web page. But he discovered it was too much work to maintain, so he shut it down. Alas, you still have a bookmark for that page, one you would woefully like to delete.

▶ **In Netscape, press Ctrl+B to visit the Bookmarks window if it isn't open already**

▶ **Locate the old or tired or stupid bookmark you want to delete**

- You can scroll through the list to find it.
- Use the Edit ➜ Find command to locate bookmarks if the list becomes tediously long.

▶ **Click on the bookmark once to select it**

▶ **Press the Delete key**

Thwoop! It's gone.

- You'll have to make the *Thwoop* noise on your own.

- You can also delete folders in this manner.
- **Warning!** When you delete a folder in the Bookmarks window, you're deleting all the bookmarks in that folder!
- I deleted all the folders in Netscape's original bookmark list so I could start my own list. No one at Netscape got mad at me for doing this.

TIP: If you delete a bookmark and then—Omigosh!—change your mind, press the Ctrl+Z keyboard combination. That's the Undo command, which undoes whatever you just did.

Changing a bookmark's name

If you added the USA Today Web page to your bookmark list, you might find yourself puzzled. Instead of saying USA Today, the Web page is listed as *Top of the news.* This isn't a mistake; the actual name of the USA Today home page is *Top of the news.* However, you may want to change that bookmark—or any other bookmark—to a name you can more easily recognize.

To change a bookmark's name, follow these steps:

▶ Find the bookmark you want to change
For example, locate the *Top of the news* bookmark.

▶ Choose Item → Properties from the menu
Click the mouse on the Properties menu item. A Bookmark Properties dialog box appears (see Figure 6-3).

▶ Type `USA Today` into the Name text box
The text appears in the Name text box, replacing the old text, *Top of the news.*

▶ Click OK
Your bookmark has been renamed.

- Feel free to rename sites so that you can remember them better. The bookmark list is *just for you.* You can do anything you like with it.
- Well, don't replace all the bookmarks with the names of Supreme Court Justices. I suppose I should say "do whatever works best for you" instead of "you can do anything you like." Semantics...

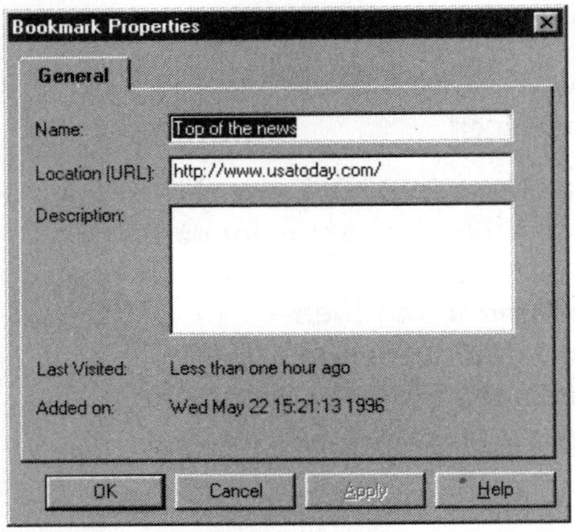

Figure 6-3. *The Bookmark Properties dialog box.*

FYI: While 98 percent of American drivers think they drive better than anyone else, keep in mind the following useless statistic: 50 percent of all drivers on the road are below average.

7 Finding the Stuff They Tell You Is Out There

http://www.loc.gov/

During a visit to Washington, D.C., I came upon the egotistical notion of finding my books in the Library of Congress. After all, there's a page in this book somewhere that says "Library of Congress card catalog information." So I wandered through the several buildings that make up the Library. When I got up enough nerve, I asked and discovered that, no, there are no "stacks" in the Library of Congress. No shelves of endless literature and reference. No books to browse. No real library.

Fortunately, searching for information on the Web isn't as disappointing as a mere civilian trying to use the Library of Congress. (Congressmen can check out books—even exhibits!) There are many tools and techniques you can use to find just about anything on the Web, and they're all free. Your only task is to have patience, since a lot of the treasures that supposedly lurk out there aren't that obvious. It's like my son who wants to be a paleontologist, yet can't find his socks in the morning: a dinosaur bone isn't just going to hit you in the head, you must *look* for it. The same thing applies to the Web: The information is there, you must *look* for it.

This chapter covers these main Web Wambooli searching topics:

- **How to search for something special on the Web using Yahoo's Search command**
- **Searching Yahoo's categories**
- **Using other Search engines, such as the Web Crawler**
- **Finding a person on the Net.**

Welcome to the Library Without a Catalog

The Library of Congress has tons of information, a marvelous catalog, but no books to check out. The Web is the opposite. It has tons of information, all of which you can check out but none of which is officially catalogued. There are no Dewey Decimal Numbers. No official registration. No Net patrol. No, nothing like that.

> YEAH, THEY WERE GOING TO CALL IT THE WORLD WIDE CHAOS, BUT THAT WOULD MAKE FOR A DULL THREE-LETTER ACRONYM.

Fortunately, many folks take it upon themselves to create their very own Web catalogs. They scour the Web as a labor of love, finding every possible Web page, and then categorize everything. The results are listed in a special Web catalog, a collection of Web pages that any mere mortal can access.

- Web catalogs attempt to list as many Web pages as they can.
- Most Web catalogs organize Web pages into categories—just like a card catalog in a library.
- A special type of Web catalog is the *search engine*. Rather than just present you with a list, the search engine will sift through all the Web pages for you, finding the information you're looking for.
- The folks who maintain these Web catalogs are amazing. They're like Web Librarians, but without the bun hairdo or the glasses on a beaded chain.

- Yes, you can "check out" a Web page just as you can check out a book in a library, keeping parts of it if you like. This is covered in Chapter 8.

Looking Up Things in Yahoo!

My personal favorite place to look for anything on the Web is the Yahoo catalog. Yes, Yahoo is really the name of it. (I certainly hope you're not the type of person who shuns something because it has a goofy name.)

► **Visit Yahoo by typing the following Web address into your browser:**

`http://www.yahoo.com`

After pressing the Enter key, you'll see Yahoo's glory unfold on your screen (see Figure 7-1). Please make note of the following things:

- A graphic "header," complete with an (ugh!) advertisement—the thing that says "Yahoo!" on top of the page.
- A *form* or box to type something in (this is the Search box).
- The major Yahoo categories, like you'd find in a library.

TIP: In Netscape, press Ctrl+D to drop in a bookmark on Yahoo's home page.

- By the way, nothing happens on the screen when you press Ctrl+D to drop a bookmark. Even so, the bookmark has been created. Refer to Chapter 6 for more information on bookmarks.
- Yahoo lists just about every useful Web page known to mankind, with dozens more added every day.
- Any time I want to find anything, I go to Yahoo. And if Yahoo can't find what I'm looking for, it directs me to the other popular Web catalogs and search engines that usually get the job done. You'll see how this is done in a few paragraphs.
- I assume it's named Yahoo after the yell—as in, "Yahoo! I found it!" This is opposed to yahoo as in "the guy our 17-year-old daughter is dating."

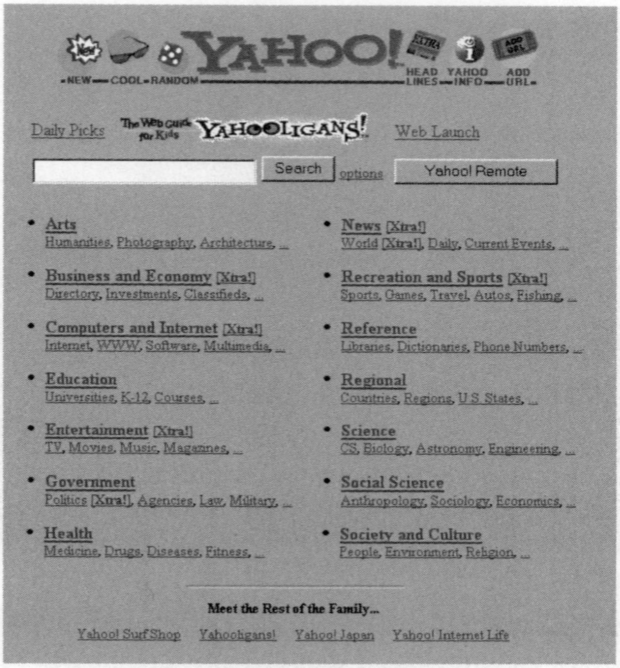

Figure 7-1. *Yahoo's opening number.*

Searching for something on Yahoo by searching for it

There are several ways to attack the massive collection of Web sites and related information listed in the Yahoo catalog. If you know exactly what it is you're looking for, then you opt for the easy way out: type that something you're looking for into the Search text box.

▶ Locate the Search text box on Yahoo's home page

It's at the top of Yahoo's main page, by the Search button.

▶ Click the mouse in that text box

A blinking cursor appears in the box, ready for you to type something in.

- If there is any text already in the Search box, use the Delete or Backspace keys to erase it.

▶ Type some text to search for into the Search text box

For example, type `Spock`.

Star Trek XII: The Search for Spock on the Net

- Try to type in something general. For example, if you want to know which type of potting soil to use, type in "gardening." You can try typing in "potting soil," but you'll have better luck searching for the more general "gardening."
- Try to search for only one word. If you type in two words, such as "pig poling," then Yahoo displays Web pages that contain "pig poling" as well as Web pages about "pig" and "poling."
- If you're searching for a person, use their last name. For example, use "Simpson" instead of "Bart" or "Bart Simpson."
- Searching for a non-famous person? See the section "Finding Humans" later in this chapter.
- If you aren't sure what you're looking for, use the Yahoo categories instead of a search. This is covered in the next section.

▶ Click the Search button

This tells Yahoo to search through its massive catalog, looking for Web pages related to the tidbit of text you typed in.

- In a few moments you'll see a page of links and some descriptions about various Web pages devoted to whatever it was you were searching for.
- If you typed in `Spock`, you'll see various Web pages about Spock—both the Doctor and Mister varieties.
- Actually, I don't see any Doctor Spock Web pages listed.

▶ Look for the results

When Yahoo finds something in its vast catalog, it displays two types of result:

- Matching Yahoo Categories
- Matching Yahoo Sites.

▶ Locate the heading: `Matching Yahoo Categories`

The first section of results lists any Yahoo categories that match what you're looking for.

- Unfortunately there aren't any matching Yahoo categories for Spock (a Yahoo boo-hoo). But for other things you search for, there might be.
- Only major topics, such as Science Fiction, have their own categories.
- The items in the Matching Yahoo Categories list are actually Web pages Yahoo devoted to your subject. For example, if you typed `movies`, you'll find several Yahoo categories devoted to the topic, such as:

```
Business and Economy:Companies:Entertainment:Movies

Computers and Internet:Software:Multimedia:Movies

Entertainment:Magazines:Movies and Films

Entertainment:Movies and Films

Entertainment:Movies and Films:Genres:Science
Fiction/Fantasy:Monster Movies

Entertainment:Movies and Films:MovieWeb-sneak previews
of various movies

News:Entertainment:Movies
```

Clicking on any one of these links takes you to another page in Yahoo—a page that lists links specific to that category.

- When more categories are available than can fit on the screen, you'll see a `Next 25 matches` link at the bottom of the page. Click it to see the next 25 matches.

▶ Locate the heading: `Matching Yahoo Sites`

The second section on your browser's screen lists some Web pages Yahoo has found. These are links that match the word you were searching for, but they are in a smattering of Yahoo categories—just as you might find books on computer graphics in the Computers, Graphics and Hollywood sections of your local bookstore.

- Yahoo displays the Web pages it found as links. Each of these links is listed below the category it was found in. For example, one of the matching sites might look like the following:

  `Entertainment:Television:Shows:Science Fiction:Star Trek`

  - `Quote from Mr.` **`Spock.`**

The first line lists the Yahoo category in which the link was found. Here, the Spock link was found in the main Entertainment category. That's followed by a chorus line of sub-categories—Television, Shows, Science Fiction and then Star Trek. That just tells you where the link was found in Yahoo's massive catalog.

- The actual link Yahoo found appears on the line after the category. Above, that's the `Quote from Mr. Spock` link.
- The word you searched for, Spock in this case, appears in bold text.
- Visit the `Quote from Mr. Spock` page if you like. It's a fun place that lists a random quote from mankind's favorite alien computer nerd. Click the Reload button to see a new quote.
- Mr. Spock frowns upon any display of emotion.

"Yahoo failed to find my special something"

Yahoo isn't exactly a full-on genius when it comes to finding things. After all, the Web is vast . . . not to mention there just might not be a Web page for every topic.

YOU JUST CLICK ON THE ALTERNATIVE SEARCH ENGINE AND IT AUTOMATICALLY KNOWS WHAT YOU'RE LOOKING FOR.

If Yahoo utterly fails to locate your special something, then it gives you a chance to use the other Web catalogs and search engines. Figure 7-2 shows what Yahoo displays when it utterly can't find anything on a given topic.

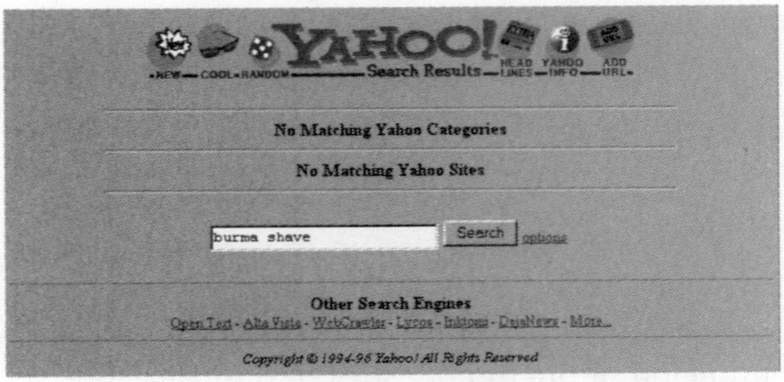

Figure 7-2. *Yahoo fails to find your special something.*

Don't despair when you see the double "No Matching" result. At the bottom of the Web page you'll find that Yahoo graciously lists some alternative catalogs and search engines for you to quickly try again. To continue looking for your subject in one of those alternative catalogs, click on its link. For example, click on the WebCrawler link and Yahoo tells, nay *demands*, that WebCrawler use its own searching techniques to locate your desired Web page(s).

- That's awfully nice of Yahoo to do this, don't you think?
- If you haven't seen Yahoo's "I can't find it" screen yet, don't despair. Just keep searching for stuff and eventually you'll see it.
- See the section "Other Places to Look: Search.Com, AltaVista, WebCrawler, Etc." later in this chapter, for more information on various Web catalogs and search engines.
- If WebCrawler (or whatever search engine you've clicked on) can't locate your information, then click your browser's Back button. This returns you to Yahoo's "I can't find it" page and you can try searching with another catalog; select one of the options at the bottom of Yahoo's utter failure page (Figure 7-2).

Searching for something by browsing the categories

Like a library, Yahoo also has its Web page catalog listed by categories. That way you can browse for something when you don't quite know exactly what it is. Yes, many refer to this as loitering. But legally speaking, a library is just about the only place anyone can freely loiter these days.

TIP: If you've been following along in this chapter, you can quickly return to the Yahoo home page by choosing Yahoo from your Web browser's Recently Visited list. In Netscape, you can also choose Go→Yahoo from the menu.

▶ Take a minute to look at Yahoo's main page and all the categories listed there

Figure 7-1 shows them, but real teensy.

Say, for example, you wanted to look for sheet music. In a library, you could saunter on over to the Music section to look for books of sheet music that you could photocopy and save a bundle off of buying the stuff at a music store. In Yahoo, the sauntering is done with your mouse.

▶ Scroll down (if you have to), to the `Entertainment` category

Beneath it you'll find listed some popular sub-categories, one of which is `Music`.

▶ Click on the `Music` link beneath the `Entertainment` category

In a few moments (longer in parts of Europe), you'll see the `Entertainment:Music` sub-category listing.

▶ Click on the `Sheet Music` link

You may have to scroll down to find it. After clicking, you'll see a page with links to various sources for sheet music and related topics.

▶ Find an interesting link and click on it

For example, click on the `GMD Music Archive` link. This takes you off to visit that site, if you like (though most of the sheet music appears to be for the violin).

WHEN YOU FIND SOMETHING THAT INTERESTS YOU, BOOKMARK IT!

- It's possible to save the information you see on your screen—but don't rush your PC's monitor over to that photocopying machine! Instead, you can use your computer to save or print whatever you see in your Web browser. This subject is covered in Chapter 8.

- Yahoo's categories are quite vast. It might help to use the Search button (as described in the previous section) to start your browsing. For example, you could search for `"sheet music"` and Yahoo would display the category for you almost instantaneously.
- "Instantaneous" is a subjective thing on the World Wide Web.
- If a Yahoo category ends with an @ (at sign), as in `Television@,` it means it's really another sub-category. Click on that link to see even more links and stuff.
- The @ is a highly over-used symbol on the Internet.
- Occasionally, you'll see Yahoo display a link called `Indices.` This is a link to Web pages that contain more links—like Web catalogs, but particular to a certain area of interest, like Phrenology.

Other Places to Look: Search.Com, AltaVista, WebCrawler, Etc.

Even though Yahoo may be the only Web catalog you need, it isn't the only Web catalog in the universe. There are several other ways to hunt down information, plus several interesting sites you can visit that store different or more detailed information than Yahoo offers. I've listed several of them on the Wambooli Find It page.

▶ Visit the following Web page

`http://www.wambooli.com/findit.htm`

Carefully type in the above address. Eventually you'll discover a Web page that looks something like Figure 7-3. Those graphics you see are all links to other Web catalogs that offer different ways to search for stuff on the Web.

- You don't have to use any other Web catalog than Yahoo. If you feel comfortable with Yahoo, then you can skip this section. However, when Yahoo fails to find a few subjects for you, consider visiting some of the catalogs mentioned in the following pages.

Figure 7-3. The Wambooli Find It page.

- The following sections offer brief descriptions of the search engines listed on the Wambooli Find It page.
- Yeah, there are even more search engines than are listed here. More of them are coming every day. In fact, some experts claim that in the future, every Web page will be its own search engine.
- Then again, there were experts in the early 1900s who claimed we'd all have flying cars in the 1960s.

C|net's Search.Com - `http://www.search.com`

There are zillions of Web catalogs. And sooner or later the idea came into someone's brain: "Hey, wouldn't it be nice to catalog all the catalogs?" That brain just happens to live in someone who works for C|net, which I think is the CNN cable network's online branch.

▶ Click on the `search.com` graphic on the Wambooli Find It Web page

Soon, yes soon, Search.com's Web page appears on your screen.

- I would pronounce it "Search-com." Some may say "Search-dot-com." Whatever.
- Search.com lists just about every search engine and Web catalog known to exist in the universe.
- So Search.com doesn't really search for anything itself, it merely sends you off to someplace else to look?
- Exactly.

▶ Down around the bottom of your screen, locate the Express Search area

This is shown in Figure 7-4. You use this part of Search.com's page to look up things in various other places on the Internet.

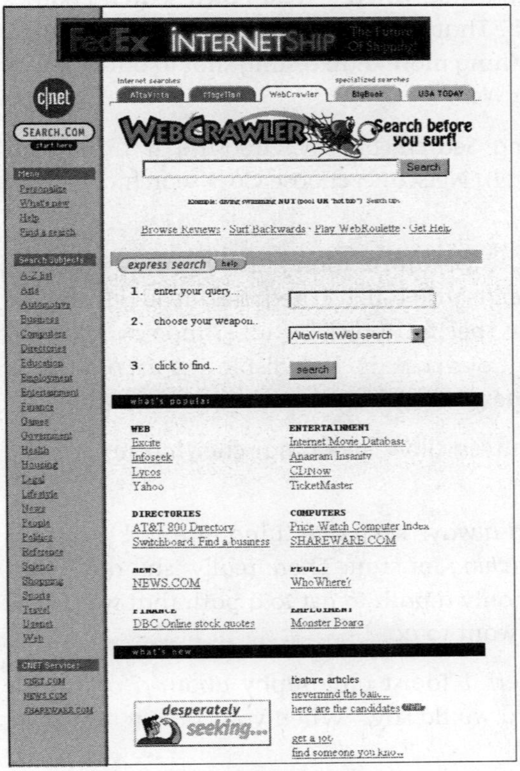

Figure 7-4. C/net's Search.com.

▶ Into the enter your query box type `Al Gore`

Click the mouse in the text box by the first item, enter your query.

▶ In the choose your weapon drop-down list, choose Excite

Pluck the word Excite from the drop-down list. (This list is actually a bunch of search engines and catalogs located out on the Net. It may or may not be in alphabetical order.)

▶ Click the mouse on the Search button

- If a Security Information warning is displayed, click the Continue button. For more information on this warning, refer to Chapter 11.

Search.com goes out and tells the Excite search engine to locate any Web Sites related to "Al Gore." In a moment, you should see 10 of them listed, with opportunities to look up even more.

- Search.com hasn't really done anything for you. It didn't find any Al Gore sites on the Web at all. Instead, it merely passed the "find Al Gore" baton over to the Excite Web thing, where Excite's own search engines were used to search the Web. That's how all of Search.com's searching tools work; Search.com is nothing more than a sling shot to other search engines and catalogs on the Web.
- You can search again using Search.com by choosing it from your browser's Recently Visited list. In Netscape, choose Go➜search.com from the menu.
- There are some categories listed down along the right side of the Search.com page. These aren't Yahoo-like categories; instead, they're links to search engines on specific topics (what Yahoo would call "indices"). For example, the `Government` link displays a list of links to various Web pages that list government-like resources on the Web.
- You know government resources: Slow, plodding, chewing up money, ineffective—like that.
- With Search.com you should always keep one thing in mind: The purpose of this Web page is *searching* for stuff. There really isn't any other information here, per se. It's only a path to get to a path that will eventually get you to where you want to go.
- I'm sure there's some wonderful Taoist philosophy about a path that leads to a path. As Yogi Berra would say, "When you come to a fork in the road, take it."

AltaVista - `http://www.altavista.digital.com`

The big boast at AltaVista is that it's the largest and fastest of all the Web catalogs. Supposedly whatever you're looking for will be found there (except for all the socks the dryer ate). Unlike Yahoo, there are no categories, simply a search box you type your query into (see Figure 7-5).

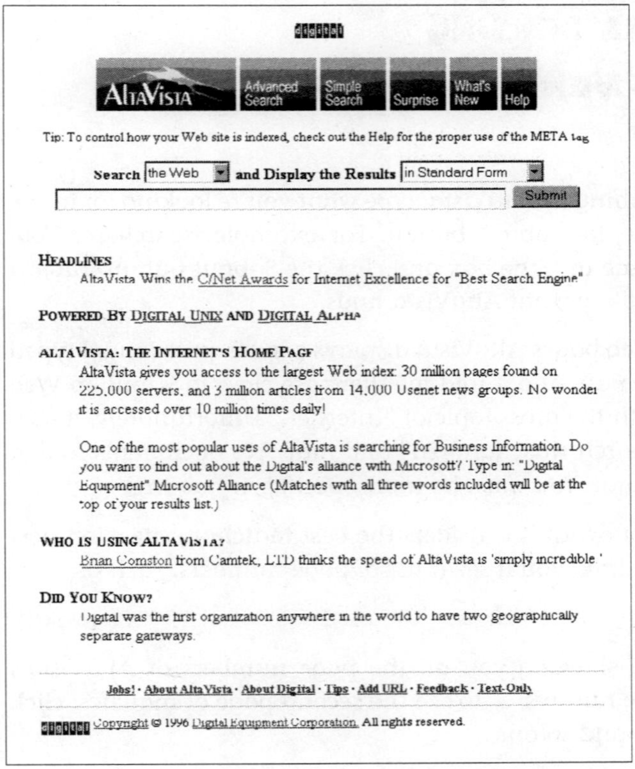

Figure 7-5. *AltaVista is yet anther search engine.*

- You can visit AltaVista from the Wambooli Find It Web page. Visit that page at the following address:

  `http://www.wambooli.com/findit.htm`

If you've been following the tutorials in this chapter, choose Go➔Find it on the Web from Netscape's menu. Then click on the AltaVista graphic.

Isn't AltaVista a Spanish term for "A pricey Southern California housing development"?

- To search for something in AltaVista, type what you're looking for in the text box and click the Submit button. For example, search for Yogi Berra. Type his name into the box and click the Submit button. After a few moments you'll see what AltaVista finds.
- The sum total of Web pages AltaVista displays can be quite long. I typed in the word `Internet` and it told me there are close to 9 million Web pages that deal with the gross topic of "Internet." Unfortunately, it also told me that the search was "Ignored" and that "No documents match the query." The moral: You must be more specific. Try again.
- AltaVista shows you what it considers the best matching sites, ten at a time. After the last link, you'll see a list of page numbers, such as:

```
p. 1 2 3 4 5 6 7 8 9 10 11 12 13 14 15 16 17 18 19 20 [Next]
```

This is an index of sorts, showing you all the page numbers of AltaVista's search results. Click on the number `2` to see the second page of matches; click on `3` to see the third page and so on.

- AltaVista doesn't list every single match it finds. It uses a best-match technique involving witchcraft and voodoo too complex to explain here. Usually, you'll be able to find what you're looking for in the 200-odd matches it might display for you. Besides, to display all gazillion matches would take eons on the Internet.

WebCrawler - `http://www.Webcrawler.com`

The WebCrawler isn't a catalog at all. It's a Web robot.

Well, the WebCrawler isn't *that* type of *robot*. Unlike the walking fish bowl on *Lost in Space*, the WebCrawler uses special programs to actively go out and hunt down things on the Web. It should be called the Web Hunter-Seeker, since *robot* is so Czech. But I digress.

DANGER!
WILL ROBINSON!
ALIENS APPROACHING!

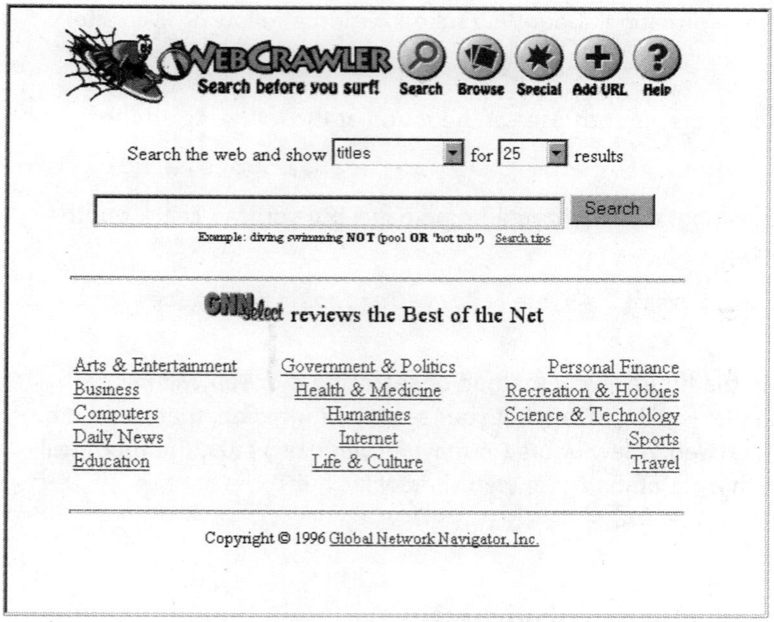

Figure 7-6. *WebCrawler crawls on your screen.*

- Personally, I prefer WebCrawler for finding things Yahoo doesn't know about. Its searches tend to be more complete and up-to-date. Heck, it's a robot!
- WebCrawler's page is very brief (see Figure 7-6). The idea here is that you're searching for some tidbit of text that *must* be somewhere out there on the Net; you don't need to mess with catalogs or "Neat-o sites of the day" or anything like that.

- The Web pages WebCrawler finds are of a different nature than what AltaVista shows you. WebCrawler goes out and finds a Web page that contains the word you're looking for, not the subject. So if you're looking for Web sites about the Dolphins football team, Web Crawler will feed you any Web page it knows about with the word "dolphin" in it.
- WebCrawler is my choice for those desperate times when nothing else seems to work.

ROBOTS! ROBOTS! ROBOTS EVERYWHERE!

If you want more information about Web robots, visit the following Web site:

http://www.Webcrawler.com/mak/projects/robots/faq.htm

A list of the Web robots you can use can be found at the following address:

http://www.Webcrawler.com/mak/projects/robots/active.htm

The *Lost in Space* robot doesn't have a home page, but you can check out the following anyway:

http://www.vader.mgmt.purdue.edu/vader/lost_in_space/lost_in_space.html

At some point in the future, every method of searching the Web will involve robots. For example, you'll give a robot your search information, then send it off to scour the entire Web. A few hours (or maybe even days) later, the robot will return to you with a list of matching Web sites. Nifty, huh?

Looking elsewhere (obviously)

The Wambooli Find It page isn't the last word in Web catalogs or in finding things on the Net. As the Web grows, more and more catalogs will appear, plus new ingenious methods of searching for stuff will crop up. Stay tuned to the Wambooli Updates page for any additional information on new and wondrous ways of searching the Web:

http://www.wambooli.com/updates.htm

Finding Humans

Finding *things* on the Web is one thing. Finding a human is quite another. No, I'm not talking about humans trapped inside a computer. This isn't *TRON*, you know. I'm taking about finding a human being's e-mail address, personal Web page, even their phone number by using various and sneaky methods on the Word Wide Web.

- You'd figure it would be a snap to locate someone online. After all, these things are *computers*, are they? But, alas, being able to ask the computer where someone is, or even who someone is, can be a minor hassle.

FYI: In the old days of UNIX, there was a program called Finger that would attempt to find someone in the electronic universe. Of course, it helped if you knew which computer system they were using. So as long as you know your sister Jody had an account at `ncsu.edu` ***(North Carolina State University) you could use Finger to "find" her account. But isn't that, like, major "duh"? I mean, if you already know where someone is, what's the point of the thing?***

- Using modern people-searching methods on the Web, you can find just about anyone anywhere. Bottom line: Forget Finger for finding folks.

Locating yourself (or anyone else) by using the Web

THE COMPUTER KNOWS ALL, SEES ALL

For a scary, *1984*-like coffee wake-up call, dial up Yahoo with your Web browser and visit its people search page. The quick way to get there is as follows:

▶ **Visit the following Web page**

`http://phone.yahoo.com/`

The Web page you see has a form that looks similar to the one shown in Figure 7-7.

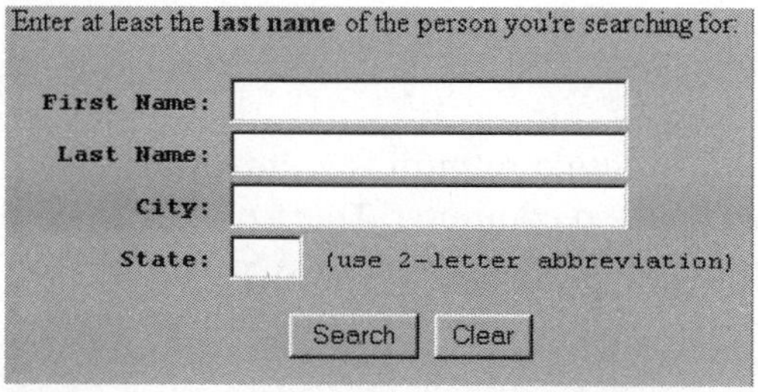

Figure 7-7. *Searching for someone with the Web.*

► Fill in the form with your own name, city and state

Click the mouse in the first text box by First Name. Type in your first name. Press the Tab key. Type in your last name.

> ***TIP: Always press the Tab key to move from one place to another in a Web form. Only press the Enter key when you're done filling in the form and ready to send the information off to who-knows-where.***

- You don't have to fill in every box to do the search. The most important things are the last name and, if you know it, the state and city.
- You can fill in anyone's name to look for them anywhere in the United States. Of course, if you forget your own address and phone number, you can always try your own name again.
- Refer to Chapter 10 for more information on forms on the Web.

Now the question is, how many people are there with your same name living in the United States?

► Click on the Search button

- Refer to Chapter 11 about the "non-secure information" warning you might see after clicking the Search button. If you see it, click the Continue button.
- Alas, there were only eight of us Dan Gookin's in the United States. Shockingly enough, one of them was me, complete with my full address and phone number.

- You won't find my address and phone number in the list anymore. I've removed it. (See the last item in this list.) Whenever someone has removed themselves from the list, the word "(suppressed)" appears.
- Yahoo's people search only locates someone in the United States. Your second cousin's brother-in-law in Bangladesh probably isn't in there.
- After you get over that creepy feeling it gives you, grant yourself a second to marvel at what a wonderful tool this is. Just about anyone who's listed in any phone book in the United States makes Yahoo's list. This is a tremendous boon for finding lost friends and arranging high school reunions.
- Of course, you still may be palpitating over the fact that your name is in there for every geek on the Internet to abuse. If so, you can remove it: Click on the link displayed that allows you to suppress your name from being listed. On my screen, the link looks like this:

  `If you have questions regarding privacy, please read this.`

Click on the `read this` part of the link, then click on the `suppression form` link on the next page. Follow the instructions on the screen and fill in the blanks as necessary to have your name removed from the database.

What about finding Web pages of friends, relatives and other weird people I know?

If you want to see if your friends, acquaintances or the geeky next door neighbor have their own Web pages, there's a Web page just for you.

► **Type in the following Web address**

`http://www.yahoo.com/Entertainment/People`

When the page displays you'll see something I call an *alphabet bar*. That's a set of links, `A` through `Z` (plus some foreign characters), that works like a reference—like a set of encyclopedias.

► **Click on the first letter of your last name**

For example, I click on `G`. If your last name is Johnson, click on `J`.

► **Stand back while a massive Web page is displayed**

- A few minutes later, you'll see a complete list of people who have Web pages and have submitted them for publication. The page will take quite a while to display since there are gazillions of people whose last name begins with the same letter.

- Now you could scroll through the list, looking for your friends and neighbors. Instead, use the browser's Find gizmo to help you search through the list. Type the name you're looking for in the Find dialog box. Click the Find Next button.

How to find someone's e-mail address

To find the e-mail address of someone you love, you need to visit another page on the Web:

▶ Type in the following Web address:

`http://www.yahoo.com/search/people/email.html`

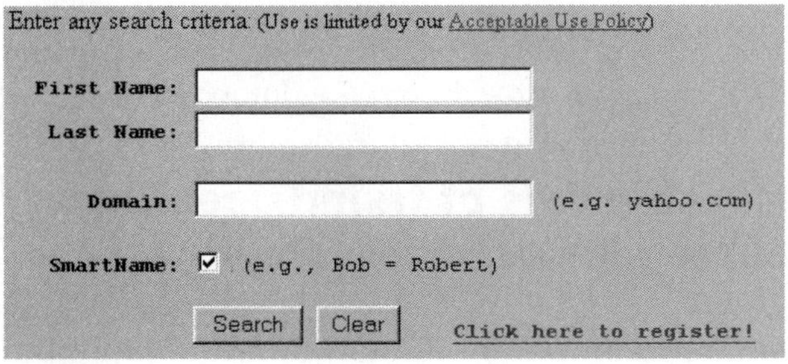

Figure 7-8. *Use this form to find someone's e-mail address.*

When the Web page appears, you'll be faced with a form you can use to search for potential e-mail addresses based on someone's first and last name (see Figure 7-8).

▶ Fill in the form

Click the mouse in the First Name text box and type in a first name—if you know it. If you don't, you can leave this box blank. Then press the Tab key and type in a last name.

- Last names are required.
- Spelling counts.
- If you know the person's computer domain name, enter it. You don't have to. This one can be left blank if you're at a total loss.

► **Click the Search button.**

Yahoo looks and looks. Eventually it may find who you're looking for.

- See Chapter 11 for more information about the security dialog box.
- Don't get all excited if a match is found: It's a good idea to send a "Are you so-and-so?" message to the person before sending off 5 megabytes of graphical images of your children and that fish Earl caught.
- Never, never use the names you find here to advertise anything. That's a big Net No-No.

TIP: If you search for yourself and find that you're not in there, click on the* `Click here to register` *link on the main searching page. That takes you to a form you can use to submit your name and other vital statistics to Yahoo for publication in their online references.

FYI: Survey says: 27 percent of male college students in the U.S. believe that life is "a meaningless existential hell." The other 73 percent don't know what the word "existential" means.

8

General Web Page Use, Abuse and Theft

http://www.fbi.gov/

Browser is too tame a word for the powerful software you have on your PC. It isn't merely a Web *browser*. It's also a Web spy and a Web thief. Browsing is just a casual activity. "Oh, I'm just looking," you tell the salesperson. Bah! The Web just don't work that way.

The truth is, anything that floats your way via the Internet, anything that winds up on your PC's screen, is yours for the taking. Not that you can grab something and say it's yours. No, no, no. But any text that floats over the screen, any graphical image, can be lifted from that Web page and saved on your computer. You can use that information later if you like, save it and compile a report, whatever.

This chapter covers several topics, each of which deals somehow with borrowing information from your Web browser:

- **Printing a Web page on your printer**
- **Printing graphics and animations**
- **Copying text from a Web page**
- **Saving an entire Web page to disk**
- **Opening a Web page you've saved to disk**
- **Borrowing graphics from a Web page**
- **Viewing graphics you've saved to disk.**

O! The Thrill of Printing a Web Page

If Edgar Allan Poe were alive today, he'd probably prefer it if you went to a store and bought a copy of *The Cask of Amontillado* (which is often called *The Cask of Armadillo*). He would want you to pay that $5.95, out of which he'd probably make a whole quarter-dollar royalty. Heck, he'd want you to buy two copies. Maybe a third one to save "just in case."

But Poe is dead and probably couldn't care less that you can have your own, personal, printed copy of *The Cask of Amontillado* in just moments.

▶ **Visit the following Web page:**

`http://www.wambooli.com/poe.htm`

This is the Wambooli Poe page. Its main purpose in life is to save you from typing in the following Web address:

`http://www.literature.org/Works/Edgar-Allan-Poe/amontillado.html`

Don't type that one in! Sheesh. Type in the Wambooli Poe page listed above it. This will save wear and tear on your fingers.

The Wambooli Poe page (Figure 8-1) is merely a place for you to go and visit various Poe places on the Web. It's just a way station.

▶ **Click on `The Cask of Amontillado` link**

In a few Web Wambooli seconds you'll see the story. But don't engross yourself with it on your screen and risk Eyeball Frazzle. Print that Web page!

MAKE SURE YOUR PRINTER IS ON AND READY TO PRINT BEFORE YOU TRY TO PRINT ANYTHING.

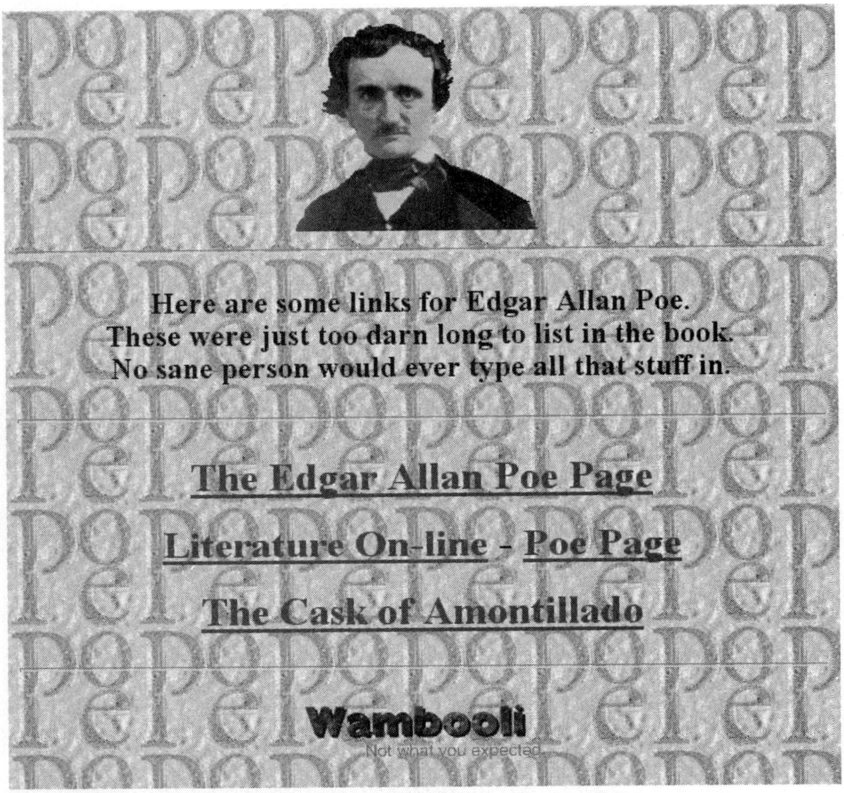

Figure 8-1. *The Wambooli Poe page.*

► **Click on the Print gizmo**

► **Click OK in the Print dialog box**

The Web page starts to print.

Musical Interlude while the page prints...

More Muzak

Soon the page appears, looking exactly like it does on the screen.

HOPEFULLY YOUR PRINTER HAS BEEN TURNED ON AND STOCKED WITH PAPER. OTHERWISE THIS COULD BE A LONG WAIT.

- The Cask of Amontillado is a text-only Web page. Your browser can also print graphical Web pages, which is covered in the next section.
- If your browser lacks a Print gizmo, choose File→Print from the menu.
- Some browsers may not display a Print dialog box. In those cases, the Web page prints the instant you choose the Print command.

TIP: Before you print a Web page, make sure the entire thing has loaded onto your screen. When your browser's busy thing has stopped twitching, then it's okay to print. If you try to print before then, you might not get the entire Web page.

FYI: Eyeball Frazzle is the unofficial term given to those folks who read too much information on the World Wide Web. Our eyes read printed text a lot easier than that glowing, quivering text you see on your computer screen. Better monitors can alleviate some Eyeball Frazzle, but not much.

Printing a Web page rich with graphics

To really see how well this printing thing works, visit a graphical Web page.

▶ **Type in the following hot Web page address:**

`http://www.hohouse.com/donho16.htm`

It's the Aloha from Don Ho Web page and, darn it, you *need* a picture of Don churning out of your printer.

▶ Use your browser's Print gizmo to print the Web page
When the page finally spews out of the printer, you'll see a black and white picture of Don Ho (plus the rest of his Web page).

- That picture of Don Ho is suitable for framing.
- If you have a color printer, you'll see a color copy of the Web page printed—just like in real life!
- If your browser lacks a Print gizmo, use the File➔Print command.
- Remember to click OK in the Print dialog box to actually print the Web page.
- No, I presently don't know of any way just to print a graphic on a Web page. Later in this chapter, you'll learn how to copy a graphic image from a Web page and save it on your hard drive. From there, you can use a graphics program to print the image. But you can't do it directly from a Web page.

Can my printer print animations?

Many Web pages feature colorful animations. You can print these as well as anything else but, as you might suspect, the animations won't be so animated on the print-out.

▶ Visit this fun page:

```
http://www.wambooli.com/anime.htm
```

The Wambooli Animations page shows a smattering of moving images.

▶ Wait for the entire Web page to load
Doh-dee-doh.

▶ Print the Web page
Make your own printing noises here.

The printed copy looks exactly like the copy on your screen. And…the graphics don't move. Now you know for certain.

TIP: Another fun place to visit is the Kodak Fun Web page:

`http://www.kodak.com/ciHome/OTUC/index.shtml`

The Kodak Fun Web thing shows lots of graphics, plus some moving images. (This Web page may change in the future; if it's not there now, refer to the Wambooli Animations page for more animation links.)

- Generally speaking, the Kodak site on the Web is really a fun place to visit. If you have the time, venture off to the following Web page:

  `http://www.kodak.com`

  The Kodak page contains lots of graphics, plus information about imaging technology, if that's something you yearn to know more about.

Copying Text Right There Off the Screen

Your Web browser is a Windows application. And just like a lot of other Windows applications, you can freely copy text from it and paste that text into any other Windows application that permits pasting such things.

▶ Return to The Cask of Amontillado page

Use your browser's Recently Visited ist. In Netscape, choose Go→*Edgar Allan Poe - The Cask of Amontillado* from the menu. Or refer to the instructions at the start of this chapter.

▶ Click the mouse on the Find gizmo

The Find dialog box appears.

▶ Type the following into the box:

```
As I said these words
```

Check your typing. What you see on your screen should look something like Figure 8-2.

▶ Click the Find Next button

Netscape locates that text and highlights it on the screen.

Figure 8-2. Locate text with the Find dialog box.

- You may need to move the Find dialog box around to see it: Point your mouse at the top part of the Find dialog box (the title bar) and drag it around.
- Oh, heck, just close the Find dialog box: Click the Cancel button since you're done with it. The text you found is still highlighted on the screen.
- If the text isn't found, Netscape displays a "Search string not found" error message. Oy. Click the OK button, check your typing, and try again.

▶ Select all the text in the paragraph

Just as you would in your word processor, *drag* your mouse over the paragraph. Start with the first word, As, and end with the last word, niche. You'll see the text become highlighted or color-reversed on the screen. That means it has been selected and is ready for copying.

SELECT TEXT ON A WEB PAGE JUST AS YOU WOULD IN YOUR WORD PROCESSOR.

▶ Choose the Edit→Copy command from the menu

There is no visual feedback, yet the text you selected has just been copied to Windows' clipboard.

You can now use the Edit→Paste (or Ctrl+V) command in any other text-friendly application to paste that selected text. For example, if you were writing a report and needed to quote that passage, you could switch to your word processor and paste the text right smack dab into it.

- Any text you see in your browser can be selected and copied. Select the text using the mouse: drag over the text to highlight it. Then choose the Edit→Copy command.
- The keyboard shortcut for the Copy command is Ctrl+C.
- The keyboard shortcut for the Find command is Ctrl+F.

TIP: You can switch between programs in Windows by pressing the Alt+Tab key combination: Press the Alt key and keep it pressed, then tap the Tab key. Keep tapping the Tab key until you see the program you want to paste your text into, then release the Alt key.

- Yeah, I know that's really a Windows tip. Forgive me.
- You cannot use this technique to copy and paste graphics. In your browser, you actually have to save a graphical image to disk as opposed to copying it as you would text. This technique is covered later in this chapter, in the section "Taking a Web Picture."

The Joys of Saving a Web Page to Disk

Why the heck would anyone want to save a Web page to disk?

The best reason to save a Web page is to read it later. For example, I have a favorite Web page just chock full of interesting movie trivia—about 480 kilobytes worth. I could read it for hours online, but why pay the extra connect charges? Instead, I saved the Web page to disk. That way I can read it any time I'm using the computer, without being connected to the Internet.

Instead of wasting precious disk drive space on movie trivia, consider saving the small Wambooli home page to disk:

```
http://www.wambooli.com
```

Here are the steps you'd take.

▶ Choose the File→Save As menu command

The Save As dialog box appears before you (see Figure 8-3).

▶ Optionally enter the name of the file in the Save As dialog box

You can type in your own name for the Web page, but I recommend keeping the name Netscape provides. Definitely don't change the file's extension (the last three letters after the period in the filename). If you change the extension, Windows won't automatically recognize what type of file you just saved.

- Making up your own name for the file may be necessary when Netscape suggests something less-than memorable. For example, a Web page with information about Dracula may be named `VLADTEPP.HTM`. Renaming it to `DRACULA.HTM` will help you remember it later.

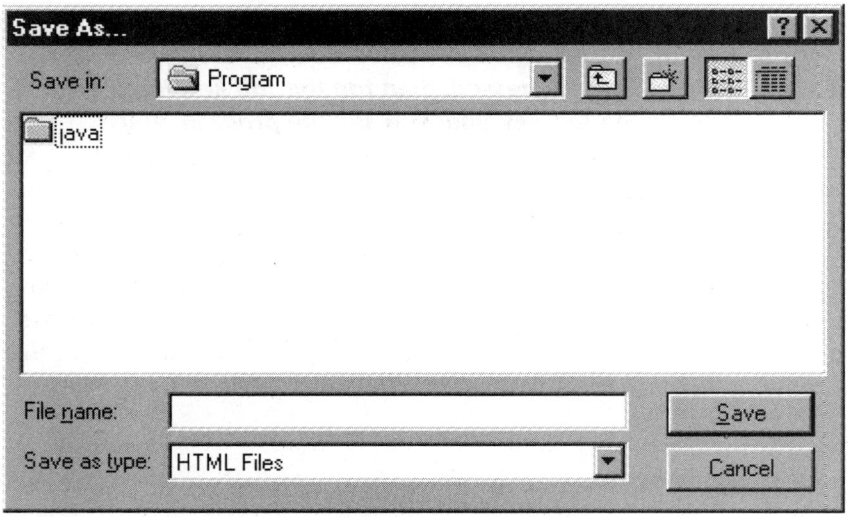

Figure 8-3. *Saving a Web page in Netscape.*

- You can flex your Windows Save As dialog box skills here to save the file to any directory or folder on your hard drive. For now, however, I would suggest saving the file in the directory or folder Netscape suggests. This makes it easier to find the file later.

► Click the Save button to save the Web page to disk

The page is saved as a file.

- As with printing, make sure the Web page you want to save has fully loaded before you save it to disk. Check your browser's little Busy thing. Only when it's standing still should you go ahead and save the Web page. If you save before then, you won't have the full text of the Web page saved to disk.

TIP: Here's a time-saving tip: All the links mentioned in this book are listed on their own Wambooli page. Here's the address:

```
http://www.wambooli.com/wamlinks.htm
```

Bookmark that page and use it to help you quickly link into the various Web pages mentioned in this and other Wambooli chapters.

FYI: The U.S. Congress employs elevator operators even though all its elevators are automated.

Now that the Web page is on disk, what can I do with it?

A Web page on your disk works the same as a Web page stored somewhere out there on the Internet. To see what the Web page looks like, you open it up using your browser. You can do this whether or not you're connected to the Internet. (After all, you don't need to be connected to the Internet just to see a Web page on your own computer.)

In Netscape you can see any Web page you've saved to disk by using the Open command.

▶ Choose the File→Open File command from the menu

Use the Open dialog box to find and open the Web page you saved to disk. (This part is boring standard Windows stuff.)

▶ Look at the Web page on your screen

Unless it's an all-text Web page, you'll notice that it looks rather odd, like a house without windows. That's because all the graphics are missing.

Quick! Someone's robbed the Louvre!

Netscape doesn't save the graphics when you save a Web page. Most of the time this is okay, since what you really need is the text on a Web page. So don't let it shock or embarrass you.

- For information on saving graphics to disk, see the section "Taking a Web Picture" later in this chapter.
- The Web page you saved to disk also contains links. Watch out: They work! If you click on a link—even on a saved Web page—Netscape attempts to contact that Web site. If you're not presently connected to the Internet, Netscape will try to dial into the Internet and connect to that link for you.
- To see a Web page you saved to disk, use the File→Open File command, not the File→Open command—which opens a Web page address and not a file on disk.
- In Netscape Navigator Gold, the menu command is File→Open File in Browser.
- For file clerks, the command is File→Open File in Drawer.

- You can also use the Ctrl+O keyboard combination to open a Web page you've saved to disk.
- Don't bother with the Open gizmo for opening a file on disk. That gizmo (button) is not the same command as the File→Open File (or Ctrl+O) command.
- If you've saved the Web page elsewhere on your hard drive, use the gizmos in the Open dialog box to go out and hunt for your file.
- If you're having trouble finding your Web pages on disk, look in the NETSCAPE directory. In Windows 95, look in the PROGRAM FILES\NETSCAPE\NAVIGATOR \PROGRAM folder
- If you're having trouble with Windows 95, buy *Real Life Windows 95* which, coincidentally, was written by the same author as this book.
- By the way, that movie trivia Web page is:

  `http://www.cis.ohio-state.edu/hypertext/faq/`
  `usenet/movies/trivia-faq/faq.html`

Opening a Web page you find randomly stuck out there on the disk

Suppose you're using the Explorer or the File Manager to look at the files on your hard drive and, lo, you come across a Web page you saved to disk. You can double-click on that file to open it and see what it contains.

wambooli.htm

- In Windows, double-clicking on a Web page icon starts your browser and loads that Web page document for viewing.
- Netscape may also attempt to connect to your Internet provider if you're not already online. Cancel that operation if you don't want to connect to the Net: Close your dialer's window or the Connect dialog box. (See Chapter 3 for more information on connecting to the Internet.)
- Web page documents you save to disk are mere text documents—nothing fancy. You can view them using a text editor or word processor, but they look rather homely that way.

TIP: Generally speaking, it's a bad idea to randomly double-click on icons to see what happens. Only try opening an icon if you know which program created it. This is more of a Windows tip than a Web Wambooli tip, but it's still good advice.

Taking a Web Picture

Copying graphics from a Web page isn't as cinchy as copying text. Even so, just as with text, you can copy any graphics the Web sends you and displays on your screen. Just like taking a picture, you merely need to point and click.

Yanking an image right off a Web page

Visit The Original (and unofficial) Elvis Home Page.

► **Direct your Web browser to the following address:**

```
http://sunsite.unc.edu/elvis/elvishom.html
```

This is but one of many houses of Elvis worship.

► **Locate the picture of the younger, cuter Elvis**

The image should be located in the upper right corner of the Web page.

► **Point your mouse at that picture**

The mouse pointer changes into a little pointing hand. Lo, you've just discovered a link. But don't click it! Instead:

► **Click the mouse's right button (not the left button you normally click)**

A pop-up menu appears, similar to the one you'll see in Figure 8-4.

- If you want to steal a picture from the Web, use your mouse's *right* mouse button to click.
- The right mouse button is the one you don't normally click all the time.
- This right-clicking jazz is really popular in Windows 95.

► **Using your left (normal) mouse button, choose Save this Image as from the pop-up menu**

A Save As dialog box appears (see Figure 8-5).

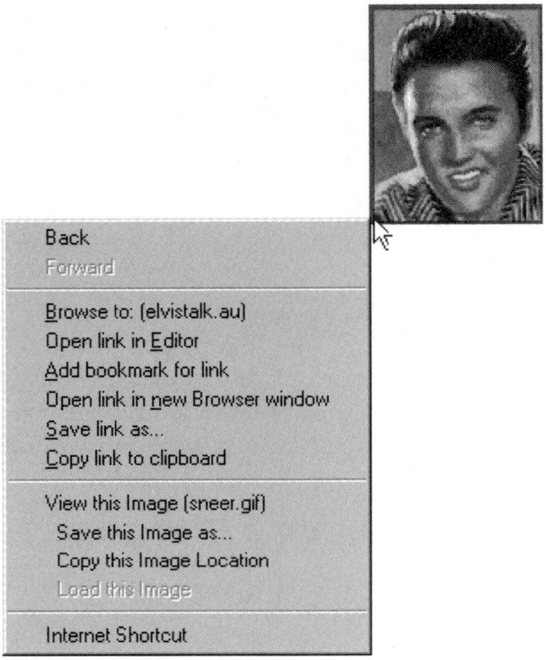

Figure 8-4. *The handy, pop-up menu.*

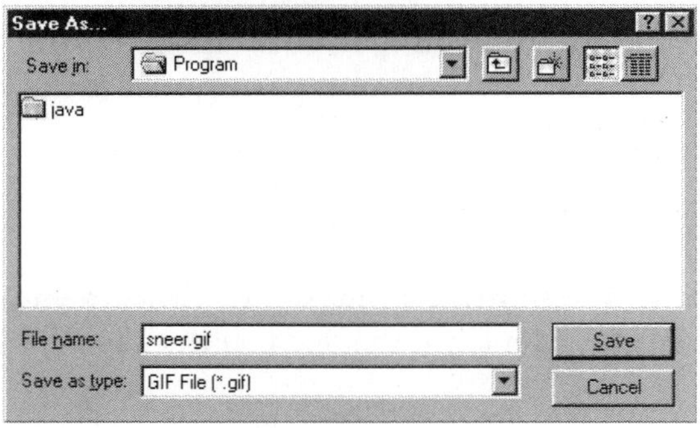

Figure 8-5. *Elvis is about to leave the Web page.*

- Notice how the Save As dialog box already contains the name of the graphic you want to save. For Elvis, that's `SNEER.GIF`.
- You can enter another name if you like, and you can use the dialog box's controls to save the file anywhere on your PC; refer to your favorite book on Windows for more information.

▶ **Click the OK or Save button**

The image is saved to your hard drive. The graphic file is ready for use by any graphics program on your computer.

- The button is labeled OK in some versions of Netscape; it's labeled Save in others.
- The techniques described in this section work only with Netscape (and the Microsoft Internet Explorer). You cannot lift pictures by using other browsers, at least not at the time this book went to press.
- Use Yahoo to find more of Elvis on the Web. See Chapter 7.

FYI: Elvis is one of those few performers to be glorified by his first name only.

Viewing the graphic images

Saving the image to disk is easy. But to look at the image later, you'll need a graphics program. Fortunately, you already have a pretty powerful graphical viewer right inside your computer. It's called Netscape (or your other Web browser).

> **YES, YOU CAN USE YOUR WEB BROWSER TO VIEW GRAPHICAL IMAGES.**

To open a graphic image you've saved to disk, such as the Elvis `SNEER.GIF` graphic you saved in the previous section, follow these steps:

▶ **Choose the File→Open File command from the menu**

The Open dialog box appears.

▶ Locate the Files of type drop-down list

- The Files of type drop-down list can be found at the bottom of the Open dialog box. This is a standard Windows thing.
- It might say List Files of type, depending on your version of Windows.

▶ Choose All Files from the Files of type drop-down list

This allows you to see every file saved on disk, including any graphics files (see Figure 8-6).

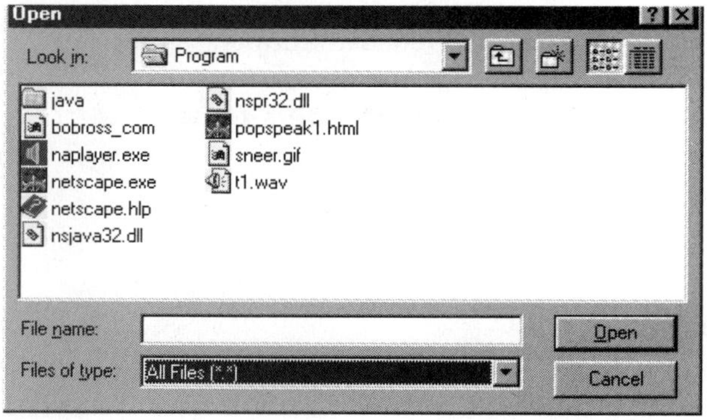

Figure 8-6. *The Open dialog box with everything properly set.*

▶ Locate the picture file you want to open

For this example, locate the `SNEER.GIF` file, which was saved to disk in the previous section.

- You should see a file named `SNEER.GIF` somewhere in the list. If not, use the scroll bar to find the file.
- With some versions of Windows, you may only see the filename as SNEER. If so, then that's your boy!

▶ Double-click on the `SNEER.GIF` file to open it

Point your mouse at the filename in the Open dialog box and double-click. The image appears in Netscape's browser window.

- This may seem like a rather convoluted way to see the images you save to disk, but it works.
- The keyboard shortcut for the File→Open File menu command is Ctrl+O—the same as when opening a Web page you've saved to disk (see "The Joys of Saving a Web Page to Disk" earlier in this chapter).

- In Netscape Navigator Gold, the menu command for opening a file on disk is File→Open File in Browser.
- If you have some graphics programs, you can load the images you stole from the Web into them just as you would load any other image on your hard drive.
- Some Internet kits come with graphical file viewers you can use to see the graphics you borrow from the Web.
- Graphical images on the Web are stored in the JPEG and GIF graphical file formats. This will only mean something to you if you're into graphics.
- Windows' graphics program, Painter (or whatever the heck it's called), does not understand the JPEG and GIF graphics on the Web. You cannot use that program to view or edit the graphical images.

A Final Few Words About "Fair Use"

While it is entirely possible for you to print, save or copy from any Web page you may view in your browser, it is not entirely true that those things you take are yours.

There is a legal something called "fair use" with regard to copyrighted material. Basically, it says that you can use some copyrighted items for your own personal use. For example, just as you can clip an image of a politician from a magazine and use it as your own dartboard, you can do the same with an image on the Web.

Generally speaking, you cannot take anything that's copyrighted and claim it as your own. This is especially true if you take something from a Web page and use it to make money—for example, copying a picture of a rock group from a Web page and then printing out copies you intend to sell at an upcoming concert. That's a definite no-no. Otherwise, use your own best judgment when you borrow anything from a Web page.

- My policy is to give credit where credit is due. If I borrow an image or text from another Web page, I will credit that Web page on my own.

- Some Web pages specifically warn you against using anything. Other Web pages may claim that the text and images are there for the taking. It's always best to ask if you're unsure.
- Oh, and you could consult with a lawyer about it, but they usually say "no" to everything.

FYI: When no one is looking, 40 percent of men—and, yes, 22 percent of you women—will drink milk straight from the carton.

Having Fun mit Sound

9

Shhh! Listen. Can you hear it? Can you hear the Web? No, it's not your modem. It's not the mouse clicking or the keyboard clacking. It's noise. Sound. Music. It's that fun part of the Web—more interesting to some than fancy graphics and animation. It's audio to go with the Web's video.

The Web can be a noisy place. There are sounds you can hear on the Web, sounds that come from the Internet, through the phone lines, into your computer and out of your PC's speaker. This chapter covers the concept in the following sections:

- Hearing sound on the Web
- Playing an AU type of sound
- Playing a WAV sound
- Saving an AU sound file to disk.

The Obligatory Reminder About Computer Sound

You cannot hear sound over the Web unless your PC is equipped with a sound card. No sound card, no sounds.

- Most PCs sold in the past three years come with sound equipment. They can play the sounds, no problem.
- If you have a multimedia PC, you can hear the sounds.
- Your PC doesn't need external speakers for you to hear the sounds. Some of the newer models play the sounds over the computer's internal speakers.
- There is no way to turn your PC's sound card off. If you have a PC sound card, it will work. And if you *don't* want to hear the sounds, don't click on any sound links on any sound Web pages.

You Can Hear It, Really Hear It

The Web has pages and pages of sounds. Most of them are from traditional, computer-nerd sources: The Simpsons, Monty Python, Star Trek, etc. And while it may seem trite to some, it's really rather impressive to have Arnold Schwarzenegger belt out, "I'll be back," every time you turn off your PC. Anyhoo...

Play me a sound

There are many Web pages with sounds on them, but they tend to come and go quite frequently. One page I know is there all the time is the Wambooli Sounds page.

► Type in the following Web page address

`http://www.wambooli.com/sounds.htm`

The Wambooli Sounds page is merely a Web page with a few sample sounds you can play on your PC. Dutifully type in the above address, and soon you'll visit a Web page that looks something like Figure 9-1.

- Some of the sounds on the Wambooli Sounds page may not play on your computer. That's because you must *train* Netscape to understand them. See the section "Attempting to Play a WAV Sound the First Time (Dealing with Unknown Types of Files)" later in this chapter.

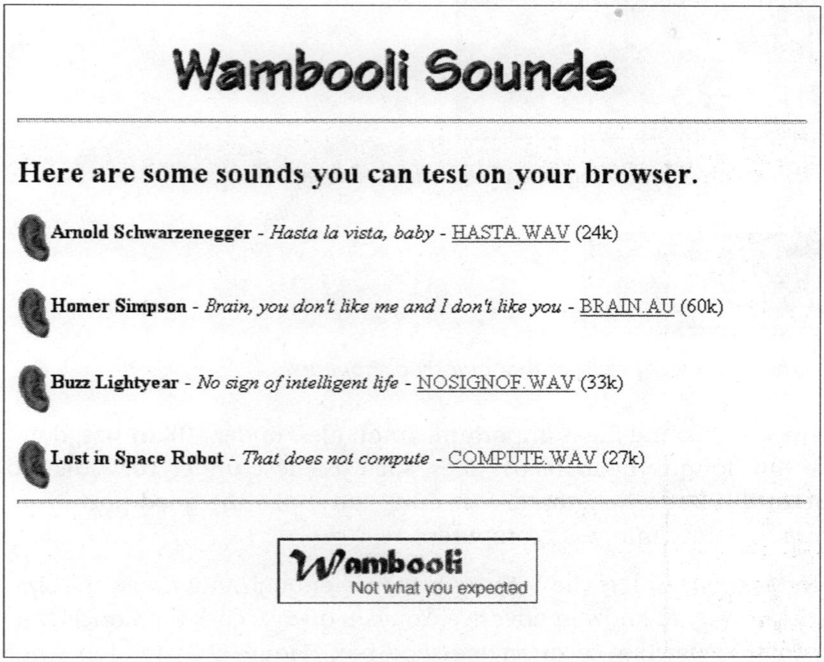

Figure 9-1. *Some Wambooli sound files.*

▶ Click on the Homer Simpson link, `BRAIN.AU`

Netscape displays a Viewing Location message box (see Figure 9-2). This tells you that a file is being transferred from the Wambooli computer into your computer.

▶ The sound file plays

After only moments, the sound file plays. Something looking like Figure 9-3 appears, and Homer Simpson begins speaking to his very own brain. Then the something looking like Figure 9-3 quickly disappears. (It was the NA Player program, which is covered near the end of this chapter.)

- Most sounds you can grab on the Web will be organized much like the smattering found on the Wambooli Sounds page. There is typically a title for the sound, maybe a description or quote, then a filename and—if you're lucky—the size of the file.

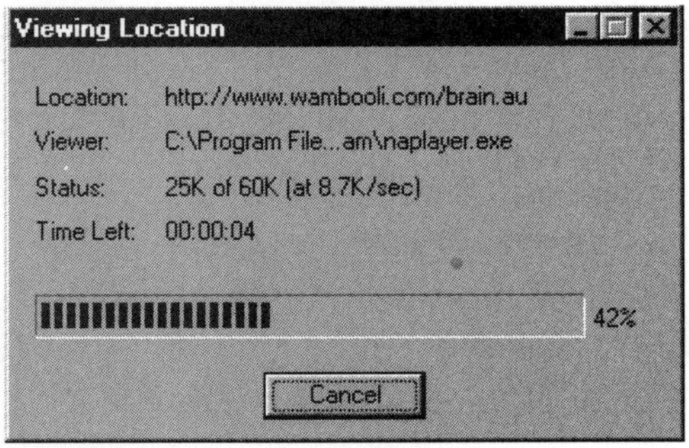

Figure 9-2. *Netscape is preparing a sound file for "viewing."*

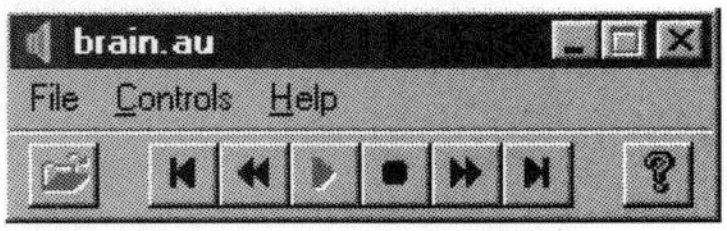

Figure 9-3. *The NA Player program that quickly disappears.*

- The size of a sound file is important. Small files, under 50K in size, don't take that long to hear. Teensy files, such as those under 10K, take no time at all. But a behemoth over 500K may take the good part of an hour to capture into your computer.
- Unfortunately, unless the Web page is nice enough to tell you the size, there's no way to know in advance. You can always click the Cancel button in the Viewing Location message box (Figure 9-2) to stop what might be a long file transfer.
- The AU sound type is used primarily by UNIX computers. It should really be AW because the sound quality is truly AWful.
- When you play longer sounds, the NA Player program won't disappear so quickly, and you can use its controls to stop, start and replay the sound if you like.
- To save the sound to disk, you'll need to refer to the section "How to Save an AU Sound File to Disk" later in this chapter. Presently, and without being told otherwise, the NA Player program merely plays a sound and then goes away.
- Gads, there are lots of sounds on the Web.
- The Wambooli Sounds page is not unique, and is rather limited in its sound assortment. There are some additional sound-page links at the bottom of the Wambooli Sounds page. And if you're interested in hearing

more sounds on the Web, use Yahoo or WebCrawler to locate lots of soundy Web pages. See Chapter 7 for more information.

- The Original (unofficial) Elvis Home Page (covered in Chapter 8) has some sounds on it. Revisit that page and click on Elvis' head to hear "Elvis" speak.

One more time!

You can hear any sound more quickly the second time you click it. Consider this a bonus.

Return to the Wambooli Sounds page if you've ventured off.

▶ Click on the `BRAIN.AU` link again
Since the sound information has already been sent to your computer, clicking on the same sound link a second time results in almost instant playback. Try it a few more times.

Attempting to Play a WAV Sound the First Time (Dealing with Unknown Types of Files)

Some sound files exist that your browser may not know about. The AU type of sounds, it understands. But the WAV type of sounds (which are used in Windows), your browser may gag at.

If you've wandered off, please return to the Wambooli Sounds page as described in the previous section.

▶ Click on the `HASTA.WAV` link
This is Arnold Schwarzenegger saying "Hasta la vista, baby" in the movie *Terminator 2*—a popular sound file. Unfortunately, when you click on this link, Netscape might display a "Huh?" dialog box, similar to the one shown in Figure 9-4.

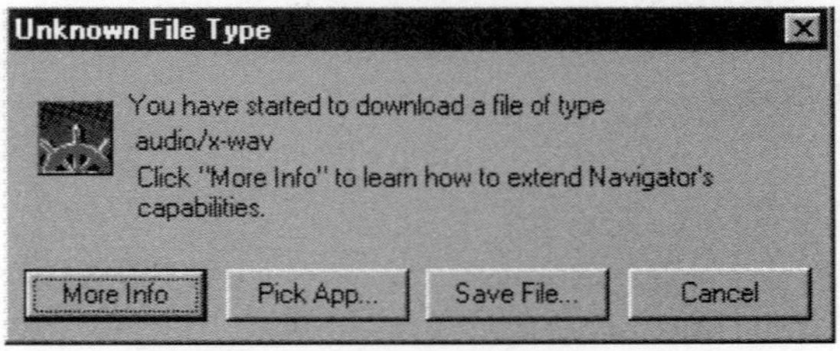

Figure 9-4. *Netscape is at a loss as to what's next.*

- On the other hand, Netscape may recognize the WAV type of sound file. If so, skim up and keep reading at the paragraph "Moving right along" on page 147.
- Netscape doesn't come out of the box recognizing WAV files, so it displays the Unknown File Type dialog box as shown in Figure 9-4. It's now up to you to find an application to play the file.
- If you're not familiar with where Windows stores files on disk, you might want to save this task for someone who does.

▶ Click on the Pick App button in the Unknown File Type dialog box

Netscape displays the Configure External Viewer dialog box. You now need to find the Sound Recorder program in Windows.

▶ Click on the Browse button

Find the Sound Recorder program, using the various tools in the Open or Browse dialog box. Here are some hints:

- The file can be found in your Windows directory or folder.
- For Windows 3.11 (and earlier), locate the file named `SOUNDREC.EXE`.
- If you have Windows 95, locate the file named `SNDREC32.EXE`.

▶ When you find the proper sound-playing program, double-click on it to choose it

The Open dialog box goes away and you're returned to the Configure External Viewer dialog box.

▶ Click OK.

You've selected a viewer for the program and now Netscape can continue.

IF THIS IS BOGGLING YOUR MIND, IT'S TIME TO HAVE SOMEONE ELSE SET IT UP.

WATCH OUT FOR THIS COMMON BOO-BOO

If you see a dialog box that says "Warning: There is a possible security hazard here," click the Cancel button. Then click the Cancel button in the Save As dialog box (if it appears). You probably made a typo when entering the name of the sound-playing program. Start over again by clicking the WAV file in the browser window.

Moving right along…

After the sound file is sent to your computer, a special player program (the Sound Recorder) appears (see Figure 9-5). Unlike the AU type of sound, the WAV sounds don't play right away. You have to click the Play button first.

Figure 9-5. *The Sound Recorder program.*

▶ Click on the Sound Recorder's play button

Click on the right-pointing arrow—the "play" button—to hear the sound.

- Play it again and again!
- To save the WAV file to disk, choose File→Save As from the Sound Recorder's menu.
- Unlike the NA Player program, the Sound Recorder window does not close when the sound is done playing. Choose File→Exit from the menu to close the Sound Recorder.
- Fortunately, since you've just gone through this exercise, Netscape now remembers what a WAV file is and what to do with it. The next time one is encountered, Netscape will go ahead and play the file for you automatically—even without asking.

WATCH OUT FOR OTHER "UNRECOGNIZED" FILES

Whenever Netscape doesn't recognize a type of file, it will ask you about it using the Unknown File Type dialog box (Figure 9-4). In most cases, you'll be at a loss as to what application it wants. In those cases, click on the Save File button. Netscape will let you save the file to disk for later manipulation, or until a time comes that you can ask someone else about which type of file it is and how to get at the information within it.

Only pick a viewer for the file—such as the Sound Recorder for WAV files—if you honestly know what type of file it is Netscape is sending.

How to Save an AU Sound File to Disk

Netscape tends to play AU sound files quickly, without giving you an opportunity to save them to disk. Heck, even if the sound does play for a while, you'll notice that the NA Player program lacks any menu commands for saving the file to disk. Oh, well.

ONLY FOLLOW THESE STEPS IF YOU WANT TO SAVE AU SOUND FILES TO DISK.

There is a way to always save an AU sound file directly to disk. Just follow these steps:

▶ **In Netscape, choose Options→General Preferences from the menu.**
The Preferences dialog box appears.

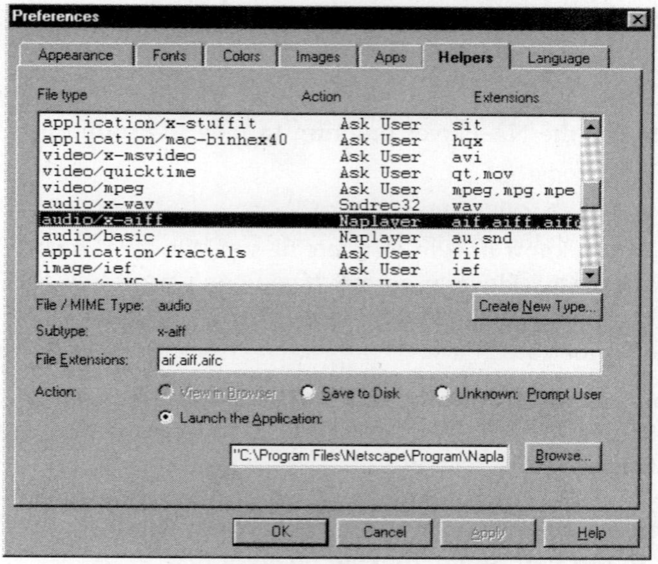

Figure 9-6. *The Preferences dialog box in Netscape.*

▶ **Click on the Helpers tab**

The Helpers part of the dialog box is shown in Figure 9-6.

- The Helpers dialog box lists a bunch of different Web file types that may be out there, and tells Netscape how to deal with them.
- There are three options for each file type encountered: View the program (or play the sound file), Save the file to disk, or choose whether to view or save.

▶ **Scroll down the list in the center of the dialog box until you see the following item:**

```
Audio/x-aifff
```

This is the AU type of sound file. Normally Netscape would just play the file, which is what it says on the screen. Your purpose here, however, is to change that.

▶ **Click the mouse on Audio/x-aifff to select it**

▶ **In the Action area of the dialog box, click on the radio button by Save to Disk**

▶ **Click OK**

You've now told Netscape to save the file to disk. Whenever you click on an AU sound link, you'll see a Save As dialog box. The file can then be saved to disk and played back whenever you want.

- You'll still need to use the NA Player program to play the sound files you've saved to disk.
- Windows may not recognize that the NA Player program is used to play AU types of files. If you know how to *associate* files in Windows, associate the AU files with the NA Player program. If you don't know how this is done, and are completely befuddled by these instructions, then bribe someone else to do it for you.
- Future versions of Netscape may come with an NA Player program that will, by default, let you save the AU files to disk. If so, then just ignore everything you learned in this section.

FYI: Twenty years after Jack Norworth wrote* Take Me Out to the Ball Game, *he saw his very first baseball game.

10 Strange Things on the Web

Be thankful you're using the World Wide Web today and not in the dark early days. Back then (say, 1991), everything was text. Your browser was text and all the Web pages were all text. It was very much like DOS, with people confused and complaining and innocent folks on sidewalks getting hit by computers tossed out windows several stories up.

A great improvement happened when graphics started showing up on the Web. Then came fancy text and colors and, thanks to Windows, all that stuff is available right there on your PC's screen. But are graphics and fun text enough? No way!

To make the Web even more interesting, Those Who Do Such Things have come up with even more Web Wambooli fun. These items, which you'll see (or have seen) on Web pages, have names such as forms, frames, animation and Java. All that madness has come to roost on the Web. This chapter tells

you what's what and whether or not it's important. Here's what you'll find on the next few pages:

- **Searching with forms**
- **Taking a quiz with forms**
- **Dealing with frames on a Web page**
- **Seeing animation on the Web**
- **The whole Java deal.**

Dealing With "Forms"

Anyone who has used Windows for more than a day will be familiar with the Web concept of *forms*. Basically, they're dialog-box stuff: Items to check, things to click on, text boxes to type stuff in—that kind of stuff. On the Web, forms are the same sort of thing.

- If you've ever searched for anything in Yahoo or any of the other Web catalogs, then you've used a form: The text box you typed your search word into was part of a form, as was the Search button you clicked to start the search.
- See Chapter 7 for more information on Yahoo and searching for stuff on the Web.

Using the Internet Movie Database search form

If you're a film buff, one of the most useful places on the Web is the Internet Movie Database. It's a completely volunteer effort to catalog and cross-reference information about actors, actresses, directors, films, studios and all sorts of wonderful, mind-absorbing, time-wasting trivia about movies.

► **Visit the Internet Movie Database search-form page**

`http://rte66.com/Movies/search.html`

Type the above Web page address into your browser. Press the Enter key to see that page appear on your screen.

- This isn't the main page for the Internet Movie Database; it's merely the searching page, which uses forms.
- On the Web, the Internet Movie Database is abbreviated IMDb. Don't think that's a new Wambooli term; it's just an abbreviation.
- The main page address for the Internet Movie Database is:

`http://www.msstate.edu/Movies/welcome.html`

Visit it later.

Down a bit on the Web page you'll see the search form, which is also shown in Figure 10-1. You work the various knobs and controls there to search for something in the database.

Say you want to look up Clark Gable.

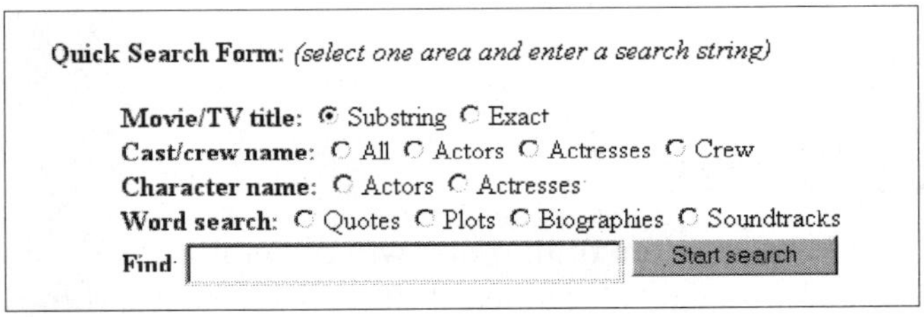

Figure 10-1. *The Internet Movie Database search form.*

► Click in the radio button by Cast/crew name: Actors

This tells the database that you're looking for actors; all other search topics are ignored.

► Type `Clark Gable` into the text box

Click your mouse in the text box and type in Clark Gable's name.

► Click your mouse on the Start search button

- You may see the Security Information dialog box displayed. If so, click the Continue button.
- Refer to Chapter 11 for more information on the Security Information dialog box.

After a few Wambooli moments, a Web page appears with the search results. It will say:

```
Actor

1. Clark Gable
```

The Internet Movie Database displays its findings. You might have expected it to display information about Clark Gable. But no, it displays what it found in the database. For example, you could have just typed in "Gable," in which case every actor who has "Gable" in his name would have been displayed.

- Click on the Clark Gable link to see information about him, the films he's done, any biographical information plus any related Web sites or images.
- You can search for movies by their titles. Type in all or part of a title in the main search form, click on the Substring search option, then click the Start search button. The Internet Movie Database displays a list of matches, one of which is probably the movie you're looking for.
- When the Internet Movie Database displays information about a film, one or more icons may appear. My favorite ones to click are Goofs, Trivia and Quotes.

- You'll notice the trendy thing now is for a movie to have its own Web page. Use the Internet Movie Database to search for an upcoming film, something you've seen in a preview. Odds are pretty good it will have its own Web page.
- More often than not, searching for something is the primary use for forms on the Web. (Remember forms, the subject of this section?)
- Other uses for forms are quizzes and games, which are covered in the next section.

FYI: "Look at those big, bat-like ears! Forget it, Lionel"—Irving Thalberg to Lionel Barrymore on seeing Clark Gable's first screen test.

A form to quiz you by

Don't be a browser! Use the Web to expand your mind! A lot of the forms you'll find out there are used to run quizzes and trivia challenges. Now you can prove to yourself what most high school students know: Quizzes are a source of angst that leads to rock and roll music, which could eventually lead to something really terrible, like dancing.

▶ **Visit the following Web page**

```
http://cnn.com/SEARCH/quiz/index.html
```

In a few seconds, the CNN daily news quiz appears.

▶ **Take the quiz, silly**

- The CNN daily news quiz is a multiple-guess quiz, where each question is followed by four choices or a true-and-false selection.
- The choices are made by clicking your mouse on the appropriate radio button.
- Read each question. Then click the mouse on the radio button you feel is the correct answer, then scroll down and answer another question.

OH, YEAH, LIKE I'M A MAVEN ON CURRENT EVENTS.

- You can always guess the right answer. There is no penalty or jail time here for not knowing who the King of Fredonia is.

▶ Click the Done button

When you're done, click the Done button near the bottom of the Web page.

- If you see a Security Information dialog box, click the Continue button.
- For more information on the Security Information dialog box, see Chapter 11.

▶ The next page shows you how well you did

After your form is submitted to CNN's big computer in Atlanta, where Jane Fonda and Ted Turner will personally laugh at your responses, you'll see a summary page describing how well you did.

- No. Seriously, Ted and Jane have better things to do than to read your responses.
- You'll probably fail the quiz unless you're a total news "dawg." My first time, I got only 25 percent right, and all those were guesses. The second time, after reading the newspaper, I got 80.
- Additional links on the results page will give you more information about the news stories—if you *really* want to know. Click on the `Answers to this quiz` link.
- And isn't knowledge what the Web is all about?
- If you like quizzes, visit the Wambooli Internetty Stuff Web page:

  `http://www.wambooli.com/internetty.htm`

Near the bottom of that page is a collection of Web sites that offer quizzes—a treasure-trove of forms to fondle!

FYI: The word quiz is one of the few made-up words in the English language.

Frames All Over the Place

Another funky Web thing you may see from time to time is *frames*. What the frames do are to split up the main browser window into two or more areas. In each area (or frame) you see something different: a menu, graphics, text and so on. It's like looking at several browser windows at once, but you're really still only seeing one Web page.

► **Visit the following Web page address:**

`http://www.wambooli.com/frames.htm`

This is the Wambooli Frames page (see Figure 10-2), a sample page I drew up because every other page that uses frames on the Web tends to do an Amelia Earhart.

***Figure 10-2.** The Wambooli Frames page looks something like this.*

- There are three frames shown on your screen and in Figure 10-2.
- You'll notice that each of the frames has a scroll bar so that you can see more information. Some frames may have a left-right scrollbar since the information in them is wide in addition to being long.

- Some folks go nuts with frames; some use them in a practical manner. Some people like frames; some people are violently opposed. I suppose the latter are just Web purists.
- Not every Web browser is capable of displaying frames on the screen. Netscape can do it, and the Microsoft Internet Explorer can. Other browsers show you the "You have a frame-challenged browser" message, leaving you to wonder what the thing really looks like.
- You can move the frames to adjust their position: Hover your mouse pointer over a frame's edge and then drag to make the frame wider or narrower, or longer or shorter.
- Another fun Web page that uses frames is the Peeping Tom Homepage—which is not what you think it is. Instead, it's a directory of all the Web "cameras" there are out there. These are various sites that contain live or almost-live images of various things around the world. Here was its address as this book went to press:

```
http://www.ts.umu.se/~spaceman/camera.html
```

This Web page may have moved by the time you read this. Check the Wambooli Updates page to find the new address if the above link yields a nasty 404 error; Web Page not found:

```
http://www.wambooli.com/updates.htm
```

Animation on the Web

Another way to wake up a dreary Web page is to sprinkle it with animations. These are graphic images that move or dance, and often amaze you the first time you see them.

Now, there are two schools of thought about animation. The first school says, "Yeah, junk up your Web page with animations and everyone will think it's really super." The other school says, "Hey, animation can get really annoying, especially when it's overused."

However you feel, I've created a silly little animation and stuck it on a Wambooli Web page for you to examine.

▶ **Try to visit the following Web page:**

```
http://www.wambooli.com/anime.htm
```

Go ahead and gawk. That's about all you do with animation on the Web.

- Please have patience when you get to any animated Web page. The graphics will take a few extra moments to load.
- There are additional links at the bottom of the page that will take you to more interesting and diverse animated places on the Web.
- Some of the links will explain more about how the animations work. I won't bore you with that information here.
- Don't confuse animation with Java. (See the very next section for information on what Java is.) Yes, Java can be used to make animations. Mostly, however, animation is done through special graphics programs.

Java and Other Weirdness

Java is the worst (or best) Web buzzword in computer history. It started a whole new, coffee-themed approach to naming new products and software. Java is so successful, it's reached the point where everyone talks about it, but only a handful of people really know what it means.

This book is not a Java book. Indeed, you really need a separate book to understand Java. Actually, you don't really need any book, since understanding Java has really nothing to do with using the Web. The following sections, however, will get you cocktail-party-conversation fluent with some Java concepts.

- If you know some tidbit about Java, casually mention it at the water cooler. People will think you're a genius.
- If you want more information on Java, use Yahoo to search that word on the Web. See Chapter 7.
- This book does not discuss any other coffee-themed products.
- Oh, what the heck: HotJava is the name of a Web browser produced by Sun Microsystems, the same company that produces Java. I mention this since a lot of people have heard about HotJava but don't know what it is.

FYI: Starbucks coffee is named after the character Starbuck in the novel* Moby Dick. *It is not the currency they used in Star Trek.

Java Q&A

Q: So what the heck is Java?
A: Java is a programming language.

Q: Oh. Is it one of those "anyone can learn it" types of programming languages?
A: No. But there is a version of Java called *JavaScript*, which is easy to learn.

Q: Are you doing to talk about JavaScript here?
A: No.

Q: So what is Java good for?
A: Java is used to write little programs called *applets*. These programs live on Web pages. You can run the applet programs when you visit the Web pages—providing your browser is Java-friendly.

Q: Is my browser Java-friendly?
A: If it's the latest version of Netscape, then yes.

Q: So what's the whole point?
A: The idea is intriguing to some in the computer industry. They envision a day when you won't really need any software on your computer other than a Web browser. You can then visit various Web pages on the Internet that contain the programs (Java applets) that you'll use instead of software on your computer.

Q: That sounds nuts.
A: Yeah, most of this stuff is.

Q: So what does Java do now?
A: Basically, it runs little programs that you can see on a Web page. Keep reading and I'll take you to a few Java-happy places.

Seeing Java in action

Do you remember the game of *Life*? It was a Milton Bradley game where you spun a big wheel and got to drive a little car through a textured game board. Remember getting a "spouse" and kids, and taking *revenge*? Well, forget all that. On a computer, the Game of Life refers to a biological simulation created by John Conway.

Oh, I don't know the details of the Game of Life. I do know that it was fun to experiment with. I must have wasted hours creating life forms on my old computer and watching them grow or die. So, out of a fond memory, I decided to use the Web to find the Game of Life to play on my new PC. And while I didn't find it, I did find a Java version of the Game of Life, which you can watch unfold on a Web page right on your PC's monitor.

▶ **Type in the following address:**

```
http://www.fusebox.com/cgi-bin/cb/lifelab.pl
```

▶ **Press the Enter key to visit that site**

You'll need to wait a while. As with animation, it takes a few moments for the Java program to wake up. When it does, your screen will come to life with a mini-version of the Game of Life. See the little dots move and multiply? That's life.

- If you want to read more information about how the computer Game of Life works, refer to the links at the bottom of the Web page.
- The game may appear jerky at times. That's just the speed of the Net, which is jerky all the time.
- Not every Web browser is capable of understanding Java. If your browser isn't, then you won't see anything dance or hear anything talk or any of that jazz. Boo-hoo. (This is why I wholly recommend Netscape as the high browser.)

FYI: In Saudi Arabia, a woman can divorce her husband if he doesn't give her coffee.

And What of Shockwave?

Shockwave is a Web add-on or "plug-in" that allows you to see movies on Web pages. It's currently one of the "hot" Web fads, though not everyone has Shockwave and only a few computers are properly configured to play the movies.

If you have the Shockwave add-on for your browser, you can visit some Shockwave Web pages and see the movies. Usually, you're given a choice whether or not you want to see the movie. For example, one link may connect with the Shockwave movie and another may offer you some tepid graphics as a substitute. Click on the proper link, depending on how your browser is set up.

Personally, I've had little luck with Shockwave. In addition to configuring my browser to understand it, I also had to set up my computer to run in a special 256-color mode. I have been unsuccessful in doing this, so my take on Shockwave isn't that grand. I'll keep you posted on the Wambooli home page for more information on Shockwave, especially if this fad turns into a trend.

11 Has This Ever Happened to You?

Nothing is perfect. If you use a computer on a regular basis, then you know this to be more than true. Even when faced with the possibility of eternal bliss, we must put up with harp music, for heaven's sake. The Web works (or doesn't work) the same way. There are moments of sheer delight and folly, dotted with episodes of frustration and terror. In a way, we're like babies on the Web. A baby can have so much fun and laugh so hard that he gets the hiccups. That's not fun.

Aside from waiting (and waiting and waiting) for things to appear on the screen, the Web—and the Internet in general—can toss up any of a number of frustrating diversions while you cruise the information superhighway. These aren't personal, so don't think the computer is out to get you. (Honestly, it's too stupid for that.) Instead, think of these minor annoyances as hiccups; they're just the computer's way of letting you know you've laughed a little bit too long.

This chapter covers several barely interesting topics:

- Things that can go weird with your modem
- Weird messages you may see in your browser
- Keeping information safe on the Web
- Seeing weird things instead of graphics.

O! Those Random Modem Things

Using a modem is like using a phone: You can get a busy signal, the other phone won't answer, you get the wrong number, everyone and anyone comes into the room and starts talking to you when you're using it, and so on.

The best thing that can happen with your modem is that the other computer answers and everything turns out fine. But there are those occasional moments when using a modem can be frustrating. Some prime examples follow, along with my advice on what to do.

Annoying modem whistling. Your modem may connect to your provider and then the modems get into an "argument." They whine and whistle and the darn things never fully agree. This could mean anything, but the solution is to cancel the call and try again. Most times this redial happens automatically—if you wait long enough.

Nothing. Sometimes your provider's modem will answer and then just sit there. Technically speaking, the provider's modem hasn't had enough time to reset since the last person called. Or the modem could have "tired blood." You'll have to try calling again later.

Everything goes okay, but still nothing happens. Even when the modems connect and everything seems to be going swimmingly, your provider's computer may be "down." In that case, the modem will answer fine, but there are no brains behind the modem to make anything else happen. You try again later.

The momentous connection and then nothing. Sometimes the connection to your Internet provider lasts about five seconds—enough to make you think everything is okay but not enough to let you do anything. Again, this is your Internet provider's computer going wacky. Try again later.

The provider becomes stony and stupid. Your Internet provider's computer relies on the phone company to send and receive information. Sometimes the phone lines will be down, in which case you and your Internet provider are all alone in the universe. This happens in the San Francisco Bay area a lot; all the Internet traffic in that area is routed through two main phone cables, one of which may go down and the other of which may be flooded with males of the species trying to log into the Playboy Web page. In these instances, you'll just need to try again much, much later.

Click! You're gone. Modems are fussy things. A number of strange occurrences—not excluding phases of the moon and voodoo—will cause your modem to drop the connection. Here are some thoughts on the matter:

- If you're using a phone that has an extension elsewhere in the house, someone can pick up the line and knock you off. My advice: Get a separate line for your modem.
- Sometimes the evil *line noise* can disconnect you. Line noise is simply pops and crackles that you wouldn't notice (or care about) on a normal phone call, but which agitate your modem to the point of getting it to hang up.
- Some Internet providers seem to randomly disconnect users after they've been on for more than three hours. I know some providers who do an "Are you there?" even after 10 minutes of inactivity. This can be annoying if you're reading a particularly long Web page.
- Whatever the reason you were disconnected, you'll want to call your Internet provider back and reconnect. If you click your browser's Reload gizmo, your computer will realize it's not connected to the Internet and your dialer program should reappear, allowing you to reconnect right then and there.

FYI: When said phonetically in Chinese, Coca-Cola translates as "Bite the wax tadpole."

Should You Phone Your Internet Provider When There Is Modem Trouble?

You know, when there's a problem with the telephone or the power, you call the phone or the electrical company. But when there's a problem with the modem and your Internet provider, who do you call?

The answer is "it depends." You can call the Internet provider and they should help you with any modem troubles, since that's part of the service and support you pay for every month. It also helps them when one of their modems is behaving oddly and they may not know it. (Tell them "the port is wedged"—they'll like that one.)

Overall, my advice is always to try dialing in a few times before you contact your Internet provider and tell them about your problem.

Strange Messages from Beyond

Like any other piece of computer software you own, a Web browser has a certain number of error messages and whatnot that occasionally wander across your screen. This doesn't mean you've done anything wrong. It doesn't necessarily mean anything is wrong with the software, your computer or the Net. No, it's more likely a combination of things. The following sections detail my favorite error messages along with occasional illustrations.

- One error message that isn't an error message deals with "security information." Refer to the section "Is the Stuff You Send Safe?" later in this chapter.

The horrid No DNS Server error

I hate the No DNS Server error message. Most of the time, it merely means you've mistyped a Web page address. This is very common. Some of those Web page addresses get long, long, long. A simple typo induces the error.

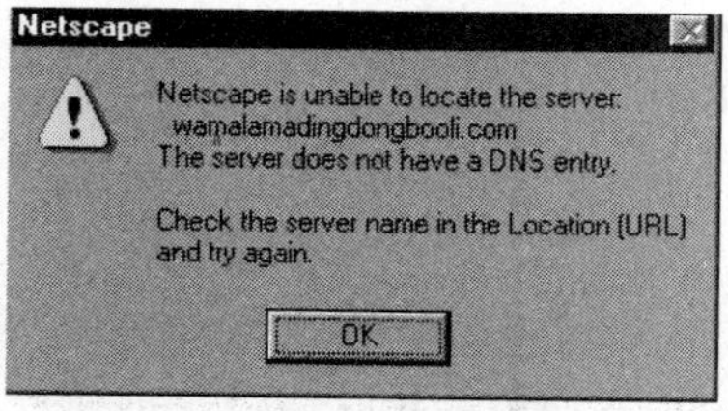

Figure 11-1. *The DNS Server error isn't as bad as it seems*

More frustrating is when you see the No DNS Server error message when you have clicked on a link or chosen one of your bookmarks. In that case, it means one of two things: The Web page is gone from the Web (which happens), or the Web page is busy. Chances are that the Web page is busy; just re-click on the link to solve the problem.

- DNS stands for Domain Name Server. It's a program on your Internet provider's computer that tells it where everything else on the Web lives.
- I'm of the school of thought that says computer error messages are the dumbest known things in the universe. If only someone could sit down and rewrite the things, maybe we wouldn't get so frustrated when we see them.

The No Response error

More ugly than the No DNS Server error message is the No Response variety (see Figure 11-2). Most of the time, this is what should be displayed instead of the frustrating No DNS Server message. However, I find the No Response error message typically means that someone (either you or the computer you're trying to contact) is not connected to the Internet. In that case, you just try again later.

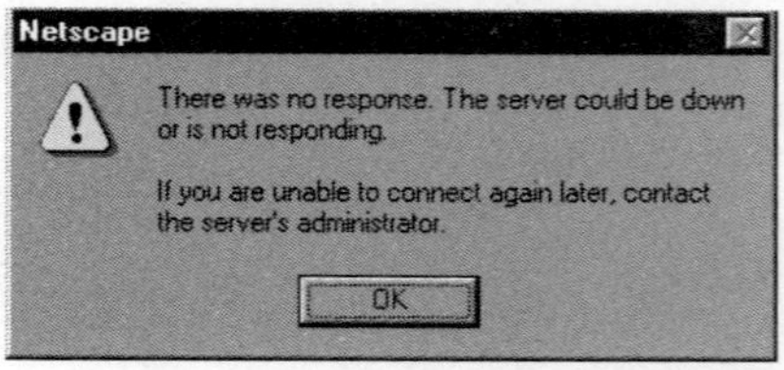

Figure 11-2. *No Response means "try again later."*

Varieties of "Not Found" error messages (and the dreaded 404 errors)

You would think one error message would be enough for a missing Web page. But, no. There are several. Here are some of the gems I've encountered:

```
Error 404; Not found-file doesn't exist or is read pro-
tected [even tried multi]
```

- Whatever. No reason to try this one again. The page isn't available. It's just not there any more. This is why the 404 error is dreaded.
- Well, you could check your typing.

```
404 Not Found; The requested URL /hurdle/myrtl.html
was not found on this server.
```

- Another 404 error, which leads you to believe in the frightening possibility of some 403-odd other errors you haven't yet seen!

```
File Not found; The requested URL /blah/blah/blah.html
was not found on this server.
```

- Don't know how this one is any different from the other two. It means the same thing, though: The URL (Web address) isn't there.

This last one is a doozie:

> **Not Found**
>
> `The request object does not exist on this server. The link you followed is either outdated, inaccurate, or the server has been instructed not to let you have it. Please inform the site administrator of the referring page.`

- A site administrator is someone who oversees Web pages on a computer.
- You can send e-mail to a site administrator by finding and clicking on a Webmaster link. Not every Web page has one of those, however.

Whoops! What the heck did I do?

One of the scariest dialog boxes Netscape displays is shown in Figure 11-3. This one shows up when you click on a link that tries to send you a file. What happened is that Netscape didn't know what to do with the file and asked you for help. So you typed in the name of a program to run, one that Netscape didn't recognize. In that case, you see the heavy-duty warning dialog box.

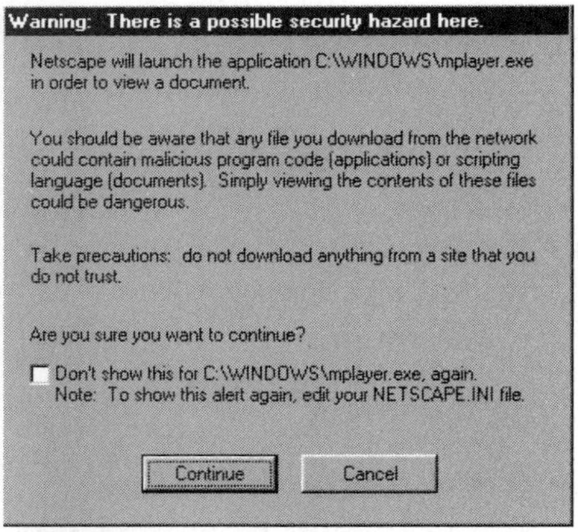

Figure 11-3. *Scary stuff about to happen message.*

What should you do? Click on the Cancel button. If you see a Save As dialog box, click Cancel to close that dialog box.

What-the-hell type of errors

There are some errors that will just plain drive you nuts. Here's one of my favorites:

```
Fatal Error; System call 'fopen' failed: Permission denied.
```

Or how about:

```
Forbidden! You do not have access to this server.
```

I thought the Web was for everybody! I guess not…

Password required

Some Web pages are password-protected. Before you can see anything on that page, you're asked to log in using a special User Name and Password (see Figure 11-4).

Figure 11-4. *Members-only allowed on the following Web page.*

If you're supposed to have access to the Web page, type in your special name and password and click the OK button. That lets you "in" to the Web page, where you can see whatever it is they're so hush-hush about.

- The name and password are different from the ones you use to connect to the Internet.

WHAT? NO FREE PORN ON THE WEB?

- Not every password-protected Web site uses the same dialog box. For example, the *Wall Street Journal* uses its own password dialog box to grant subscribers access. Even so, the same rule applies: you must have an account before you can get in.
- What types of Web pages require passwords? Anything that contains information for which there is a fee. Unless the password protection is on a very private Web page (such as one on a large company's server for employees only), then it's usually some type of Web page that people subscribe to.
- What's there to subscribe to? Why, pornography of course.
- Actually, there are a lot of questionable pictures on the Web. But if you want the (wink, wink) *good stuff*, you'll need to subscribe—as in, pay for access. This is the best way to ensure that you can see the stuff (since you know the password) but your kids cannot (since they don't know the password).

Is the Stuff You Send Safe?

Time and time again you may see a warning when you fill in a form on the Web. For example, you may be innocently searching for something on the WebCrawler, when you see a warning appear, similar to the one shown in Figure 11-5.

Without scaring the pee out of you, the message basically tells you that sneaky hacker types could, possibly (but probably not), read that information and somehow use it to an evil end. It probably won't happen, but it could.

- Most of the time, sending information on the Web is trivial. For example, you type in a gardening question on Ask Earl, the Yard Care Answer Guy's Web page. You click the Send button and you see the Security Information dialog box. Whoah! Someone may grab your "Do gardenias work well in clay?" question and use it to embezzle funds from your Christmas fund. Golly.

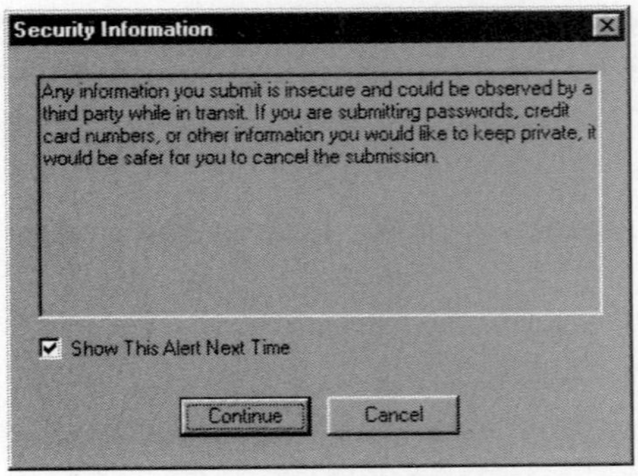

Figure 11-5. *Do you really want to tell this to the world?*

- A more realistic problem happens when some Web page asks for a credit card number. *Don't send it!* Only send information if you're told it's secure *and* you believe, trust and know the organization asking for it. That's a tall order, but not when you consider what could happen should someone get a hold of something important. After all, you don't mutter your bank card's PIN out loud when you use an ATM machine.
- Whenever you see the Security Information dialog box (or one similar to it), pause and think about what you're sending.

TIP: Always keep the Show This Alert Next Time box checked; you want Netscape to always remind you about the information you send on the Net.

- Refer to Chapter 10 for more information on forms.

The Secure Browser Business

With some browsers you can safely send important information. There's no need to worry that the French will steal your baked chicken recipe or that young Brandon down the street will find out about your tummy tuck. No, with a *secure* browser, you can send anything you like on the Internet and no snooping eye will ever know what it is.

Presently, only Netscape (version 1.2 or higher) and the Microsoft Internet Explorer (version 2.0 or higher) are true secure browsers. With those browsers you can send information out on the Net and know that it rests safe from enemy hands. Of course, this only happens under certain circumstances.

► **Next time you're using Netscape, locate the little broken key in the lower left corner of the window**

The broken key means that all information you send and receive is not secure. Computer geeks with the proper knowledge could snoop in on you. It's unlikely, but they could.

When you contact a secure site, however, you'll see a solid key. That means all the information sent and received is confidential; the computer encodes it so only you and the party you're sending it to can see it.

When you send information to a secure site, and you see the solid key in Netscape, a dialog box is displayed similar to the one shown in Figure 11-6. This is the flip side of the Insecure dialog box (Figure 11-5). It means you can send the information without worrying that *anyone* could get a hold of it, anyone other than the party you're sending to.

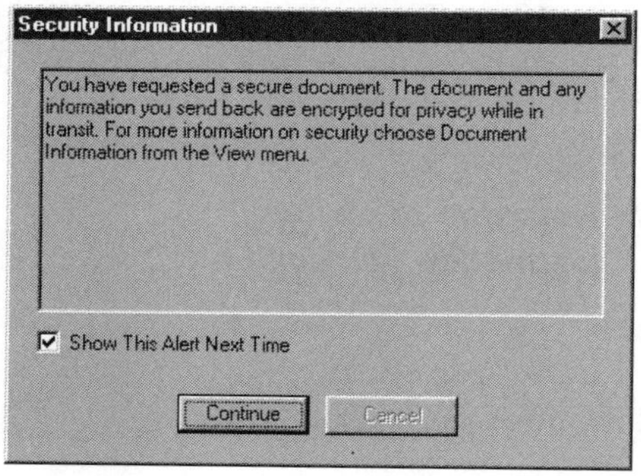

Figure 11-6. *The information is safe, and so is democracy.*

- In the future, security may not be such a touchy issue. Those Who Are In Charge are currently working on ways to make the Web secure all the time. Supposedly it will be okay in the future to send sensitive information without worrying about who's looking in on you. Even so, be wary of who you're sending information to.

TIP: Some information, such as your Social Security number, Driver's License number, and the numbers along the bottom of your checks, should never be given out.

- Secure browsers, such as the recent versions of Netscape, are technically called SSL-compliant. What this means and how it works, I have no idea. Sounds impressive, though.

FYI: Talk about security problems: Every day, U.S. Government computers authorize payment of over $5.5 million—without any human supervision.

Shattered Pictures

When a Web page isn't available, your browser displays an error message. When a picture isn't available, a cute little broken picture appears in its place (see Figure 11-7).

Figure 11-7. *Ooops! Picture missing (or just broken).*

A variation on the broken picture is the unbroken picture (see Figure 11-8). You'll typically see that one when you click the Stop button to halt a Web page from displaying.

Figure 11-8. *Ooops! Picture never got loaded.*

- A missing picture doesn't necessarily mean something is wrong. Most of the time, it means whatever computer is providing that picture isn't available. For example, the picture may actually be on a computer in Japan or somewhere else on the globe. If that foreign computer is down, the picture won't appear on the Web page.

- Oftentimes you can use the Reload button to try to grab the picture again. (Don't know why that works, but it does.)
- Different browsers show different graphics for missing pictures. Figures 11-7 and 11-8 are for Netscape.

FYI: "Reader, suppose you were an idiot. And suppose you were a member of Congress. But I repeat myself."—Mark Twain.

12 The Fine Art of W-W-Waiting

How fast is the Web? Even though you may have the fastest modem in the galaxy, the Web moves a lot slower. It's not you, your modem, your Internet provider, their modem or the phone company. It's just the incredible *volume* of information on the Web—just as too many cars on the freeway during rush hour drags everything to a halt.

Presently, the average speed of the Web is about 32 bytes per second. That's slow. It would take the Web longer to send you this sentence at 32 bytes per second than it would take you to read it aloud. And the stupid part is that the Web is getting slower.

This chapter covers a few of the things you can do to cope with the sluggish speed of the Web. Here are the major topics:

- **Gauging how fast the Net is**
- **Things to do while waiting for the Web**
- **Opening a second browser window in Netscape**
- **Viewing things text-only**
- **Information about off-line browsers.**

How Slow Is That?

The Web has a speedometer of sorts. It's located along the bottom of your Web browser. It shows up whenever the Web is sending you a chunk of information. For example, you might see something like this:

```
67% of 94K (at 836 bytes/sec)
```

What this means is that the Web is taking its own fair share of time getting the information to you. Those bytes, which should be squirting through the phone line like water through a fire hose, are merely dribbling into your PC. Unfortunately, there's very little you can do to speed up the process.

- You'll see that display whenever your computer is receiving a large Web page, and especially when viewing graphics.
- Sometimes the display flickers, changing values wildly. Nothing is wrong—Netscape is just keeping track of several graphics that are being sent at the same time.
- The sad part about the display is the *bytes per second* part. Your modem is capable of sending and receiving anywhere from 9,600 to 28,800 bytes per second. Yet a lot of the time, your browser may tell you you're getting only 32 bytes per second or even less. That's not the modem's fault; it's just part of the waiting aspect of the Web—the fourth W.
- Welcome to the Computer Age. Now sit back and wait.

What to Do While You're Waiting for Something to Happen

To make Web waiting more pleasurable, I recommend preparing something else to do while you're waiting. Here are my ideas:

- Turn on a small TV by the computer while you're browsing the Web. That way you can be mindlessly entertained while waiting for a Web page to appear. If the TV bugs you, just turn it off.
- Start up a game of computer Solitaire in another window and use the Alt+Tab key combination to switch back and forth. Web page still coming? Alt+Tab back for another round of old Sol.
- Read a magazine while you're waiting for a Web page to show up.
- Switch to another window and read your e-mail. (See Chapter 15.)

- Switch to another window and read some newsgroups. (See Chapter 22.)
- Shave. You may have to.

Opening a Second Browser Window in Netscape

Netscape has the ability to show you more than one Web browser window at a time. That way you can double-time it—or even triple-time it—on the Web, reading one Web page in one browser window while you're waiting for a second or third page to show up in another. Yes, it's called *multitasking* and it can really save time.

To start a second Web browser window in Netscape, follow these steps:

▶ Choose File→New Browser window from the menu

This throws up a new Netscape window on the screen, in which you'll see your home page. You'll get a new browser every time you press Ctrl+N. Figure 12-1 shows four browser windows all jammed onto the screen.

Figure 12-1. *Press Ctrl+N and see more Netscape browsers on your screen.*

- The new browser windows start all over again with your home page. But don't just sit there! Go ahead and visit somewhere else: Click on a link or type in a Web page address.

- You can use the second browser window just like the first one. Nothing has changed: you just have two windows onto the Web instead of one.
- The keyboard shortcut for starting a new browser window is Ctrl+N.
- You can open as many Web browser windows as your PC has the memory (or the guts) to handle.
- What you do in one browser window does not affect what happens in another.
- Text and graphics in one browser window will continue to appear even if you're looking at another browser window. This is how you can save time waiting: While a slow page is crawling up on the screen, press Ctrl+N and go visit someplace else that isn't so slow. Then return to the first browser window to check its progress every so often.
- To switch from one browser window to another, use the Alt+Tab key combination.
- In Windows 95, you can click on the various Netscape buttons on the taskbar (at the bottom of the screen) to switch from one browser window to another.
- When you're done with one of the browser windows, choose the File➜Close command, or press the Ctrl+W key combination. This closes that one browser window, and doesn't affect anything else you're doing.
- Do not accidentally choose the File➜Exit command, as this closes *all* Netscape windows on the screen.

Add Speed by Viewing Things Text-Only

A nifty way to speed up the Web is to dispense with all the superfluous graphical garbage. After all, pictures take time. And in most cases, you don't really need to see the pictures to get the information you want. Why not do away with them?

▶ Turn off the loading of images in your browser

In Netscape, choose Options➜Auto Load Images from the menu. This removes the check mark from that menu item and tells Netscape not to load any graphical images.

► **Now visit the following page:**

`http://www.primenet.com/~mwc/`

This is Alfred Hitchcock's home page on the Web, or at least a page devoted to him. Your screen should look something like Figure 12-2.

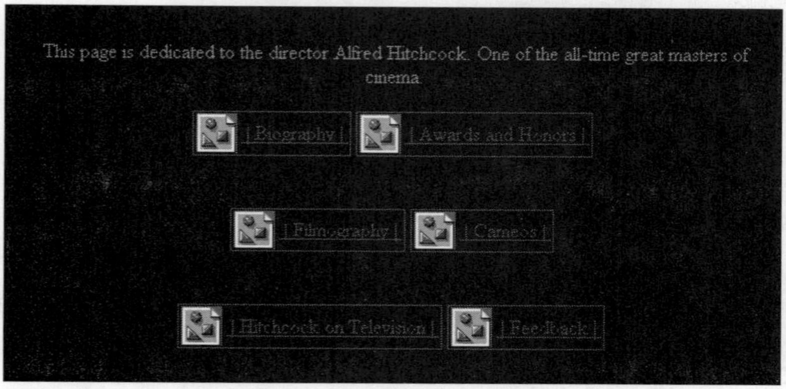

Figure 12-2. *A Web site without graphical images loaded.*

- Did you notice how quickly the page appeared? Graphics are what consume the most time when receiving a Web page. Without the graphics, the text loads in a snap.
- If you do see the graphics (and not the little "missing picture" icons), then you've probably been to the Hitchcock Web page before. Try visiting some other, new Web page to see how fast the Web page loads without the graphics.

► **Click on the Images gizmo**

The Images gizmo is located on your browser's button bar or gizmo area, right by the Reload button (typically). Clicking that gizmo tells your browser to load the graphics. This takes longer but you'll end up seeing a whole Web page, as in Figure 12-3.

Q: So this allows you to manually choose when you want to load graphics instead of it happening automatically?

A: Exactly.

Figure 12-3. *Same Web site with its graphics*

► Select the option to automatically load graphics again

- In Netscape, choose Options → Auto Load Images from the menu again. This tells the browser to, once again, automatically load graphics. However, if you find the Web really slow and unresponsive, and it takes weeks to load one page, consider switching this option off again.
- The Images gizmo only works when you've told your browser not to automatically load graphics.
- The Images gizmo may be called Load Images on some browsers.
- Most of the time, you'll discover that you don't really need the graphics. Typically, there's enough text to make things understandable.
- Even with the Load Images item switched off, you may still see some graphical images. That's because your browser remembers some of the images and stores them on disk. When you re-visit a Web page, it may pull up the images from disk instead of showing you the little "missing picture" icons.

Some of That "Off-Line" Browser Software

There are some interesting software packages out there that let you browse the Web without being connected to the Internet. Sounds strange. And, honestly, I haven't checked it out fully. But what these things do is phone up the Internet for you, visit some favorite Web pages, steal new information, then store it in your computer. Then you can read that information off-line—when you're not connected to the Internet—to save yourself some time. At least that's how the company propaganda reads.

If you're interested in this concept, check out one of the following Web pages. I cannot vouch for any of this, but it seems to be the rage among a handful of Web addicts.

Milktruck:

`http://www.milktruck.com`

Freeloader:

`http://www.freeloader.com`

SurfBot:

`http://www.surflogic.com`

WebWhacker:

`http://www.ffg.com/whacker.html`

- What you do here is to download special demo software from the above Web pages. That software enhances your browser, allowing it to visit Web pages ahead of time so you can look at things later.
- After you use the demo software, you'll have to buy the real software. Yes, this costs money. Doesn't everything?
- Again, I can't vouch for any of these services, but they are available if you want to check one or more of them out.
- Why can't I vouch? I find the speed of the Web consistent with the amount of time I tend to waste on it.

- Additions and updates can be found on the Wambooli Updates page:

  `http://www.wambooli.com/updates.htm`

NOW BE CAREFUL WITH THIS OFF-LINE BROWSER STUFF. YOU MAY FORGET THE PURE JOY OF CONNECTING TO THE INTERNET AND ACTUALLY GET A REAL LIFE.

FYI: "I just kept looking around me, remembering that everything in the capsule was supplied by the lowest bidder"—Alan Shepard's thoughts as he awaited the countdown for America's first ride into space.

13 Off into the Wild Web Yonder

Time to wrap up this exciting Web stuff. I have only a few parting thoughts as you prepare to venture off on your own—just a few tips and some warnings and Q&A. There's really nothing else that waits for you out there that's too much to handle.

This chapter sends you off into the Wild Web Yonder by covering the following topics:

- **Some tips for using your browser**
- **Warnings about what you may find on the Web**
- **Some Wambooli Q&A.**

Great Browsing Tips

Actually, just about anything you've read in the last several chapters counts as a great browsing tip. There are still two more to offer.

Editing the command box

You may have discovered this on your own, but any Web address you put into your browser's command box can be edited—just like any text in Windows. If you make a typo, you can click the mouse in the command box and use whatever editing keys you want to change what's there. Then press the Enter key to visit that Web page.

A popular variation on this theme is as follows:

▶ **Type the following Web page address into your browser's command box:**

```
http://cnn.com/SEARCH/quiz/index.html
```

▶ **Press the Enter key to visit that Web page**

This is the CNN news quiz (from way back in Chapter 10). But when the Web page appears, you don't have to take the quiz. Instead:

▶ **Click the mouse in the command box and edit the address to read as follows:**

```
http://cnn.com
```

That's CNN's home page on the Web. The Quiz is merely a sub-page (if you will). By editing the address in the command box, you can visit the main Web page—the first part of the Web address.

▶ **Press the Enter key**

This zooms you off (or "up") to the main Web page at CNN computer central in Atlanta.

- You can also copy and paste to and from the command box. For example, you might see a Web page listed somewhere in Windows. If so, select it by using your mouse, then press Ctrl+C to copy it. In your browser, click the mouse in the command box, then press Ctrl+V to paste. Press the Enter key to visit that Web page.

- In addition to the Backspace and Delete keys, you can use the left and right arrow keys to move the text cursor back and forth one character in the command box. You can also use the Home and End keys to move to the start and end of the line, respectively.

Keep a timer going

TIP: There's nothing wrong with wasting time on the Web. After all, consuming information, even of trivial value, does exercise the mind. And we all could use less fat in the brain. In any event, it helps to keep a grip on the amount of time you spend browsing. Honestly, it can be time-consuming.

Keep a timer going!

If you have a stopwatch, use it. Or at least look at your wristwatch or a clock when you start your Internet day. Try to set aside a certain amount of time for your browsing.

- If you notice the room starting to get lighter, then, well, it's too late: It's morning and you've been on the Web all night.
- If you're using Netscape's dialer program, it has a little clock letting you know how much time you've spent on the Internet. Refer to it often.
- For Windows 95, the wee li'l "Connection" window tells you how long you've been online, staring bleary-eyed at the Internet. Refer to it often as you're out and about the Web. Think about returning to the real world after a few hours. Or so.

Some Warnings About the Web

Traditional publishers stay in business by publishing what people want. Web publishers, on the other hand, don't worry about staying in business. While useful and needed information is what the Web mostly consists of, there are those who publish stuff that is of a personal or potentially irritating nature. After all, anyone can do this. And anyone does.

Warning! There be perverts out there! Lots of Web pages have, well, some truly raunchy graphics on them. Some of these are hard to stumble into. Others will hit you in the face. Beware! There is no regulation or routine method of warning potential viewers about this.

Warning! While pornography may not bother you, you may take offense at some of the religious, political and racist pages on the Web. Again, there is nothing that says these pages have to put up warnings or be delicate before presenting some outlandish views. Just be aware that such things exist, and realize that you can go elsewhere on the Web.

Warning! Many companies use the Web as a marketing tool. Though I won't name any of the pages here, there are some pages that mix obnoxious advertisements with good information. Personally I find this truly disgusting.

- Software does exist to prevent tender eyes from seeing some of the harsher Web pages. Refer to the following Wambooli page for more information:

  `http://www.wambooli.com/noperverts.htm`

Check your spelling when you type that in. It's noperverts as in "no perverts."

All Important Web Wambooli Q&A

Some questions are probably zipping through your mind like electrons around a molecule in the old Monsanto InnerSpace ride at Disneyland. And if you've never been on that ride, let me tell you: those electrons move dangerously fast, often colliding with each other and leading to an utter breakdown in the fabric of the universe. Or something like that.

Anyway, the following Q&A stuff may help get some nagging questions out of your mind. This is not optional reading.

Q: I tried to get on the Web but I got a "no carrier" message. What happened?

A: You were trying to connect to a Web page aboard the USS Nimitz and it was out at sea. Seriously, it's just a modem bug. Try the call again. (And see Chapter 11 for more modem troubleshooting information.)

Q: Can anyone put anything up on the Web?

A: Anyone with access to a Web server (which is one of the services your Internet provider should provide you with) can put something up on the Web. In fact, some people who don't even have access can put things up on the Web: comedian Harry Shearer has his own Web page and he doesn't even own a computer!

Q: Can I add something to someone else's Web page?

A: No. Since they own the Web page, only they can publish things there. You are merely a browser, an information consumer.

Q: Where can I find some interesting places to visit?

A: Start with the Wambooli Internetty Stuff Web page:

```
http://www.wambooli.com/internetty.htm
```

The first dozen or so links on that page will take you to collections of fun, interesting, good and truly awful places on the Web.

Q: Is there any one big list that has everything on the Web?

A: They try to create one all the time, but the Web is constantly changing, with old pages disappearing and new pages changing and so on. Also, a lot of Web pages are private and don't want to be listed.

Q: There I was, connected to the Internet, minding my own business reading the Web, when all of a sudden, for no reason whatsoever, I got an error message and all my windows closed. What happened?

A: It's a bug with Windows. You should disconnect from the Internet (if your dialer program didn't hang you up), and then quit Windows and restart your PC. I must do this maybe two times a week—even on my Windows 95 computer.

Q: Sometimes I type in a Web address one way, but when I finally get to the Web page, the address in the command box changes to something longer or different. Why?

A: Because what you see in the command box isn't always a Web page address. That's only one type of information that can go in there. The ugly truth is that the command box contains a URL, which is a way of communicating on the Internet. Those URL commands can be quite long and tedious, and that's often what you see in the command box.

Q: How do I program my VCR?
A: Chant.

Q: Can I send and receive mail through the Web?
A: You can send mail using your Web browser. The sending mail command is a URL, just like HTTP is a command for viewing a Web page. You cannot, however, receive any mail. For this you need a separate mail program. Netscape comes with a built-in mail program, which is discussed later in this book.

Q: How do you learn to do all those graphics and animations?
A: With a computer, of course! Graphics come from one of three places: You make them yourself or you borrow them from a disk of "clip art" or you steal them from the Web. If you opt to make them yourself, you'll need graphics software for your PC. Animations are made the same way, with animation software. The animations made on the Wambooli Animations page were created using the GIF Construction Set. A link to that company's Web page appears on the Wambooli Animations page.

Q: Where are the newsgroups?
A: Newsgroups are a separate part of the Internet from the World Wide Web. Part 4 of this book covers newsgroups in shallow detail.

Q: Where do I find the naked ladies?
A: If you want to view naked ladies, you should go to the obvious sources: the *Playboy* or *Penthouse* magazine home pages. There are also ads in the back of computer magazines for Web pages that offer collections of graphic images.

- In the old days on the Web you could see the naked ladies as easily as you could lift the magazine from a magazine rack. Today, with all the cybersmut hounds and legal maneuvers, you generally must apply for an account or special ID to see the naked ladies. This protects the magazines and publishers from being sued and keeps the eyeballs in the heads of wandering teenage boys.
- The major newsmagazines, in periods of national slow-news weeks, often come up with covers decrying how the Web is rife with filth and pornography. Well, golly, then *where is it?* Most of the Web is silly and it takes effort to find the naked ladies and such.
- If you're a parent and this issue concerns you, please refer to the following Wambooli page:

  `http://www.wambooli.com/noperverts.htm`

Q: Where can I find the naked men?

A: Use the same searching techniques as you would for naked ladies, but substitute "men."

Q: What's a "mirror site?"

A: Knowing that their Web pages may crawl to a halt because of high traffic, many businesses and organizations often create duplicate Web pages. Those duplicate pages are called *mirror sites*. So if you visit the Internet Movie Database and find it's busy, you can check out one of their mirror sites. This is typically done by clicking on a "mirror site" link that's very obvious on the page. (If it doesn't say that there's a mirror site, there probably isn't one.)

Q: It's easy to get sidetracked, eh?

A: Ho-boy, being sidetracked is what the Web is all about. I sat down and read for three hours the other day, and it was just meaningless trivia about my favorite TV show. Talk about sidetracked . . .

Q: What's your favorite TV show?

A: *Babylon 5.*

Q: My question wasn't here. What should I do?

A: Please send me your question, and I'll answer it as best I can. My e-mail address is `dgookin@wambooli.com`, which you can also find in this book's Introduction as well as on the Wambooli home page and various other Wambooli Web pages.

New Questions and Answers can be found on a special Wambooli Web page. The address is listed below, should you want to see more Q&A:

```
http://www.wambooli.com/more Q&A.htm
```

Refer to the instructions at the start of this chapter for information on getting to this Web page.

Q: So, will you ever tell us a what a Wambooli really is?

A: No, not in this book. But maybe at the following Web page:

```
http://www.wambooli.com/what.the.heck.is.a.wambooli.htm
```

FYI: Col. Sanders, patron of the Kentucky Fried Chicken franchise, was actually from Indiana.

PART THREE

CONQUERING E-MAIL

14 E-Mail Madness

`http://www.usps.gov/`

There is only one reason for electronic mail: To make stamp collecting a thing of the past. Anyone who uses electronic mail (*e-mail* for short) is bound to think so. Stamps are indicative of the sluggish Post Office. E-mail is instantaneous. Send an e-mail message now and it's sitting in the recipient's electronic mail box in just a few nanoseconds. (Of course, they may not answer right away, but the message has been delivered.)

Next to the Web, the most exciting part of the Internet has to be e-mail. O! How I could wax on about the efficiency of e-mail, not to mention the utter prestige of having a `yourname@somewhere.com` thing on your business card. Heck, a personal pager, cellular phone—even your own 800 number—all of that pales in comparison to your own e-mail address.

This chapter covers the following introductory points about e-mail:

- **Understanding your e-mail address**
- **Using your e-mail password**
- **Some e-mail questions and answers**
- **General e-mail advice.**

Anatomy of an E-Mail Address

Yes, you have an e-mail address. It's one of those services your Internet provider provided you with. (Refer to Appendix A if you need to know *exactly* what your e-mail address is.) That, combined with your e-mail password, is what lets you send and receive electronic mail on the Internet. And, unlike sending a letter, there's never anything to lick.

All e-mail addresses follow a similar pattern. Take the time to identify the following tidbits in your e-mail address:

yourname	This is your e-mail name, a unique identification for you on your Internet provider's computer.
@	The "at" sign, probably also known as "about" to some oldsters. In e-mail, it's pronounced "at."
somewhere	This is the name of your Internet provider, or your company or some organization.
.	The period, pronounced "dot" by everyone in the universe (well, at least everyone who speaks English).
com	The last part of your e-mail address is a three-letter word, most typically *com* (rhymes with *com*) though others are used as well.

Hopefully your own e-mail address won't look too insane; I've seen some dreadfully long e-mail addresses in my time. But no matter what, your e-mail address will typically have the above three parts, plus a smattering of unusual characters.

- If you didn't get a chance to choose your own e-mail name, then it might be some combination of your first and last names, or a nickname—unless you use CompuServe or Prodigy, in which case you're a number (like the way the government sees you).
- Your e-mail name may or may not be the same as the name you use to log into the Internet. Just don't get them confused.
- The *somewhere* part of an e-mail address (right after the @ sign) can be one or more words. If it's more, then each word will be separated by a period. Each word is required.

- The last part of the e-mail address isn't necessarily the word `com`. It's technically the *domain name*, which again is up to your Internet provider. It could be `com` or `org` or `net` or `edu` (see Appendix C).
- Overseas e-mail addresses often end with a two-letter country code. See Appendix C for more information. Within your own country, the two-letter country code isn't required.
- People on other planets also have a four-letter planet code at the end of their e-mail addresses: `moon` for the moon, `mars` for Mars and so on.
- The previous point may not be valid for a few decades.
- When you think about it, this mumbo-jumbo is actually a lot easier than your street address, which has numbers and words you have to spell. (I have a history of living in cities and on streets that always need to be spelled into the phone: Coeur d'Alene, Issaquah, Pilchuck, Repecho, El Cajon, Et Cetera.)

> **COMPARED TO STREET NAMES, NUMBERS, CITY NAMES AND ZIP CODES, AN E-MAIL ADDRESS ISN'T THAT COMPLEX.**

- There are no spaces in an e-mail name.
- Sometimes you'll see underlines used as substitutes for spaces in an e-mail name, as in:

```
joe_blow@kokomo.org
```

I've also seen dots:

```
dorothy.freckle@polka.com
```

FYI: On the* Larry King Live *TV show, late-night talk-show host David Letterman gave out the following as his e-mail address:

`wwww.com.com.com.dot.dot.dot.com.com.diggedy.diggedy.dank.dot.com.diggedy.www.com.Dave.com.com.dot`

The e-mail password

Since you want to be sure you are the only one reading your e-mail, your electronic mailbox has a password. This is the electronic lock and key you use to keep weirdos, corporate spies and your spouse from reading your e-mail.

The password is a special word or code you type in that proves you are who you say you are. You need both your e-mail name and password to read and send e-mail on the Internet.

- You chose your e-mail password when you signed up with your Internet provider. Either that, or a password was assigned to you.
- Your e-mail password should be listed in Appendix A.
- Your e-mail password will be different from the password you used to log into the Internet.
- In some instances, you'll have two sets of names and passwords: One name and password to connect to the Internet and another name and password for your e-mail. Maybe you'll be lucky and have only one set, but my Internet provider doled out two.

Wambooli e-mail Q&A

Q: Is e-mail part of the Web?
A: E-mail is actually part of the Internet, though you can use your Web browser to send an e-mail message. You really need a separate e-mail program, though—one that both sends and receives electronic mail, lets you store and organize messages as well as keep an address book of all your e-mail friends and associates.

Q: What if I don't have any friends?
A: Try going outside once in a while.

Q: Do I have an e-mail program? Is it part of the browser?
A: Netscape comes with an e-mail program in addition to a Web browser. So if you have Netscape, you already have an e-mail program—and a good one at that. If you don't have Netscape, you'll need to use another e-mail program.

Q: Are you going to talk about non-Netscape e-mail programs in this book?
A: Nope.

Q: Where is my e-mail?
A: E-mail is stored on your Internet provider's computer until you run a program that picks it up for you. That program copies each message to your computer, where you can read and respond to it.

Q: How do I get e-mail?
A: Someone on the Net sends you e-mail and you receive it, just as someone from the IRS would send you a letter.

SAVING E-MAIL NAMES IN YOUR ADDRESS BOOK IS AS IMPORTANT AS DROPPING BOOKMARKS ON THE WEB.

Q: How do I know who to send mail to?
A: You'll eventually collect a list—called an *address book*—of your friends on the Internet and their e-mail addresses. You can then send them a message anytime, or you can always reply to an e-mail message they send to you.

Q: How long can an e-mail message be?
A: As long as you want, providing your e-mail software can accept a message that large. For example, if you wanted to send a chapter of a book, you probably could. However, it would be better to send the file as an attachment, which is covered in Chapter 17.

Q: Can I send packages through e-mail?
A: Not really, but you can send files through e-mail. This means you could send your mom a graphical picture of you and the dog. I use e-mail to send chapters of my books to various publishers across the land.

Q: How can I send a picture of myself and my dog (even though I only have two cats)?
A: You need some way to get the graphic image into your computer. This can be done with a device called a scanner. If you don't have one, then you can go to some place like Kinko's or any high-tech copying center and they'll create a graphics file from one of your photographs. This is off the subject, but you asked about it anyway.

Q: Is there such a thing as "junk" e-mail?
A: Most definitely. It's called SPAM mail for various reasons unknown to me. This is when someone you don't know sends you (and a whole bunch of other people at random) an advertisement or any other unwanted e-mail. Internet oldtimers really, *really* hate spamming and they'll pounce on anyone who tries it (usually by flooding their electronic mailboxes with tons of nasty hate mail).

Q: Obviously I'm not going to SPAM anyone.
A: Wise move.

Q: What about chain letters?
A: They, unfortunately, exist in cyberspace as well as the real world. Don't feel compelled to answer any of them (unless it makes you feel good).

Q: I have an account on Prodigy as well as an Internet account. Will I get mail in both places?
A: Yes, but not the same mail. The mail sent to one account will not appear in the other account's mailbox. So if you send mail from one place (say Prodigy), the reply (if any) will come back to your account on Prodigy—not your Internet account.

It's difficult to keep multiple accounts straight. If you have more than one way to get mail on the Internet, I highly recommend using only one account for your electronic mail. This avoids any problems you may have later on.

Q: So what's the point of having Prodigy or AOL if I can get e-mail from my Internet provider?
A: This is a question Prodigy and AOL stockholders are currently wondering about.

Q: Can someone from AOL or Prodigy send me e-mail on the Internet?
A: Yes they can, and you can send e-mail back. For more information, see Chapter 19 on keeping an e-mail address book.

A Few E-Mail Homilies To Live By

After nearly 16 years of doing this e-mail thing, I have collected some interesting tidbits of advice.

- Now that you're a human with an e-mail address, tell your friends about it. My wife and I put our e-mail addresses into our Christmas letter every year, just in case we have any geeky friends or relatives who will bother to write.
- Don't worry if you don't get mail when you first hook up to the Internet. Keep in mind you must send mail to get it. For example, I cruised around some Web pages and complimented the people who created them on what they had done, by sending them e-mail. This meant they sent me mail back. Had I merely sat on my butt and *lurked* (not sent mail), then I'd still have an empty mail box and would probably eat another pint of Haagen Dazs in despair.
- If you truly want to get a full mail box, consider subscribing to a mailing list. This is covered in Chapter 21.
- Don't forget to put your e-mail address on your business card. It's a very "in" thing to do.

FYI: After finishing the U.S. Constitution, the Founding Fathers celebrated by going out and getting drunk. I'm not making that up—the liquor bill is in our national archives.

15 Message for You, Sir!

Nothing can make your day like new messages in your electronic mailbox. But don't think you need to get tons of e-mail to be a happy person on the Internet. Sure, some people boast of their "full mailboxes," but there are ways to get full mailboxes and not be Mr. or Miss Popular (Chapter 21 tells you how to get lots of mail every day). Most often, you'll get mail when you send mail. And since this e-mail stuff is much easier to reply to than regular mail, all you need are a few friends on the Internet and you'll be getting more and more mail every day.

This chapter covers the core of e-mail—sending and receiving electronic messages. The following fun concepts are covered here:

- Getting mail
- Checking for new mail automatically
- Reading your mail
- Receiving an attachment
- Quitting the mail program.

Stop! Oh, Yes! Wait a Minute, Mr. Internet Mail Software

To see if you have any mail, run your mail program. Open your mail program's window if it isn't already open on your screen.

▶ In Netscape, choose Window→Netscape Mail from the menu

The Netscape Mail window opens and the program attempts to get any new mail for you. If you have any mail waiting, it's listed in the top part of the window, on the right (see Figure 15-1).

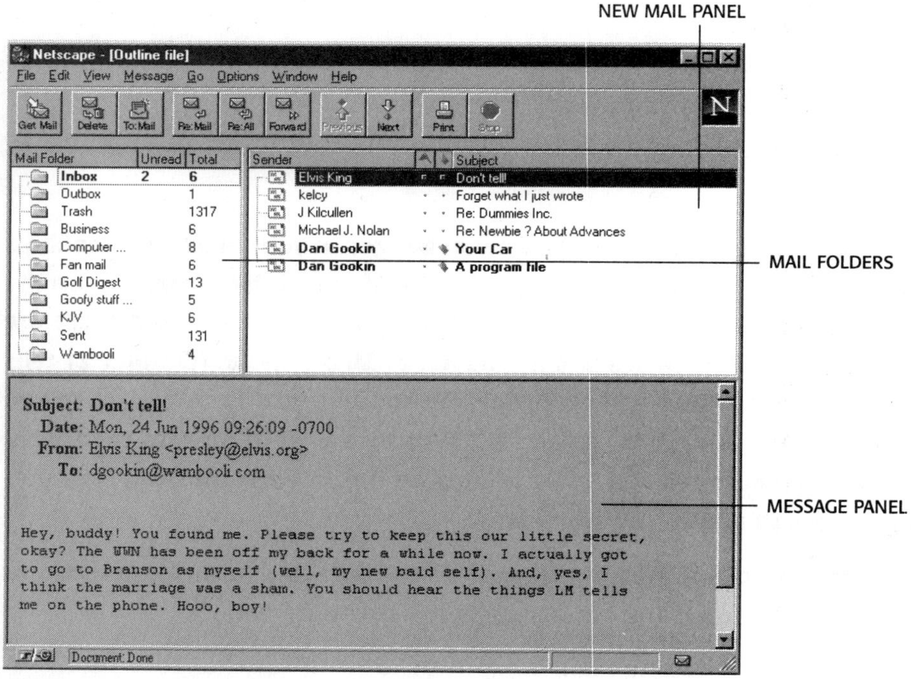

Figure 15-1. *The Netscape Mail window.*

- If you have mail, jump for joy! Mail is what makes life worth living on the Internet.
- Refer to the section "Reading your mail" for what to do if you have any mail waiting.

- If you have too much mail, scream in agony! Some Internet book writers get upwards of 500 messages a day. Yikes!
- If you have no e-mail waiting, hide your face in shame!
- Seriously, when there are no new mail messages waiting, you'll see an annoying message telling you "No new messages on server." Scrunch up your face in a puzzled sort of way and that moment of discouragement will soon pass.

IF YOU'RE FAMOUS, OVER-PAID OR OVER-EXPOSED, YOU'LL GET A LOT OF E-MAIL, TOO.

TIP: Keep in mind that you generally have to send mail to get mail.

- You'll read more about the folders part of the mail window in Chapter 18.
- The new mail part of the window contains any messages you've received recently.
- The message part of the window shows the actual contents of the highlighted message.
- If you haven't used the mail program before, you might be asked to type in your e-mail name and password. If so, try to choose the option that forces the mail program to remember your e-mail name and password. That way you won't have to type them in every dang doodle time you check for mail.

- If you skipped over e-mail setup during installation, Netscape may want you to configure the mail program when it starts. Refer to Appendix A for the various and sundry bits of information you'll need.
- If you're not using Netscape, you'll need to start your separate mail program, such as Eudora or whatever other e-mail program your Internet package came with. Most of them work similarly, so you can follow along here (which is like trying to sing a song you're hearing for the first time, but you'll eventually get the idea).
- If you're using an online service to get mail, you'll need to use the service's mail package.

How to order Netscape to automatically check for mail

There's no sense in opening your mailbox if there's no mail in it. This is kind of a pickle for most people. You love to get mail, but don't want to seem despondent checking your mailbox every two minutes. (Heck, if the mailman didn't come to our house at the same time every day, I'd check for paper mail three or four times myself!)

▶ In Netscape, choose Options→Mail and News Preferences from the menu

The Preferences dialog box appears. Like a creepy neighborhood, this isn't the kind of place I'd want to loiter.

▶ Click on the Servers tab

▶ Look for the text that says Check for Mail

This is shown in Figure 15-2.

▶ Make sure the Every item is selected

Click the mouse in the radio button by the word Every if that button doesn't presently have a dot in it.

▶ Press the Tab key

This moves the cursor into the minutes text box.

▶ Type in the number `10` (don't press the Enter key yet)

You've just instructed Netscape to automatically check to see if you have any new mail. This will be done every 10 minutes after you first log on to the Internet.

▶ Click the OK button

Netscape will now alert you when you have mail waiting.

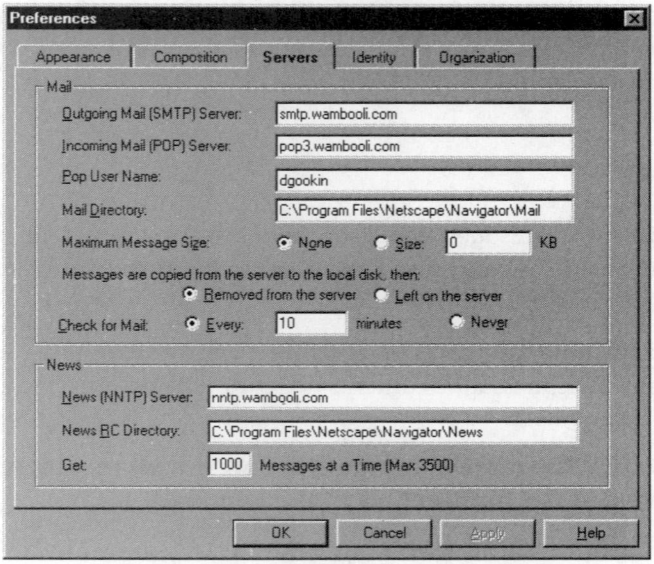

***Figure 15-2.** Netscape is configured to check for new mail every 10 minutes.*

AND JUST HOW DOES NETSCAPE LET ME KNOW I HAVE MAIL?

Look in the lower right corner of Netscape's window. There you'll see a little envelope. When you see the exclamation point by the envelope, it means Netscape has checked and, by golly, you have mail waiting. Then double-click on the envelope to quickly open Netscape's Mail window and read your new e-mail.

-  When you first open Netscape, a question mark appears by the envelope. That means that Netscape hasn't checked your mail yet. So just wait. (Or you can open the mail window right then, in which case Netscape will be forced to check automatically.)
- Nothing by the envelope means you don't have any new mail—at least none since Netscape last checked. Just wait a few minutes and Netscape will check again.
- You can type a value other than 10 into the Preferences dialog box if you want Netscape to check for mail at other intervals. For example, type 5 into the box to have Netscape check your e-mail every five minutes.

- 

If Netscape's Mail window is open and the little envelope has an an exclamation point by it, you'll need to click the Get Mail gizmo to have Netscape go out and fetch your mail.

Reading your mail

After Netscape fetches any new messages, you'll see them listed in the top right part of the mail program's window. The new e-mail messages appear in bold type and at the bottom of the list.

▶ To read a new e-mail message, click on it using your mouse
You only need to click once. The message's contents appear in the bottom (message) part of the e-mail window.

▶ You don't need to click the mouse on the *first* new e-mail message; that one already appears in the bottom half of the window.

- New e-mail messages are listed in **bold** type. Messages you've already read are in plain type.
- You may need to use the scroll bar to find new messages at the end of the list.
- Old mail messages (those not in bold type) can be stored in folders or deleted. Chapter 18 goes into more detail on this e-mail organization madness.

▶ Read the message
Uncle Vern has survived his hernia operation. Kim has sent you a picture of young Henry's doodling. And the latest football pool has arrived from the office. Where would we be in society if it wasn't for e-mail?

- You may need to use the scroll bar to read a particularly long e-mail message.
- Some messages are long left-to-right (sent by weird mail programs, no doubt). You may have to scroll left and right to read them.
- Refer to the section "Responding to Your Mail" in Chapter 16 if you want to answer the e-mail message.
- Some messages may contain graphics or files or "attachments." Refer to the section "Receiving a File (Attachment) from Someone Else" for more information on what to do with them.

TIP: If the person sending you mail has typed in any Web page addresses, they appear as links within the mail message. Click on those links and Netscape opens your browser window (if it's not open already) and visits the corresponding pages.

- If you want to print the e-mail message, make sure your printer is on and ready to print, then click on the Print gizmo.
- To save an e-mail message to disk, press the Ctrl+S key combination. A Save As dialog box appears, allowing you to save the message to your hard disk. (Mail message files are text files, which can be read by your word processor or any program that can swallow text.)

The Ugly Mail Header

At the start of each e-mail message is something called the Ugly Mail Header. Like the information you'd find on an envelope or at the top of a corporate memo, the Ugly Mail Header tells you about the message:

Subject: The message topic (typed by the person who originally sent the message)

Date: The date and time the message was composed

From: The person who sent the message, usually their real name followed by their e-mail address

To: Your name and e-mail address. (There might be more than one person here if the message has been sent to several people.)

CC: People who have been "carbon copied" the message. These people aren't as important as the folks on the To line, though they don't feel badly about it.

Other items may appear in the Ugly Mail Header from time to time. These are merely additional tidbits of information you most likely can ignore.

(If you really want to scare yourself, take a gander at the Very Ugly Mail Header: Choose View→Document Source from the Mail program's window. This displays the "raw" message sent over the Internet—with a Massively Ugly Mail Header at the top of the list. Yikes! Close that window before that Medusa turns you to stone!)

Moving along...

After you're done reading a message, you move on to the next message. You can do this by clicking the mouse on the next message in the list (in the upper right part of the mail window), or you can use the Next gizmo in the mail window.

- After reading a message, it changes from bold to normal text in the upper right portion of the mail window. That just means you've read the message.
- You can re-read any message by clicking on it with your mouse. It doesn't matter if the message is bold or not.
- Most people delete messages they've just read, or they drag the messages (using the mouse) to a special folder. This subject is covered in Chapter 18.
- When you first delete a message, Netscape creates a Trash folder, into which it places those messages you deem unworthy.

Receiving a File (Attachment) from Someone Else

Occasionally, someone may have the gall to send you something other than text in an e-mail message. This happens in one of two ways:

- Someone sends you a graphical picture
- Someone sends you some other type of file.

If they send you a graphical picture, you'll see it displayed at the bottom of the message. This is because Netscape is smart and will show you pictures instantly (other mail programs, stupid ones, don't do this). Figure 15-3 shows a picture that was sent to me by my wife.

Figure 15-3. *My wife, showing off in an e-mail message.*

Any other type of file sent to you appears as an attachment, an example of which is shown in Figure 15-4. The attachment shows you various and sundry information, every part of which is unimportant except for the underlined text.

> **SAY! THAT UNDERLINED TEXT LOOKS LIKE A LINK!**

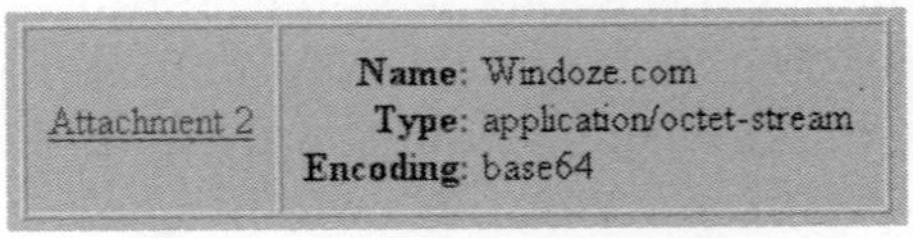

Figure 15-4. *Someone sends you a file; it looks like this.*

▶ **To retrieve a file sent to you in an e-mail message, click on the `Attachment` link**

A Save As dialog box appears, which allows you to save the attached whatever to disk.

▶ **Mess with the Save As dialog box**

Use your Windows Save As dialog box skills to find a proper directory or folder for the file on your PC's hard drive. This is an optional step; you need only do this if someone has beaten the facts about organized hard drives into your head.

You probably won't need to type in a new name for the file. Chances are the filename is already listed properly in the Save As dialog box. If not, type in a name for the file, such as `MESSAGE` or something more creative.

▶ Click the OK button

The file is saved to disk. There's no feedback, so you'll have to trust me on this.

▶ Continue reading your mail

Later, when you're done with the Internet, you can examine or use the file, as necessary. For example, when I receive a word processing document from my editor, I save it in my Wambooli folder on the hard drive, then I go back to reading the Cindy Crawford home page on the Web. The word processing document can wait for later.

- Most e-mail messages are just plain text. Only a handful of Internet users actually know how to send files. Fewer still actually need to send files.
- You can join the ranks of those who know how to send files. Read Chapter 17.
- Netscape Mail lets you view JPEG or GIF graphics files. So if you have friends who want to e-mail you pictures, have them send them in either of those formats. (This is something for them, not you, to fuss over.)
- If you want to save the graphics file, use the same trick you would for saving an image from the Web to disk. Refer to Chapter 8, "Taking a Web Picture."
- Mostly, you'll know what to do with a file when it's sent to you; people just don't randomly send files back and forth through e-mail. For example, someone may send you a word processing document, a database file, a game, whatever. This works just like copying the file from a floppy disk, though the file is sent through the Internet instead.

TIP: Be wary of program files sent from someone you don't know. The program could be a virus that may erase important files on your hard drive. Use anti-virus software to scan any unknown programs before you run them. (The programs are harmless until they're run.) Graphics files and plain text messages cannot contain viruses, so you don't need to scan them. Virus-scanning programs are available any place you can get software. A good scanner can be found by visiting the following Web page:

`http://www.mcafee.com/`

I'm All Done Reading My Mail

When you're done reading your mail, you can close the mail program window. Choose File→Close from the Netscape Mail window. There. You're done.

- You don't really have to close the mail window. You can leave it open and switch back to your browser for more surfing. Press the Alt+Tab key combination in Windows to switch back to your browser, or press the Ctrl+N key combination to start a new Netscape Web browser window.
- By leaving your mail window open, you can quickly switch back to it should Netscape alert you to any new mail messages. (Use the Get Mail gizmo to have Netscape pick up any new messages.)

TIP: Don't choose the File→Exit command from the mail window unless you want to quit all your Netscape programs! Use the File→Close command instead.

- Refer to Chapter 3 for more information on quitting your Internet software and saying bye-bye to the Net.

FYI: Mail service in the United States was free prior to 1863.

16 Sending Mail Here and There

If it's true that it's better to give than receive, then you should please yourself to death by sending tons of e-mail. Send it fervently. Send it broadly. Send it regularly. E-mail your friends and family, and even uncover the secret e-mail addresses of your federal and state representatives. Then e-mail them, too. And try not to start each letter with "Just because I'm writing you in e-mail doesn't mean that I'm a kook."

When you have an Internet mailbox you can send e-mail to anyone on the Internet. All you need to know is their e-mail address. After that, composing the new message is a cinch.

This chapter tells you how all that's done, in the following entertaining sections:

- **Writing an e-mail message**
- **Canceling a message**
- **Writing a response**
- **Responding to a gang-message**
- **Forwarding a message**
- **Quoting from a message**
- **E-mail etiquette.**

Composing an E-Mail Epistle

To create an e-mail message, you need to know only two things: the address of the person to whom you're sending the message and the subject you're going to write about. Never write a message saying, "Oh, hi Bob, I forgot what I was going to say." That just isn't properly representative of the fast-paced electronic age in which we live.

▶ Open the mail program (if it isn't already open)

In Netscape, choose Window→Netscape Mail from the menu to see the Mail program's window. If you're not using Netscape, start your mail program, whatever it may be.

▶ Click on the To: Mail gizmo

A window appears where you can create a new e-mail message (see Figure 16-1).

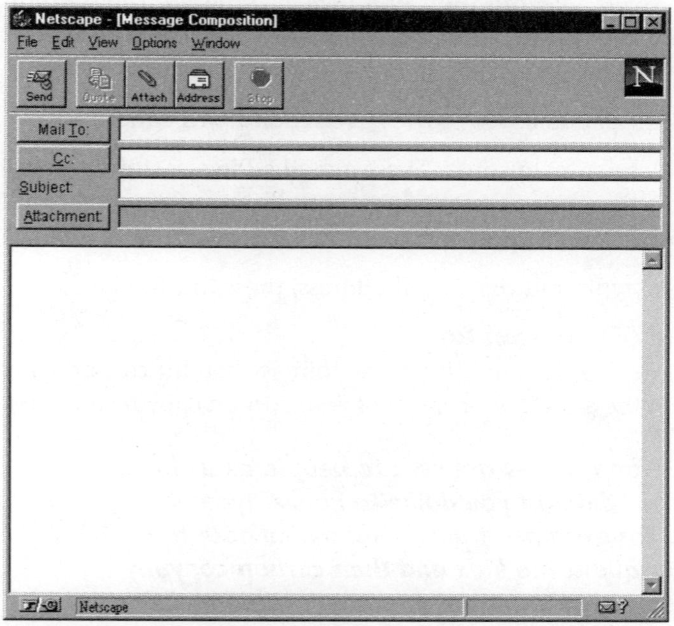

Figure 16-1. *Netscape's mail composition window.*

- In Netscape, use the To: Mail gizmo to compose a new message. Or you can use the Ctrl+M keyboard shortcut.
- Avoid the temptation to choose the logical Ctrl+N key combination to create a new mail message. In Netscape, Ctrl+N starts up a new Web browser window (see Chapter 12). Think Ctrl+M, *M* for Mail. Or *MMMM*, good, Maybe I'll Make More Mail.
- If you're using the popular Eudora mail program, you can press Ctrl+N to start a new mail message. (Unfortunately, that's all the info I have on Eudora.)
- Some mail programs have a Compose or Prepare gizmo that lets you create a new mail message.

▶ Fill in the Mail To: field

Type in the address of the person to whom you're sending your e-mail. For example, if you're sending mail to me, you would type in:

```
dgookin@wambooli.com
```

- Don't click the Mail To: button in the mail composition window (the button to the left of the address text box). That displays your e-mail address book, which you shall read about in Chapter 19.
- To send the message to more than one person, separate their e-mail addresses by commas. For example, here is what you would type to send e-mail to both the President and Vice President of the United States:

```
president@whitehouse.gov,vice.president@whitehouse.gov
```

Notice how those are titles and not people? These e-mail addresses stay the same before and after the election. (If you want to send mail to a politician out of office, you just need to know the e-mail address of the prison they were sent to.)

- After you're done typing in the e-mail address, press the Tab key.

▶ Fill in the Cc: field (if you want to)

The Cc: (carbon copy) field is optional. If you're going to send a carbon copy of your message, type in the e-mail address(es) of your carbon copy recipient(s).

TIP: Carbon copies are sent to people as a "by the way" or "thought you'd like to know" type of thing. For example, I may send a nice note to my mother about the kids and then carbon copy my wife on it. She's not the message's main recipient but would like to read it anyway.

- E-mail addresses in the Cc: field appear just as they do in the Mail To: field. You should separate multiple carbon copy e-mail addresses with commas.
- You don't have to send carbon copies at all.

▶ Press the Tab key to move down to the Subject field

▶ Type a subject into the Subject field (this is required)

The subject should be descriptive, telling the person who's getting the message what it's about. Here are some good subjects:

```
I crashed the new car
Where I found the cat this morning
Here's that new nerve gas recipe
Places to get mugged in NYC
You're fired
```

Here are some bad subjects, along with the reasons they're bad:

`Stuff`	Doesn't tell you anything.
`Nothing`	An empty message? Surely they must have something to say.
`Hello from Steve`	Since you can already see Steve sent the message by reading the mail window, this subject is redundant.
`I was drunk when I wrote this`	Drunks don't compose good e-mail.
`Report from the John Tesh concert`	Egads!

The idea is to put *information* into the subject. I know some e-mail writers who, when they can't think of a subject, actually put the first few words of the message into the subject line.

▶ Press the Tab key and start typing your message

Try to remember all those letter-writing skills you were taught long, long ago. There isn't a need to be totally formal, since e-mail is rather informal. But you shouldn't write like you talk. Refer to the section "General E-Mail Etiquette," found later in this chapter, for more e-mail composition tidbits.

- You can use the arrow keys, Delete, and Backspace to edit your message.
- You can select and cut and copy text.

- There is no limit to how long you can make the message, but there is an eyeball-frazzle limit for reading long messages; try not to be overly long-winded.
- You don't really need to "sign" (or type) your name at the end of the message. People can tell who the mail is from by reading the message header. But you can have something called a *signature*. See the section "The All-Important E-Mail Signature" in Chapter 18.

► Review your message

Re-read what you wrote. Check your spelling. Check for misused words.

- Netscape has a "plug-in" program that will check your spelling. If you ordered the Netscape Power Pack, then the spell-checker is on that disk.

► Click the Send gizmo to send your message

Off it goes!

- A copy of each message you send is kept in the special SENT folder in the mail program's window. Refer to Chapter 18 for more information on folders.

Tip: If you have relatives on the Internet, write to them! For some reason, communicating with your kids—even if they live down the hall—seems to be more successful with e-mail. I got this advice from an 80-year-old reader who says her grandkids write to her all the time now that she's on the Internet.

FYI: After putting rubber reptiles on or near roads to study driver reactions, biology professor David Shepherd concluded the following: "There are apparently very few animals hit accidentally on the highway."

I Changed My Mind and Don't Really Want to Send the Message

If you've already sent your message, then you can't change your mind. Like screaming at your wife in an airplane cabin because you have the headphones on and don't know how loud you're talking, there's no way to take it back. No way.

However, if change your mind before clicking that fatal Send button, you can cancel your message.

▶ **Choose File→Close from the menu.**
Netscape ponders if that's really what you wanted to do, displaying an "Are you sure?" type of dialog box.

▶ **Click the Yes button**
Yes, it's the Yes button you click to avoid sending the message. Tricky wording in that dialog box...

Responding to Your Mail

One of the cinchiest ways to send mail is simply to respond to an e-mail message you've received. When you reply to an e-mail message, the mail program automatically fills in the To: and Subject: fields for the new, out-going message. Figure 16-2 shows my reply to my wife's message from Figure 15-2.

To reply to any e-mail message in Netscape, take these steps:

▶ **Select the message you want to reply to**
Normally, the message you're replying to appears in the bottom part of the mail window. If not, choose the proper message from the upper right part of the mail window.

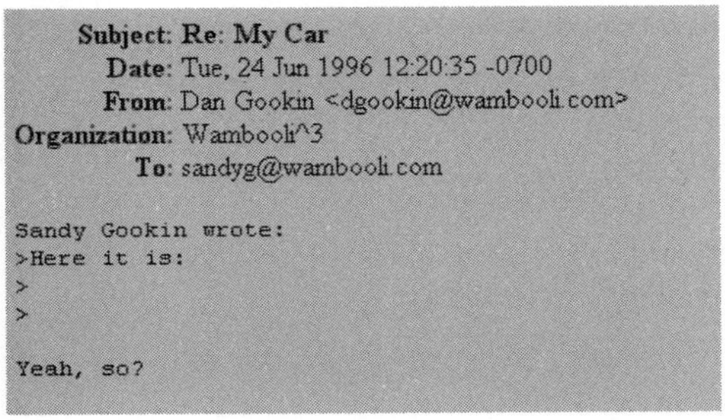

Subject: Re: My Car
Date: Tue, 24 Jun 1996 12:20:35 -0700
From: Dan Gookin <dgookin@wambooli.com>
Organization: Wambooli^3
To: sandyg@wambooli.com

Sandy Gookin wrote:
>Here it is:
>
>

Yeah, so?

Figure 16-2. *Responding to e-mail is the easiest way to send a new message.*

▶ Click on the Re: Mail gizmo

Or you can press the Ctrl+R key combination, where R stands for Reply. This opens a mail composition window with the To: and Subject: fields already filled in (see Figure 16-2).

- The To: field contains the name of the person who originally sent the message.
- The Subject: field contains the original subject, prefixed by "Re:."
- Re comes from the ablative form of the Latin *res*, which means "in reference to" or "concerning."

TIP: Yes, you can and should edit the Subject: field, especially if the subject has drifted. People may be replying back and forth, hitting that Re: Mail gizmo without thinking about the message's subject. For example, suppose the original subject was:

```
Yachting
```

But after a few exchanges the subject changes to humorous drowning incidents. Even so, the subject would still read:

```
Re: Yachting
```

This is why most savvy e-mail users would change the subject to the following:

```
Humorous drowning incidents
(was "Yachting")
```

▶ Is the original message quoted?

Netscape is set up to "quote" the original message, including its contents, in your reply. Something like:

```
Rush Limbaugh wrote:
```

This is followed by the original message text, which has > (greater-than signs) on the left margin:

```
>  You're right. I've been a fool all these years.
>  There really is something to being a liberal.
>  Something human that I've somehow overlooked. Thanks
>  for your note. I start a new me this instant!
```

This is simply the traditional Internet method of quoting an original message.

- All of the original message is quoted.
- Refer to the section "All About Quoting E-Mail" for more information on what to do with the quote.

▶ Write your reply

Compose your clever and witty reply to the original message.

- Heed the same rules as you would for creating a fresh, new message; refer to the section "Composing an E-Mail Epistle" earlier in this chapter.
- Actually, you can do anything with the reply that you can do with a message you make up out of the blue: You can add more people to the To: or Cc: fields and you can change the subject. You don't have to, but you can.

Tip: Few e-mail–savvy humans bother to reply "OK" or "Thank you" to e-mail messages. For example, if someone writes to you, "Thanks for all your good advice," you don't have to send a "You're welcome" reply. Oh, you can if you want to. But don't expect such short replies from the majority of the people who send e-mail.

▶ Send the message

Click on the Send gizmo and off it goes!

- Replying to a message does not delete the original message from your mailbox. That message stays there until you delete it. See Chapter 18 for more information.

Replying to One of Those Gang-Messages

It's possible to send one message to several people. You do this by putting more than one person's e-mail address in the To: or Cc: field when you create the message (this was covered earlier in this chapter). Commas separate the addresses.

For example, suppose you get a message with the following Ugly Mail Header:

```
Subject: Who turned off the hot water?
Date: Wed, 29 May 1936 17:00:31 PDT
From: moe@stooges.org
To:curly@stooges.org,larry@stooges.org,shemp@stooges.org
```

When you reply to this type of message, you really have two choices.

First, you can click on the Re: Mail button to reply to the person who sent the message (on the From: line). In the example above, that would be moe@stooges.com.

Second, you could click the Re: All button. In this case, your reply will be sent to everyone the original message was sent to. Now Moe, Curly, Larry and Shemp would get copies of your message.

- After clicking the proper button, you would fill in the mail message just as you would when replying to one person. The only difference is that it will be sent to several people.

- People who were carbon-copied on the original message will be carbon-copied in your reply.

ONLY SEND A GANG REPLY IF EVERYONE IN THE GANG SHOULD READ IT. OTHERWISE, SEND INDIVIDUAL REPLIES.

FYI: Shemp Howard was one of the original Three Stooges. He was Moe's brother in real life. Their younger brother Jerome joined the group after Shemp left, using the stage name "Curly."

Forwarding an Interesting Message

Some messages are just too good to waste on only yourself. For example, suppose someone sends you a sheet full of dumb blonde jokes.* Those are just too good to waste, so you decide to send some to Earl. In that case, you would "reply" to the message by forwarding it.

▶ **Click the Forward button.**

After clicking the Forward button you'll see a mail composition window, just as if you were creating a new mail message.

▶ **Fill in the To: field**

For example, type in Earl's e-mail address or the address(es) of whomever you're forwarding a copy of the message to.

* And keep in mind here that dumb blondes can be either male or female

▶ Optionally fill in the Cc: field

Hey kids! Did you know the "carbon" in Carbon Copy used to be this stuff called "carbon paper?" Ask your folks about it—as well as other stuff from the olden days, like mimeograph machines, rotary phones, shoelaces and leaded gasoline that cost $.23 a gallon!

▶ Gander at the Subject: field

You'll notice that the subject is already filled in. You'll see something like this:

```
Fwd: Dumb Blonde (male or female) jokes
```

The `Fwd` means Forwarded. The message you were reading will be sent to the people whose e-mail addresses you typed in the To: and Cc: fields.

▶ Optionally type in a short message

- You can type your own message if you like, maybe describing what's being sent. This isn't really necessary though.
- You won't see the forwarded message in the mail composition window. Don't worry, it's there; the people to whom you're sending the forwarded message will see it. (Some e-mail programs may show you the text of the forwarded message; Netscape doesn't.)

▶ Click the Send button to send the message

In few brief Internet moments, your friends will receive copies of the message.

All About Quoting E-Mail

E-mail is rather conversational. It's relaxed. But unlike a conversation, sending e-mail back and forth can take place over a series of days. Don't expect the people to whom you send your e-mail replies to always remember every tidbit of their original messages. To help them out, you can include a quote in your reply.

For example, you may get lots of e-mail every day and then Jerry sends you the following reply:

```
Why did you do that? I would be embarrassed but I'd
never crawl out the window.
```

The Ugly Mail Header tells you that Jerry has written a reply to a message you wrote, but what did you write?

Now what the heck is Jerry talking about?

If Jerry had been thinking, he would have thought to *quote* your original message—which Netscape does automatically each time you reply to an e-mail. So after reading your message and clicking on the Re: Mail button, Jerry would have seen the following as his message:

```
Dan Gookin wrote:
> I went over to my boss's house for dinner last night.
> After using the bathroom the toilet just wouldn't
> stop flushing so I crawled out the window and ran home.
```

That's Netscape automatically copying the entire contents of the original message into the reply—what's known as a quote. It starts with So-and-so wrote:, followed by the message with greater-than signs on the left side.

Now Jerry (or you) can write your reply and keep the original message in there for reference. His message now reads as follows:

```
Dan Gookin wrote:
> I went over to my boss's house for dinner last night.
> After using the bathroom the toilet just wouldn't stop
> flushing so I crawled out the window and ran home.

Why did you do that? I would be embarrassed but I'd
never crawl out the window.
```

This shows that you wrote the original message, which is quoted, and then Jerry wrote his reply. You can now more easily keep track of the conversation, thanks to the quote.

- You can place your new text above or below the quoted e-mail message. It doesn't really matter, though sometimes having the quoted text first makes more sense if you're replying to something the other person said.

- You can even split the quotes, editing your new text between the quoted text:

```
Chris Wagner wrote:
> We took your suggestion and went to Cholesterol Heaven
> for dinner last night. Hated it. Sorry.

That's okay. It really depends on who's cooking.
It must have been Ben's night off.

> But we did have fun later watching the homes on the
> cliff slide into the canyon. Is it like that after
> every big rain?

Ever since I've been a kid it's worked that way.
You'd think people would wise up about living on Canyon
Drive, but no.

Cheers!
DAN
```

- In the above example, I've put my comments between Chris's comments, so the final e-mail message reads more like a conversation. There is nothing wrong with doing this.

Tip: For brevity's sake, don't feel like you have to quote the entire message just to reply to one part of it. You can edit the original message and keep only the quote you're replying to.

- A lot of the Internet Lords prefer it if you quote as little as possible. For example, they consider a long quoted message with a reply of only one line as a "waste of bandwidth." What that means is that you sent a message that was far longer than it needed to be.
- If you don't like the quote, press the Ctrl+A key, then the Delete key. This selects the entire message and deletes it, removing the quote. (Do this *before* you compose your reply.)
- When you quote a message with attachments, the attachments are not included with the quote.
- The same techniques for quoting from e-mail can also be used in newsgroups. See Chapter 22 for more information on newsgroups.

General E-Mail Etiquette

You and I live in a society where, thanks to the telephone, most instant communication is vocal. You can hear what the other person says, divine meaning through intonation and easily catch sarcasm or giggles. The same cannot be said of written communication.

People often forget that writing an e-mail message is written communication. We do not write the same way we speak. Or, at least, we shouldn't. Especially in business situations, where writing is always formal, the informality of e-mail can lead to a lot of trouble. Therefore, I offer you the following rules and suggestions for composing friendly e-mail.

- When you're having fun in an e-mail message, let the other person know. It's entirely okay to put "Ha ha" into a message. Or you can use *smilies* to denote a lighter tone:

```
:-)
```

Turn your head 90 degrees to the left to see the happy face. Litter your lighter messages with those guys to let the reader know you're just poking fun.

- If you're replying to someone, quote the original message to help them remember what you're replying to. See the section "All About Quoting E-Mail" earlier in this chapter.
- Try not to ramble.
- If you need to emphasize a word, put asterisks on either side:

```
Please! I'm *begging* you!
```

Some people use underscores instead:

```
I told you, Marty, it's _over_ between us.
```

- Never send e-mail when you're mad. It's okay to write it when you're mad, but wait until you cheer up and get a chance to read what you wrote before sending it. (Just like Post Office mail, you can't un-send an e-mail message.)

- Be very careful when sending business e-mail. Treat it as a business letter even if it's just a casual or personal message. Written communication is far easier to misunderstand than verbal communication. Not only that, it's easier to make a hard copy of the message or store it on a hard drive for all eternity.

REMEMBER THAT THERE ARE NO TRUE RULES FOR USING THE INTERNET; MERELY SUGGESTIONS.

- Everyone play together nice.

FYI: "For thou art not so long by the head as honorificabilitudinitatibus." William Shakespeare,* Loves Labour Lost, *Act V, Scene I.

Sending a File (Attachment) to Someone

In addition to zipping off some snappy text to someone, you can use e-mail to send a file. This works just like sending someone a file on disk—without the disk, of course. The person receives the file, saves it to disk, and then it's theirs for them to cherish for the rest of their days.

Of course, most often you'll receive a file with an e-mail message in a work situation. Your boss, too busy playing *Wing Commander* to do his real job, will send you a report or spreadsheet and bellow "Fix this!" without any other clue as to what needs to be done. But that's really the subject of a Dilbert comic strip and has nothing to do with this chapter, which covers the nuts and bolts of sending files with e-mail messages in the following, down-to-earth sections:

- **E-mail file sending overview**
- **Getting a graphical image to send**
- **Sending a file (attachment).**

The Big Picture

Sending someone a disk file is really a snap with Netscape's e-mail. The file is hooked onto your e-mail message as an *attachment*, just like you'd hook a boat onto your truck so you could drive for miles before you realize you live nowhere near the water.

The nifty thing about e-mail attachments in Netscape is that it handles all the ooga-booga parts for you automatically. You don't have to encode anything, count bytes, convert, insert or pervert.

- Before you can send someone a file, you need to know what to send them.
- Write to your intended recipient in advance to find out if they can receive the file. If they have Netscape, it's okay. But if they're using another program, or they access the Internet through Prodigy or CompuServe, they may not be able to receive the file.
- Sending a small, insignificant, test file first might be a good idea.

From whence cometh thine graphical images?

While Netscape can send any type of file, a graphics file is really near and dear to the hearts of anyone who owns a computer. The big problem is getting the image off of that Fuji paper and into your computer.

It would be nice to press a photograph up to the computer screen, have the computer go "Uh, okay," and then see a graphic image of that photograph appear on the screen. Unfortunately, the folks who design computers haven't thought of that one yet. Still, there are several schemes for getting a graphical image from a photograph into a file on your PC. Here are a few you can try:

- Take your photograph to a high-tech copy center, like Kinko's. They usually have the equipment there to convert the image into a computer file. The type of file you want is a JPEG or GIF file. That's for them to worry about, not you.
- You can buy a device called a scanner and attach it to your PC. The scanner will take photographs, scan them (just like a photocopier) and convert them into graphics files on your PC's hard drive.

- You can take photographs with a digital camera, which you can then connect to your PC and use to "beam" the pictures into the computer.
- You can also send a file you might have taken from elsewhere on the Web. Refer to Chapter 8 for information on taking a Web picture.
- Remember in which directory or folder you saved the file. This will help later when you try to find the file on disk.

IF YOU WANT TO MAKE THINGS EASIER, SAVE THE FILE IN THE NETSCAPE DIRECTORY.

- Generally speaking, keep the size of your graphical images to about 400 by 300 pixels or smaller. Anything larger than that takes too long to send.
- A pixel is a small dot on the computer's screen.
- A pixie is a mischievous elfin creature with pointed ears and wings, usually naked.

Zipping that file off through e-mail

You have the file. You have the e-mail address of the person to whom you're sending the file. All you need to do now is follow these steps:

▶ Write your e-mail message as you normally would

Start by writing your message as described in Chapter 16. It can be a new message or a reply to some other message.

▶ Click the Attach gizmo

Netscape displays the Attachments dialog box (see Figure 17-1).

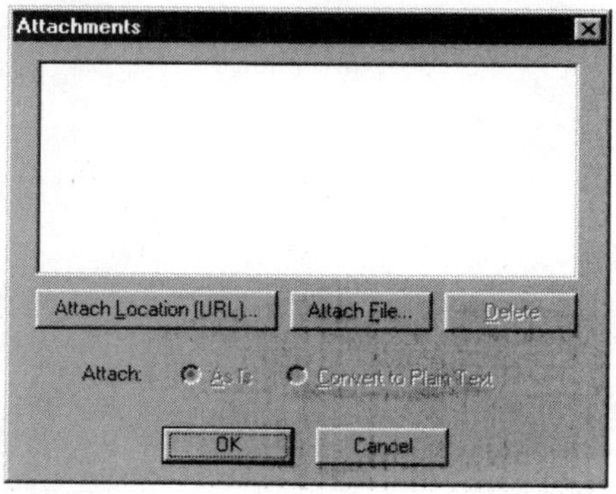

Figure 17-1. *The Attachments dialog box.*

▶ Click the Attach File button

A browsing dialog box appears.

▶ Use the dialog box to go out and fetch the file you want to attach

Use your Windows dialog box skills here. Locate the file you want to attach. When you find the file, double-click on its name. This closes the dialog box and inserts that file's name into the Attachments dialog box.

▶ Make sure that the As Is radio button is selected

Do not choose the Convert to Plain Text option. This usually results in chaos for whomever is receiving the message.

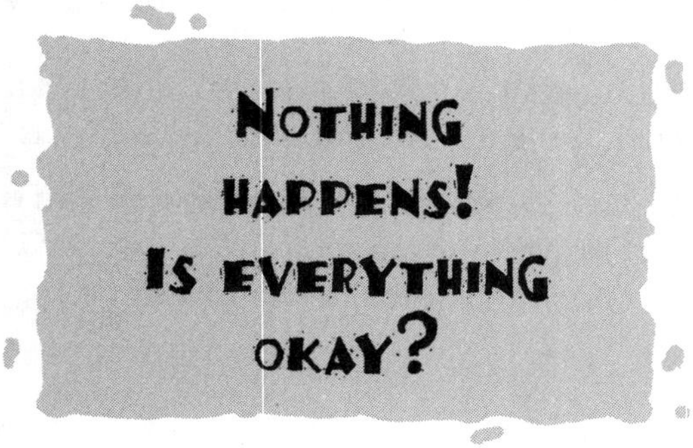

▶ Click OK

You won't notice any changes to your message in the message composition window. You will, however, see the filename added in the Attachment text box. That's your only sign that you've successfully attached a graphic image or file.

Netscape will send that file when you click the Send button, as described in Chapter 16.

- Refer to the section "Receiving a File (Attachment) from Someone Else" in Chapter 15 for information on what happens when you receive an e-mail message with an attachment.
- Sending a graphics file works the same as sending any file on disk. Unlike when receiving the graphics file, however, you will not see the image in the message on your screen before you send it.
- The person you're sending the attachment to can best receive that file if they're using Netscape's Mail program. Be sure to ask if they have Netscape before sending the file, or send a test file to make sure they receive it okay and can do something with it.

***FYI: William Shakespeare made up many words in the English language. In addition to honorificabil-itudinitatibus, he also coined the word* bump.**

18 SPIFFING UP YOUR E-MAIL

http://the-tech.
mit.edu/Shakespeare/

People on the Internet actually spend more time with e-mail than they do browsing the Web. Face it, getting e-mail is fun. It's a great way to stay in touch with people you otherwise might not. So if it hasn't already, someday soon the e-mail bug will bite you. When it does, you're going to be thankful you've read this chapter, since it deals with e-mail organization and efficiency—something you'll need to know about when all those messages start pouring in.

This chapter covers the following random points:

- Starting Netscape with the e-mail window
- Creating an e-mail signature
- Sending mail from the Web browser
- Organizing your e-mail.

Starting Your Internet Day with E-Mail

Unless you tell Netscape otherwise, it starts up by displaying a browser window, complete with your very own personal home page. But Netscape doesn't have to start with a home page or even a browser window. If you're addicted to e-mail, you'll probably want Netscape to start with an e-mail window full of fresh messages for today.

Follow these steps if you want Netscape to start up each day with the mail window:

► In Netscape, choose Options→General Preferences from the menu

The Preferences dialog box appears.

- It doesn't matter if you're in your browser window or the mail window. The Options→General Preferences command is on both windows' menu bars.

► Click on the Appearance tab

Look for the middle area in the dialog box, titled Startup.

► Click in the box by Netscape Mail

Below the text On Startup Launch you'll find three items. The middle one is Netscape Mail. If you click the mouse in that box and put an X there, it tells Netscape to start with the mail window instead of the Web browser.

► Click the OK button

Now Netscape is configured to start with the mail window—and fetch any new messages you may have—each time it starts.

- The browser window still appears when Netscape starts, but the mail window appears on top of it. To switch back to your browser window after Netscape starts, press the Alt+Tab key combination.
- Refer to Chapter 5 for more information on home pages.
- You can use these steps to order Netscape to start any of its three major programs: the Web browser, mail program or newsgroup reader.

FYI: When it was first created, Coca-Cola was colored green.

The All-Important E-Mail Signature

Computers are all about saving time. And, of course, the Internet is all about wasting time. So if you put the two together, you would probably create some kind of huge space-time vacuum. Mr. Spock would peer into it and say, "Fascinating." Then a ton of car keys, misplaced eyeglasses and socks would pour out of the opening. The EPA would probably fine you a ton to clean it up.

Alas, the combination of computers and the Internet doesn't result in anything that catastrophic. Instead, you get some nifty tricks for saving yourself typing time while doing your e-mail.

For example, at the end of every e-mail message you type, you probably put something like the following:

```
Sincerely,
Kathleen
```

This is, of course, assuming your name is Kathleen and that you're being sincere.

Or perhaps you've seen other electronic signatures:

```
- - - - - - - - -
Written by Norton Blortz
Making the Net a Better Blace Bor Blortz
Visit my Web page: http://www.blortz.net
- - - - - - - - -
```

The secret to this electronic signature is that Norton Blortz does not type that in every time he sends a message. No, Norton Blortz only typed that in once, in a separate file on his hard drive called a *signature file*. He then told Netscape about it. So now, every time Norton Blortz sends an e-mail message, Netscape automatically tacks on the above Norton Blortz signature to his mail.

You, too, can create your own custom signature file. It's real cinchy. You need to take only two fun steps:

- Creating a signature file
- Telling your mail program about it.

- And I never did type in Blortz all those times. I had a special keyboard macro in my word processor do it for me. See? Computers are all about saving time.

FYI: The first computer took up nearly a city block. Today's computers on the Internet only take up the rest of your life.

Creating your very own e-mail signature file

Your e-mail signature file is a text file on disk. You can create this using a text editor, such as Windows' Notepad program, or you can use your word processor. Or you can pay someone else to do it for you.

▶ Start Notepad or your word processing program

Take whatever steps you normally take to fire up the Windows Notepad program or your word processor. It doesn't matter which you use; Notepad is really designed for this task, though starting your word processor should be a lot more familiar to you.

- Windows Notepad is a program named `NOTEPAD.EXE`. It can be found in your Windows directory or folder on drive C.
- If you use your word processor, take whatever steps you use every day to start that program.

▶ Type in the text you want to use as your e-mail signature

You should be brief and to the point, though many people like to put their home-page address and maybe a clever quote in their signature. Generally speaking, don't write a signature file longer than four or five lines of text.

- Try to keep each line short, about half the width of your screen.
- Press the Enter key at the end of each line.
- Use only characters you can type at the keyboard; no graphics or "extended ASCII" characters (like the happy face or other dingbats).
- Dingbats: ✱ ❄ ✪ ✷ ❧ ❀ ✙ ✠ ♣ ➠ ❦ ❣ ♦ ✿ ➢
- Some people use "text graphics" to make simple images. The _ (underline), - (hyphen), | (pipe) and / \ (slashes) can be used to make crude pictures. Personally, I think they look cheesy.
- If you're using your word processor, set the font to `Courier`. This will help you line things up properly on the screen.

- All these items are merely suggestions. Some people go really whacko when designing their e-mail signature. There's no harm in that, unless you don't want everyone to think you're a dork.

▶ Use the File→Save As command to save the signature file to disk

Use the Save command in Notepad or your word processor to save the file to disk. If you can, try to save the file in your Netscape directory or folder. Save it under the name `SIG.TXT`.

This is important: Tell your word processor to save the file as a *plain text* file. That may also be called an ASCII file, MS-DOS Text or Text-with-line-breaks. Choose whichever of those options are available, to save the file as a plain text file. This signature trick will not work if you save the file to disk as a word processing file.

SAVE YOUR SIGNATURE AS A TEXT FILE.

- Saving the signature file in your Netscape directory makes it easier to find later.
- Refer to your favorite book on Windows for more information on saving files to disk.
- My favorite book on Windows is *Real Life Windows 95.*

Now that you've created the signature file, named it `SIG.TXT` and saved it in your Netscape directory, you're ready to tell Netscape's Mail program about it. This is covered in the next section.

TIP: Your signature file doesn't have to remain the same forever. You can change it as often as you like; just re-edit the signature file on disk.

- Too much, well, *crap* in a signature file is the sign of a new Internet user—a newbie. I remember from school, you could always tell when the sophomores had discovered their Internet accounts because they'd have these massive, half-page signature files. Imagine graphics of the Starship Enterprise and three or four quotes from Dr. Who in a box of asterisks three deep. Sheesh.
- Presently, there is no way to add a graphical copy of your real signature to your e-mail messages. In the future, this might be a possibility.

WHAT TO STICK IN YOUR SIGNATURE FILE

A signature file is really open turf. You can stick any text in there you want. There are some things that are more important than others:

- Do stick in your name, since this may not be immediately determined by looking at the start of the message.
- Don't bother sticking your e-mail address in the signature file; they already have your e-mail address at the top of the message.
- If you work for a company, you'll probably want to put the company name there.
- If you're a mucky-muck, you'll probably want to put your title there.
- If you have a Web page, put its address in there.
- Quotes are always acceptable in a signature, even dumb quotes.
- Recipes: A no-no.
- The date and time are unnecessary since this information is already in the mail header.

Letting your e-mail program know about your signature

To have Netscape automatically add your signature (carefully tucked away in your `SIG.TXT` file created just paragraphs ago) to each of your out-going e-mail messages, follow these steps:

▶ In Netscape, choose Options→Mail and News Preferences from the menu

A Preferences dialog box appears, looking big and ugly like a speeding semi coming at you on an icy road.

▶ Click on the Identity tab

The center part of this dialog box is where you tell Netscape about your signature file.

▶ Click the Browse button

The Browse button can be found at the end of the Signature File text box. Clicking that button causes a browsing dialog box to appear.

▶ Use the dialog box to locate your signature file on disk

Use whatever skills you can muster to force this dialog box to find your `SIG.TXT` file.

- If you followed instructions earlier in this chapter, your signature file will be found in your Netscape directory (or folder).
- You might have saved the file in your word processor's directory, or in Windows' directory.
- You know, there's a great "How to use the Save As and Open dialog boxes" tutorial in *Real Life Windows 95*.
- When you find that directory in the Browse dialog box, look for the `SIG.TXT`. Double-click on that file to select it.

► Click OK to close the Preferences dialog box

Unfortunately, there's no solid feedback to let you know everything went okee-doke. You will, however, see the signature appear the next time you create or respond to some e-mail.

- If you see an error message box, claiming that your signature exceeded the recommended four lines, ignore it. Your humongous signature will be attached to your e-mail messages, no problem.
- Remember that your e-mail message will have a signature! There's no need for you to type one in yourself. This takes some getting used to. For a while, you may send messages that end like this:

```
Sincerely,
Bobby

Sincerely,
Bobby
** Internet LORD! **
Visit my NIFTY Web page: http://www.nifty.nifty.net
"I'm a doctor, not an Internet Guru"—Dr. McCoy
** Internet LORD! **
```

The Internet Lord forgot about his signature file.

- To stop Netscape from using your signature file, follow the above steps to make the Preferences dialog box appear. Then, in the Signature File text box, delete `SIG.TXT`. This tells Netscape not to use any signature file. (This does not delete the file from disk, it just tells Netscape that you don't want to use a signature file.)

Yes, the Web Browser Can Be Used to Send Mail

You can use your Web browser to send mail. This is thanks to the *mailto* URL. That's an Internet command, just like *http* is a command for Web pages. In this case, the mailto URL is used to send mail.

There are two ways you can use the mailto URL. The first is to use the command box. The second is by clicking a `mailto` link on a Web page.

- You can only send mail from your Web browser. You cannot receive mail.
- Refer to Chapter 4 (the sidebar "You. You Are. URL.") for more information on what a URL is.
- Yes, I lied in Chapter 4. A URL is not just a Web page address. Actually, the http URL is a Web page address. The mailto URL is a command to send mail. I hope you can forgive me for getting technical.

Using the mailto URL directly

Just for fun, with your Web browser up on the screen, try the following:

► **Type a mailto URL into your Web browser's command box**

```
mailto:president@whitehouse.gov
```

Unlike a Web page address, there is no slash-slash. Type in `mailto`, a colon, then the e-mail address of the person you want to send mail to. Above, I've inserted the e-mail address for the President of the United States. On your screen, you can type in anyone's mail address, or type in your own if you don't feel like bugging anyone. (Yes, you can always send mail to yourself.)

► **Press the Enter key (if you haven't already)**

This tells the Web browser to help you compose a new message. In mere picoseconds you'll see a window appear where you can create a new mail message.

► **Fill in the mail message**

Type in a subject and the body of the message—just as you always do for e-mail. There is no difference here.

- See the section "Composing an E-Mail Epistle" in Chapter 16 for details on sending mail.

- Be polite when sending mail to the President. If you have a complaint, don't be nasty, as your letter will have little effect.
- If you're sending mail to yourself, you can be nasty if you like.

► **Click the Send button to send your e-mail message**
The message floats off into the electronic ether.

Sending mail by clicking on a link

The second way to send a message from your Web browser is by clicking on a mailto link. These look just like any other link, but instead of taking you to another Web page, they send mail to a specific person.

Most people put these mailto links on their home pages. So if you're visiting a friend's page, you may see a link like the following:

    Please send me e-mail. I'm desperate.

Click on the `me` link and a window appears where you can send that person e-mail.

- Sending mail by choosing a mailto link (or URL) on a Web page works just like sending mail from your mail program. The only difference is that the "to" part of the message will already be filled in. (The mailto URL does that for you automatically.)
- Most Web pages have a mailto link for the Webmaster, who is the person in charge of that Web page. You should use that link to tell the Webmaster of any problems with the page—missing links and other weirdness (beyond normal weirdness) that you may encounter.

What to do with Your Old E-mail

Too much e-mail can be a curse. Since it's easier to write, and it causes less wear and tear on the tongue than sealing an envelope, e-mail tends to be generated higher and deeper than regular mail. Therefore, something must be done with it.

In Netscape, as with other major e-mail programs, you can place old e-mail into *folders* for long-term keeping. Netscape does this automatically for you, although you can be even more organized by creating your own folders and moving messages in and out of them according to your needs. This is all covered in the following sections.

- You don't have to use the folders to organize your e-mail. And you don't always have to hang your car keys on a little hook in the kitchen. But if you do, then you'll always know where they are. The same logic applies to your e-mail messages.
- All mail you receive is kept in Netscape's INBOX folder.
- All mail you have sent is copied to the SENT folder. (Before the mail is sent, it lives in the OUTBOX folder, but after that it moves over to the SENT folder.)
- The TRASH folder contains any mail you've deleted. Why it does this, I have no idea. Though, I suppose, you can rummage around and get old messages out of the TRASH—especially if you're in a dumpster-digging mood.
- After a time, these folders get full and rather cumbersome. When that happens, Netscape will ask if you want to "compact" them. Click the Yes button with your mouse to compact the folder when asked. This helps save disk space on your PC and keeps Netscape from bugging you about compacting every two hours.

FYI: "E-mail is a lot like a major output of a cattle feed lot–if you don't get rid of it quick, you will be buried in it." –Vinton G. Cerf, President of the Internet Society; Father of the Internet.

Deleting your e-mail

Some e-mail messages are keepers; some are stinkers. If you read a keeper, you might want to stick it in a special folder—a folder you can create using the steps provided in the next section. But if the message is as meaningful to you as a joke on a cocktail napkin, you can zap its electrons to ethereal oblivion.

After reading the message you want to delete, click the Delete gizmo. This doesn't really delete the message. Instead, the message is moved from your INBOX folder to the TRASH folder. So there is still a copy of the message available "just in case," but at least it's not cluttering up your INBOX folder.

- To delete any message, click on it first using the mouse, then click the Delete gizmo.

- You should delete any old messages you don't want to keep. It's always nice to have an empty INBOX.
- If you don't want to delete a message, you can store it long-term in another folder. The following section tells you how to create a new folder; the section "Moving things into various folders" tells you how to move a mail message from one folder to another.
- You can use the Delete gizmo on any message in any folder.
- You can delete several messages at once by selecting them with the mouse. Press and hold the Ctrl key and click the mouse on each message you want to delete. Release the Ctrl key, then click on the Delete gizmo to delete the selected messages.
- To delete all the messages in a folder, press the Ctrl+A key combination (which selects all the files in a folder), then click on the Delete gizmo.
- If you delete a message in the TRASH folder, it's gone for good.
- A way to clean up the entire TRASH folder is to choose File→Empty Trash Folder from the menu. That permanently removes all the messages in the TRASH folder, which can save you a lot of disk space. You should do this every month or so.

Creating a new e-mail folder

Netscape lets you create a nearly unlimited number of folders into which you can place your e-mail messages. In addition to the standard INBOX, OUTBOX, TRASH and SENT folders, you can create folders for work correspondence; folders for any mailing lists you belong to; folders for messages from friends, for special projects, for funny stories—whatever folders you like. The idea here is organization: by putting e-mail into specific folders, you'll be able to find it more quickly later.

Here are the steps you would take to create a new e-mail folder.

▶ In the Netscape Mail window, choose File→New Folders from the menu

A boring dialog box appears.

▶ Type a name for your new folder

For example, type in `Family` for a folder you would use to store messages from your family.

- You can name your folders anything, though I'd keep the names short and descriptive.
- You cannot give your new folder the name of a folder that already exists. You wouldn't want to, anyway, since that would confuse things.

▶ **Click the OK button**

The new folder appears in the upper left part of the mail program's window.

- You can use the folder to store mail messages you've read. Moving those messages into the folder is covered in the next section.
- To see the contents of the new folder, click on it using the mouse. Any messages you have stored in that folder then appear in the upper right part of Netscape's Mail window.
- New messages are always initially put into the INBOX folder, no matter how many other folders you create or what you name them.
- If you use the Delete gizmo on a message in one of your own folders, that moves the message into the TRASH folder.
- If you don't like your folder, you can choose Edit→Delete Folder from the menu to get rid of it. But first, you have to delete all the messages in the folder.

Moving things into various folders

To move a mail message from your INBOX folder (or from any folder) to another folder, just drag it using the mouse. Point the mouse at the tiny envelope by the sender's name (see the margin) and drag that envelope to some other folder.

- If you drag a message to the TRASH folder, it's the same as deleting that message.
- Drag those messages you want to keep to their own special folders.

FYI: You must apologize for eructation, but for sternutation you are blessed.

19 The Joys of Keeping an E-mail Address Book

If you have an IQ of 350 or greater, you probably won't need to keep an e-mail address book. For you, memorizing all those names and numbers will make perfect sense. After all, you can access all 30 billion of your brain cells. Why not just set aside a few thousand for some e-mail addresses? Then again, if you're like me, you'll probably want to take advantage of your e-mail program's address book to remember e-mail addresses for you. It just seems a lot easier.

This chapter tells you several engaging things about your e-mail address book. Among the techniques covered here are:

- Using your e-mail address book
- Looking at your address book
- Manually adding names
- Automatically adding names
- Creating a list of e-mail names
- Using the address book to send mail.

An Address Book of Your Very Own

Your e-mail address book is an electronic Rolodex of names and e-mail addresses. Whenever you decide to send a message to someone, you can quickly look up their name in your handy address book. Your mail program will then automatically paste their e-mail address into your message.

You can also pull e-mail names from the messages you get, neatly stuffing them into your address book for further use. You can even store separate addresses into groups for sending e-mail to a whole bunch of people at once.

- The idea behind an e-mail address book is actually rather evil. You see, the people who design e-mail address books hate sunflowers. And a monitor that has 100 sticky notes, with various e-mail addresses on each of them, kind of looks like a sunflower. When you copy those names into your address book, you pull off all the sticky notes. This annoys sunflower growers no end.

Viewing Your Address Book

Whether you use it or not, Netscape's Mail program has an address book, one just for you and your online cronies. Why not use it?

▶ Choose Window→Address book from the menu

The Address book window appears, looking like Figure 19-1 (though your address book may be empty).

- The names in the address book are alphabetized by first name. I know, that's stupid. Doesn't look like there's any way to change it, either.
- To add someone to your address book, refer to the next two sections in this chapter.
- To delete someone from your address book, click on their name and press the Delete key.
- To change someone's information in the address book, click on their name and then choose Item→Properties from the menu. This displays a Properties dialog box, which is discussed in detail in the next section. Make your changes and click the OK button.

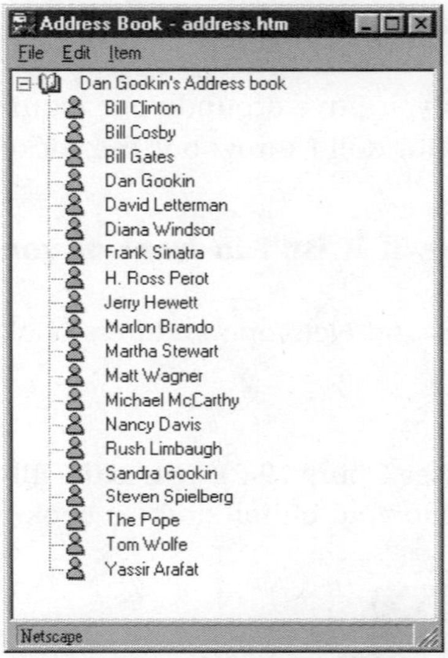

Figure 19-1. *A sample address book.*

- To instantly send mail to anyone in your address book, double-click the mouse on their name. (There is another way to access the names; see the section "Sending E-Mail to Someone in Your Address Book" at the end of this chapter.)
- Other mail programs also have e-mail address books. They all work similarly, though this chapter is specific to Netscape's Mail program.
- To quit the address book, close its window. Choose File➜Close from the menu.

Adding Names to Your Address Book

An empty e-mail address book shows the world one of two things: Either you really don't have any friends, or you just haven't yet figured out how to add names to the address book. Hoping it's the latter, you have two choices for adding names to your address book. You can do it manually, or you can have Netscape do it for you automatically. Though the automatic way sounds easier, you'll probably end up using both methods.

Manually adding a name to the address book

Forget all those sticky notes of e-mail addresses you have around your monitor. It's time to let the computer do the work. (But don't throw out the sticky notes just yet!)

▶ Make the Address Book window appear, if it isn't in front of you right now

Choose Window→Address book from the menu, and Netscape's address book appears.

▶ Choose Item→Add user from the menu

An Address Book Properties dialog box appears (see Figure 19-2). This is the fill-in-the-blanks form you can use to add someone to your e-mail address book.

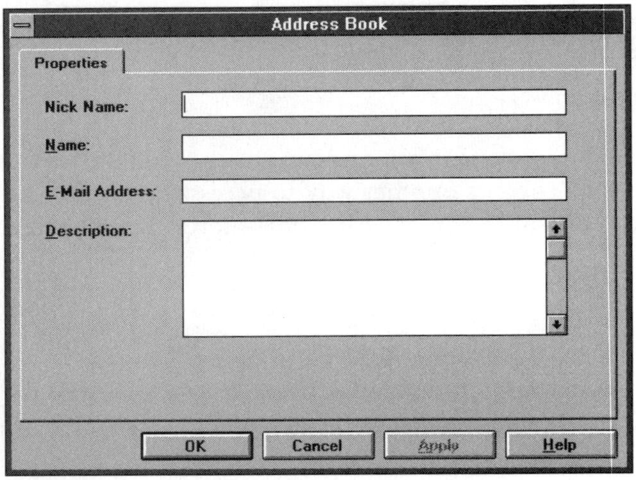

Figure 19-2. *The Address Book Properties dialog box.*

▶ Press the Tab key

You don't need to bother with the Nick Name.

▶ Type the person's real name in the Name field

Press the Tab key when you're done typing in the name.

▶ Type the person's e-mail address into the E-mail Address field

Jot down their e-mail address, exactly as you would type it if sending them a message.

▶ Click the OK button

That person and their e-mail address have been added to your address book.

- The new name appears in the address book window—in alphabetical order by first name.
- These steps describe the manual way you add information to your e-mail address book. This is okay for adding names and addresses you've already collected. A quicker way to add new names is covered in the next section.
- Now you can throw away those sticky notes.

Automatically adding a name to the address book

Any time someone sends you an e-mail message, you can instantly add their name and e-mail address to your address book. There's no need to write anything down any more.

You should heed these steps only when you have mail from someone and you want to add their name to your address book. Only then will the following steps actually do anything for you.

▶ Read a message from someone you want to add to your address book

Say The Queen writes you a letter. You'd like to keep in touch, so you decide to keep her name in your address book.

▶ Choose Message→Add to Address Book from the menu

The Address Book Properties dialog box appears (see Figure 19-2), but it's already filled in. All the important information—name and e-mail address—is ready to be added to your address book.

▶ Click the OK button

Done! That person's name and e-mail address have been added to your address book.

- If you need to, close the Address Book window: choose File→Close from the menu.
- There are some instances when you'll need to go back and edit the name just added. For example, some people's e-mail systems may not automatically insert their first and last names. In those cases, highlight the name in your address book, choose Item→Properties from the menu, then make any necessary changes in the Properties dialog box. Click the OK button when you're done.

- Another instance when this trick may not work is when you want to respond to an individual on a mailing list. This subject is covered in Chapter 21.

Adding the name of an AOL, CompuServe or Prodigy user

When it comes to the Internet, anyone who has an account on AOL, CompuServe or Prodigy can send you e-mail. How that works, exactly, is a puzzle for *them* to figure out. All *you* need to do is get their e-mail message. When you do, simply add them to your address book as described in the previous section. Netscape takes their bizarre e-mail address and neatly stores it in your address book.

- In some cases, when you add a Prodigy or CompuServe user to your address book, it lists both their name and e-mail account as the same. In those instances, go into your address book, highlight their name, and choose Item➜Properties from the menu. In the Properties dialog box, change their name from the account number back into their real name. Click the OK button to make the change permanent.
- When this book went to press, AOL and Prodigy users could send e-mail to anyone on the Internet by typing in their full Internet e-mail address. On CompuServe, you were required to type the word `Internet` and insert a colon before the Internet address. This may change in the future.
- A CompuServe e-mail address has a comma in it, which isn't allowed in an Internet e-mail address. If you manually add someone's CompuServe address to your address book, change the comma to a period. For example, the following is my CompuServe address:

```
73055,1405
```

Here is how you would write that address on the Internet:

```
73055.1405@compuserve.com
```

Creating a List of Folks to Send Mail To

Suppose you have a list of people you always send messages to. For example, your bowling team, or people from your church. You can gather up all their e-mail names into a single list for easy e-mailing. That way, when you need to send a message to the group, you just tell Netscape to use the list and then Netscape sends the message to everyone on the list automatically and you can bug a group of people at once.

Follow these instructions when you need to create a list of people to send mail to. (This won't work if you don't have anyone in your address book yet.)

▶ **In the Address Book window, choose Item→Add list**

An Address Book Properties dialog box appears (see Figure 19-2).

▶ **Type in a shortcut name for the list**

For example, `Bowling`, or `Church`, or `Group` for a group of people at work. Something short and sweet. This is the shortcut name you'll use when sending e-mail.

▶ **Press the Tab key**

▶ **Type in a name for the list**

This name appears in the Address Book window, representing the list. It can be the same as the shortcut name, or a bit more descriptive.

▶ **Click OK**

After the Properties dialog box goes away, you'll see the name of the list appear in your address book window. It has an open book by it, which works like a folder but looks like a little blue book. I call that open book a *list icon*.

▶ **To add someone to that list, drag their name to the list icon**

- For example, point the mouse at your boss's name and drag it down to the list icon. That adds him to the group (though don't do this if it's a weekend hunting group and your boss is a vegetarian).
- Dragging names to the list creates duplicates; it does not erase the original entries.
- Using the group is a cinch. When you're sending mail to it, all you do is type in the shortcut-nickname in the Mail To: field of the message. For example, you could type in the word `Church`, press the Tab key and Netscape would automatically change that shortcut word into a code name for your mailing list. When you send the message, that code name would change into the e-mail addresses of everyone in the list. Nifty, eh?

Sending E-Mail to Someone in Your Address Book

When you start a new mail message, Netscape displays a blank mail message form (see Figure 16-1). Normally you would fill that form in manually. But since you have an e-mail address book, you can force the computer to fill it in for you.

▶ Start creating a new message

Refer to Chapter 16 for more information on how to start sending a new message. Return here, though, for information on how to fill in the Mail To: field with an e-mail address from your address book.

▶ In the Mail Composition Window, click the Mail To: button

The Select Addresses dialog box appears, as shown in Figure 19-3. This is a special variation of your address book.

Figure 19-3. *Gather up e-mail addresses from here.*

▶ Click on the name of someone you want to send mail to

You may need to use the scroll bar to find the person on the list.

▶ Click the To: button on the bottom of the Select Addresses dialog box

This places that name into the Mail To: field in the e-mail composition window.

▶ Repeat the previous two steps to add more people to the Mail To: list

This is an optional step.

▶ Click the OK button

You're done adding names from your address book, and you can now continue creating the message.

- To send carbon copies, choose the Cc: button in the dialog box instead of the To: button.
- The Bcc: button is used to send a *blind* carbon copy of the message. That works just like sending a carbon copy, except the other recipients of the message won't see the blind-carbon copy recipient's name. So, for example, if Hillary and I were in on a scam, I could send mail to Bill and blind-carbon-copy Hillary. Both Bill and Hillary would get the message, but Bill wouldn't know I sent a copy to Hillary. Sneaky.
- The only funky thing about using the Select Addresses dialog box is that you have to click the OK button when you're done.
- You might also think that double-clicking someone's name adds them to the Mail To: list. It does not. You must click a name in the address book, then click the To: or Cc: buttons to send mail to that person.
- You can continue reading in Chapter 16 if you need help with the rest of the mail composition window.

FYI: Since 1916, it's been illegal to mail an entire building in the US. That's when a Utah man mailed a 40,000-ton brick house across Utah to avoid high freight rates.

20

Get Mail all the Time on a Mailing List

The odds are pretty good that people who get a lot of e-mail are either (A) lying or (B) subscribing to one or more mailing lists. Of course, some people get lots of e-mail because they're very public. People who write a lot of e-mail get a lot. People who work at companies with e-mail systems get a lot of e-mail (it's the e-mail snowball effect). Obnoxious people on the Internet get e-mail by the bucket. But one of the quickest, most effective and productive ways to get a lot of mail is to subscribe to a mailing list.

This chapter covers the following mailing-list topics:

- Understanding what a mailing list is
- Using Yahoo to find mailing lists
- Finding mailing lists on the Web.

What's a Mailing List?

A mailing list is basically a huge group discussion. But instead of being in a room together, everyone e-mails everyone else a copy of the same message. In a way, it's like being in on a party line; several people may be writing each other back and forth, but a whole lot more people are reading the messages and not sending anything (they're called *lurkers*).

- There are mailing lists for everyone, on just about every topic available. I belong to several myself, one for computer-book authors, another for people who are fans of the *Babylon 5* TV show, and several other lists on other lurid topics.
- There might be a mailing list of interest to you, but most likely there won't be. This chapter tells you where to find the lists. But keep in mind most lists are of a technical nature and are not on general-interest subjects.
- To join a mailing list, you *subscribe*—just like you'd subscribe to a magazine or newspaper. There is no fee involved, and you can unsubscribe at any time. Subscribing is covered in Chapter 21.
- Don't feel under any pressure to contribute to the lists. In fact, a lot of the lists are "digests," which are collections of information drawn from other sources. These are read-only lists for the most part.
- Of the five lists I read, I only send messages to one of them. That's because only one of them makes me mad enough to write. The others are for information or entertainment value only.
- Some mailing lists are private, invitation-only things. Obviously, you'll never hear about any of these unless you're invited to join.
- Mailing lists are created using special software, which you'll hear referred to as something like "list serve" or "major domo." It's that special software that sends mail messages out to a whole group of people.

Finding a Mailing List Just for You

Before you can join a mailing list, you have to find it. These things aren't very obvious, so like all the other good information on the Web, you'll have to hunt for it.

- Most mailing lists are advertised on related Web pages. If you find a Web page that contains lots of information about some subject, odds are pretty good they'll also tell you about any related mailing lists.
- For example, the "Lurker's Guide to Babylon 5" Web page lists other *resources* on the Internet available to *Babylon 5* fans. One of the resources lists all the various *Babylon 5* mailing lists. Similar Web pages for *Star Trek* (and other popular TV shows) also list related mailing lists, plus information on how to join them.
- You can search Yahoo and other Web catalogs for mailing lists. This is covered in the next section.
- A great Web page for finding mailing lists is the Liszt Web site. See the section "Liszts of mailing lists" later in this chapter.
- Many lists are announced in newsgroups. If you read any newsgroups, you may find information there on how to subscribe. Chapter 22 covers the subject of newsgroups in general.
- When it comes to getting information on the Internet, your first source will be the Web. Following that will be newsgroups (covered in the next part of this book) and then e-mail and mailing lists.

Searching Yahoo for mailing lists

A handy way to find a mailing list just for you is to search Yahoo. All you need to know are two words. No, no—not "please" and "thank you." The first word is "mailing" and the second is the topic of the mailing list you want to find.

For example, if you really wanted to join a *Star Trek* mailing list, you would search for the following in Yahoo:

```
mailing star trek
```

Entering the above line and clicking Yahoo's Search button yields a bunch of matching Yahoo categories and sites for *Star Trek* mailing lists.

If you were interested in genealogy, you would type the following for Yahoo to search for:

```
mailing genealogy
```

- The most difficult thing about genealogy is knowing how to spell it correctly.
- The sites Yahoo displays have more information on joining the mailing lists.

- See Chapter 7, "Looking up Things in Yahoo" for more information on searching for stuff in Yahoo.
- Yahoo may not find your mailing-list information. If so, that's okay. There are other places on the Web you can look. The following sections give you more information.

Liszts of mailing lists

Some Web pages are devoted to searching for mailing lists and helping you join. One such site is the Liszt Directory of E-Mail Discussion Groups (mailing lists). This is named after Franz Liszt, who was probably the best piano player of all time and would probably have been on the Internet had he not died in 1886.

▶ **Whip out your Web browser and visit the following site:**

`http://www.liszt.com/`

Behold the Liszt Web page—a search engine for finding various mailing lists on the Internet (see Figure 20-1).

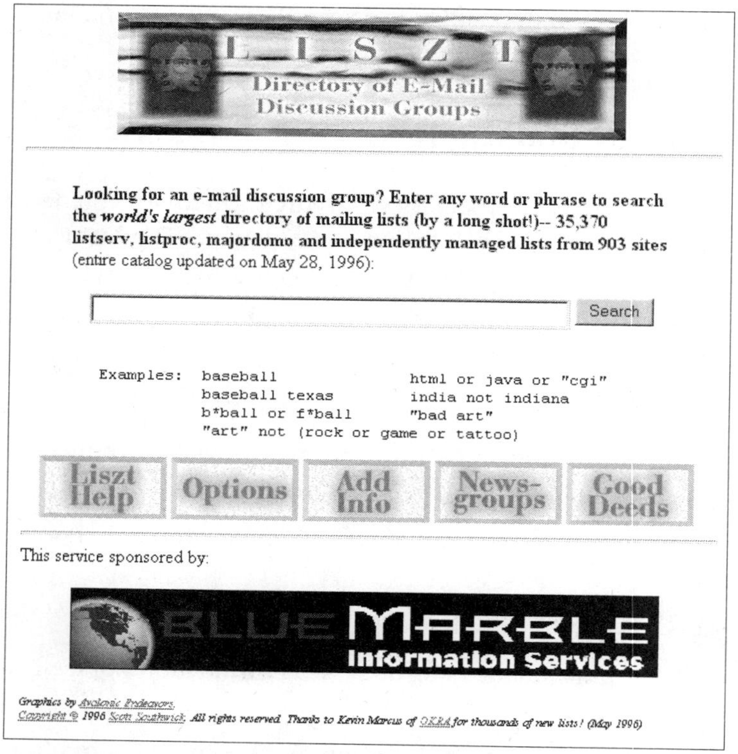

Figure 20-1. *The Liszt Web page will help you find a mailing list.*

Tip: Drop a bookmark! Press Ctrl + D in Netscape.

- See Chapter 6 for more information on Bookmarks.

▶ Type a subject into the text box

Click the mouse in the text box in the center of the Web page. Type in a subject you're interested in. As an example, type in the word `golf.` You're going to search for mailing lists pertaining to the sport (pastime, annoyance, etc.) of golf.

▶ Click the Search button

A network security dialog box may appear. If so, click the Continue button to submit the search request to the Liszt Web page.

▶ The Liszt page goes out and finds any mailing lists pertaining to your search word

If you're searching for golf, the list will find several matches, which are shown in Figure 20-2. Those are all mailing lists pertaining to the subject you were searching for.

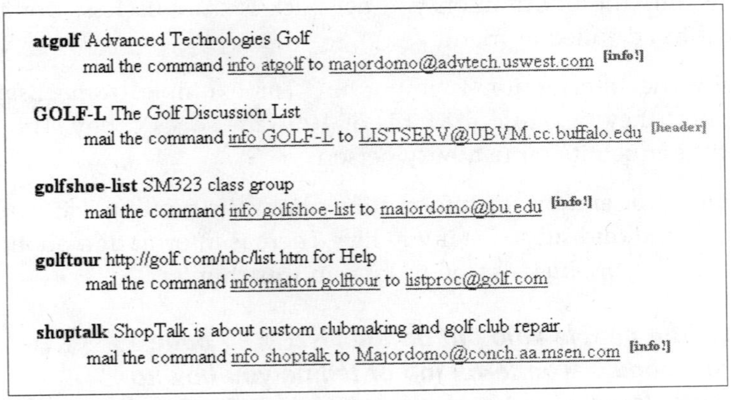

atgolf Advanced Technologies Golf
mail the command info atgolf to majordomo@advtech.uswest.com [info!]

GOLF-L The Golf Discussion List
mail the command info GOLF-L to LISTSERV@UBVM.cc.buffalo.edu [header]

golfshoe-list SM323 class group
mail the command info golfshoe-list to majordomo@bu.edu [info!]

golftour http://golf.com/nbc/list.htm for Help
mail the command information golftour to listproc@golf.com

shoptalk ShopTalk is about custom clubmaking and golf club repair.
mail the command info shoptalk to Majordomo@conch.aa.msen.com [info!]

Figure 20-2. *Various mailing lists found by Liszt.*

- Liszt displays two links for every match. The first link contains information about the mailing list. That's the one you want to click for more information.
- The second link Liszt displays is a mailto URL for the mailing list—the actual send-mail command you should use to subscribe to the mailing

list. Don't click that link until you've read the instructions from the first link. Or just wait and read the information about subscribing to mailing lists in Chapter 21.

▶ Click on the first information link

The next Web page you see describes how to subscribe to the mailing list.

- The Liszt people recommend first getting information about the list, then deciding if you want to subscribe.
- Not every mailing list will have such information.

▶ Locate the Get more info before you attempt to subscribe heading on the Web page

You may have to scroll down a bit to find it. When you do, follow the instructions there. They tell you how to send an "info" request to the list. Since this is subtly different for each list, I can't document it all here; the information on your screen is okay for this purpose.

- The information you get on the list tells you a few tidbits about what you're going to subscribe to. You can then decide whether or not the list is for you and whether or not you should subscribe.
- Most of the time the information you get back is truly useless. Don't expect anything detailed or friendly.
- Occasionally the information is important. For example, some lists warn you that they generate upwards of 100+ messages a day. That may be a little much if you're a busy person.
- You don't have to send off for information about the mailing list; you can just go ahead and subscribe if you like. There is information about this on the Liszt Web page, as well as later in this chapter.

Tip: The people who put up the Liszt Web page have done a wonderful job of telling you how to locate, learn about and subscribe to various mailing lists. Always be sure to read that Web page carefully before you do anything. Yeah, I know they get a little snippy about not sending subscribe messages to the wrong place, but it's still great information and not that hard to follow.

I Have the Information. Now What?

Now you get to decide whether or not you want to subscribe to the mailing list. I'll bet you do, so continue reading in the next chapter for the specifics on subscribing to a mailing list, as well as other informative tidbits.

FYI: You and I may call it "the bird" but to the Romans it was digitus impudicus, or "the finger without shame."

I WANT TO START MY OWN MAILING LIST

Mailing lists can be fun—a great way to bring together a group of people with a common interest and share information. If you like, you can start your own mailing list. This is yet another service your Internet provider may provide you with. Alas, there is a cost involved. Since mailing lists need to be maintained, you'll need to pay a monthly fee for the service, as well as a per-head subscription charge. I know this sounds awful, but that's the way Internet providers make money. Ask your provider for the details.

Another option besides creating a true mailing list is to just create a list of the people you want to send messages to, as described in Chapter 19. You collect various e-mail names and addresses and store them in your address book. Then you can e-mail to everyone at once without having to type in a gang of names every time. This works fine for a few dozen people, but gets cumbersome after that. Also, it's impossible for anyone else to "subscribe" unless they're invited in.

Oh, you would think things would be easier with computers. Sometimes they just aren't.

21 Taking the Big Step and Subscribing to a Mailing List

When you've found your mailing list, the next step is to subscribe. But brace yourself! The mail will start *flowing* into your mailbox. As a golf enthusiast (I'm an enthusiast since what I do on the course doesn't in the least resemble playing the game), I subscribed to the Golf-L digest. Whoah! Two hundred messages a day. Far too much information to read. So I had to unsubscribe. But that's the whole beauty of this: you can always test the waters and unsubscribe later if you need to.

This chapter covers the ins and outs of subscribing to a mailing list, reading and replying to the list, as well as unsubscribing later—after you post something so personal and embarrassing to the list that you feel like tossing your PC out the window. Here are the sections in which you'll find that information:

- **Subscribing to a mailing list**
- **Reading and Replying**
- **Sending mail to someone on the list**
- **Unsubscribing from a list.**

Signing Up for a Mailing List

Subscribing to a mail list involves sending the word `subscribe`, followed by the mailing-list name, to the mailing-list computer. Oh, there are variations, but that's basically how it's done.

So to subscribe to any mailing list, you need two pieces of information:

- The mailing-list address
- The mailing-list name.

Finding the specifics is covered in the previous chapter. You can use Yahoo or the Liszt Web page to discover both the above tidbits of information for whichever mailing list you want to subscribe to.

- When you have the specific information, send mail to the proper address to subscribe to the list.
- I usually put the subscribe information both in the message's subject line and in the message itself.
- Sometimes you also have to include your first and last names in the message text. For example, the subject may be:

```
subscribe LISTOMATIC
```

And the first (and only) line of the message should be:

```
subscribe LISTOMATIC Dan Gookin
```

Where, of course, "Dan Gookin" would be replaced by your own first and last names. Unless you're named Dan Gookin, too.

- Yes, many times you need to send only one line in the message. I press the Enter key at the end of that line.

You're subscribed!

A few minutes after sending off your subscription message, you'll probably get a reply. Most of the time, it will be a welcome message telling you how to send information to the mailing list and how to unsubscribe.

Tip: Save that message! You'll need to refer to it later if you need to unsubscribe or if you need additional information from the people who run the mailing list.

- The section "Two mailing-list tips" below tells you how to save the subscription message in a special folder in your mail program.
- Expect to get your mailbox flooded with messages in just a matter of hours.

You're asked to send a confirmation message

In some cases, the reply you get back from the mailing list may ask you to send a confirmation message. Don't sweat over this. Confirmation messages are usually sent by especially busy lists. They want to make sure you're totally committed to getting a full box of e-mail everyday.

In most cases, all you need to do is send a reply to the message with only one line of text:

```
ok
```

Don't quote the original message text—if Netscape has automatically quoted it for you, delete what Netscape inserted—and don't write anything else or change the subject. Just send a reply with "ok" as the only text. Then you'll be subscribing and getting that mountain of e-mail you've always wanted.

- Refer to Chapter 16, "Responding to Your Mail," for more information on how to send a reply to an e-mail message.
- To delete the quoted original message, press Ctrl+A, then the Delete key.
- And don't get all cute on me and send "okay" instead of "ok."

Two mailing-list tips

The mailing list you subscribe to is a special thing and may contain information you want to keep. So as not to clutter up your INBOX with that information, you should create a separate mail folder just for your list. Here are the steps for doing that in Netscape's Mail program:

▶ Choose File→New Folder from the menu

Netscape displays a dialog box where you can type in the new name for your folder.

▶ Type in a name for the mailing list

For example, I have a folder named GOOFY STUFF FROM JERRY because he sends me goofy stuff all the time.

▶ Click the OK button

Netscape creates the new folder, putting it in the list with your other folders, similar to what you see in Figure 21-1.

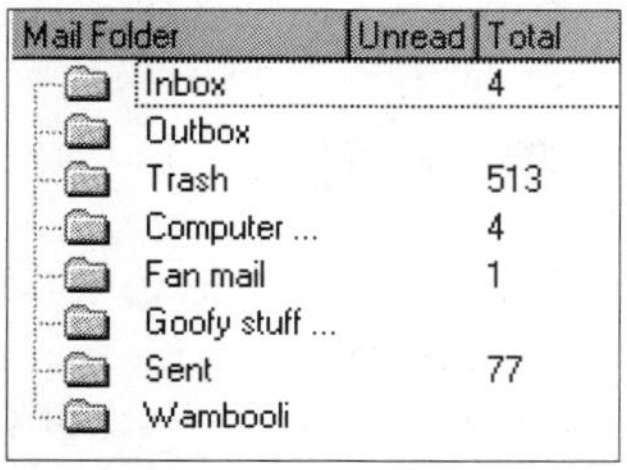

Figure 21-1. *Different folders for different things in the mail program.*

You can now drag mail messages pertaining to the list into that folder, for organized, long-term storage.

- Refer to Chapter 18 for more information on working with folders in Netscape's Mail program.
- Your mail program won't save mailing-list messages into your new folder automatically; you must *drag* them there using your mouse after the mail messages are received.

TIP: The first mailing-list message is most important! After subscribing to a mailing list, you'll get a reply that describes how the list operates. It's important that you savor that message's contents. It tells you exactly how the list works and what your duties are. When you get that message, drag it from your INBOX folder to the mailing-list folder.

In addition to creating a folder for your mailing-list messages, you should also add the name of your mailing list to your address book. Do this right after subscribing and moving any "you are now subscribed" messages to the new mail-list folder.

▶ **Open your mail-list folder**

Open the folder containing any mailing-list messages you've saved. Click on the folder's name once with your mouse. The contents of that folder appear in the window on the right side of Netscape's Mail program.

▶ **Click on one of the mail messages**

Click the mouse on one of the messages you've received from the mail list. This highlights that message as well as displays the message's contents in the big window at the bottom of Netscape's Mail program.

▶ **Choose Message→Add to Address Book**

The Address Book dialog box appears, partially filled in.

▶ **Press the Tab key to move the mouse into the Name text box**

Presently, the Name and E-Mail Address text boxes contain the same information. That isn't necessary; only the E-Mail Address text box needs that information.

▶ **Into the Name text box, type a more memorable name for your mailing list**

For example, if the mailing list name is `ESOUP@VETS.NCSU.EDU,` you might want to type in `Elephant Soup` for the Name instead. Type in whatever name reminds you that the address is a mailing list—and not your Aunt Edna from Minnesota who surfs the Web on Prodigy.

▶ **Click the OK button**

There. The name is now in your address book for later use.

Participating (or not) in Your Mailing List

E-mail messages from the list will show up in your mailbox almost as soon as you subscribe. Some lists have low-volume traffic, some are horrendous. However fast they come in, you read the messages just like you read any of your mail. The only difference is that you're reading a message that has been sent out to everyone who subscribes to the list.

Sending a message to the list works just like sending normal e-mail as well. All the information about replying to a message presented in Chapter 16 applies to mailing lists as well. The only thing you need to remember is that a copy of your message is sent to everyone who subscribes to the list.

As a subscriber, you'll also get a copy of each message you send. When you do, the message header may look something like this:

```
 Subject: Elephant Soup with Peas or Carrots?
    Date: Thu, 27 Jun 1996 10:20:34
    From: Dan Gookin <dgookin@wambooli.com>
      To: ESOUP@VETS.NCSU.EDU
Reply-To: ESOUP@VETS.NCSU.EDU
```

- The message is sent to the list, not a specific person.
- Also note the Reply-To line. That's the information your mail program will use if you send a reply. In this case, remember that the reply would be sent to the mailing list, not to the person who originally wrote the message. (To reply to that person, see the section "Saying a Private 'Hello' to Someone on the List" later in this chapter.)
- The following are some of my happy Internet mailing-list reading and responding suggestions:

Pay attention to the subject line. Mail-list topics tend to diverge. You see a message and want to respond immediately with some clever quip. However, the message's original subject doesn't change, leading to confusion down the line. Because of that, always check the subject line when you respond to a message. If the subject doesn't apply any more, change it.

For example, assume someone is responding to a message with the following subject line:

```
Subject: Grain futures
```

The reply turns out to be a joke made on a subject mentioned off-handedly in the original message. Therefore, the person replying may edit the subject line as follows:

```
Subject: Soybean humor (was "Grain futures")
```

The `(was "Grain futures")` addition to the subject lets people know the message's history, which is nice. But some folks will merely change the subject line to `Soybean humor` and leave it at that. Either way it's better than leaving the subject line unchanged and leaving everyone confused about the message's true subject.

Be brief when you quote. It's a good idea to quote the original message so that everyone remembers what you're talking about. But, without trying to repeat the good information in Chapter 16: Quote only the relevant parts of the original message. Netscape quotes the entire original message; you can edit that text if you like, getting quickly to the point.

Try not to drift too far from the subject. All too many times, a conversation will drift away from a topic relevant to the mailing list to some esoteric conversation between two people. Be aware of this! Inside jokes and joshing between friends is great, but does it need to be broadcast to everyone on the mailing list?

BE BRIEF WHEN YOU QUOTE!

Usually when this happens, the person in charge of the list will e-mail you, suggesting you just send private e-mail back and forth instead of wasting everyone's time on the list. (Yes, there is usually someone in charge of the list.)

Sometimes subscribing to a newsgroup is a better alternative. Mailing lists are a lot like newsgroups, but more private. If your mailing list is swamping you with hundreds of messages a day, most of which you never read, you'll probably be a lot happier reading a newsgroup on a similar topic. Chapters 22 to 24 cover newsgroups.

Saying a Private "Hello" to Someone on the List

Privately replying to someone on the mailing list requires a few hoops to jump through. Mainly, you can't use the Re: Mail (or Reply) gizmo in your mail program, since that sends your message to *everyone* on the mailing list. Instead, you'll need to manually enter an e-mail address. This isn't as hard as it sounds, just bothersome.

To personally respond to someone on a mailing list, follow these brief steps:

▶ Reply to the message

In Netscape, press Ctrl+R and a mail composition window appears. Unfortunately, the Mail To: text box contains the name of the mail list, not the person who wrote the message.

▶ Press the Alt+Tab key combination

This switches you back to the original message window.

▶ Use your mouse to select the name of the person you want to send mail to

For example, the mail list message may start out as follows:

```
 Subject:  Using Rhinos as a substitute for Elephants
    Date:  Wed, 29 May 1996 14:40:22 -0400
    From:  Conan <conan@barbarian.com>
      To:  ESOUP@VETS.NCSU.EDU
Reply-To:  ESOUP@VETS.NCSU.EDU
```

Drag your mouse over the e-mail name in the From: field. Don't select their real name or the angle brackets; select everything between the angle brackets. In the example above, that would be `conan@barbarian.com`.

▶ Press Ctrl+C

This copies the text you've selected.

▶ Press Alt+Tab

This switches you back to the mail composition window.

▶ Double-click the mouse in the Mail To: field

In the new message, point the mouse at the Mail To: field—which contains the mailing list's e-mail address—and double-click. This selects that address.

▶ Press Ctrl+V

The e-mail address of the person you want to reply to is pasted into the new message's Mail To: field. Everything is now set up for you to finish writing a private message.

- Yeah, this is a hassle, but it's the only way to reply to an individual on a mailing list.
- Remember that *replying* to a message sent from a mailing list sends that reply to everyone on the list. Follow the steps above to send a reply to an *individual* on the list.

Canceling Your Mailing-List Subscription

When you no longer wish to be a part of a list, you can unsubscribe from it. This is a snap. All you need to do is send an unsubscribe message to the mailing list.

This is typically a message with the subject `unsubscribe` and the word `unsubscribe` as the only item in the message's text.

```
   Subject: Unsubscribe
      Date: Wed, 17 Jul 1996 08:30:16
      From: Dan Gookin <dgookin@wambooli.com>
        To: ESOUP@VETS.NCSU.EDU
  Reply-To: ESOUP@VETS.NCSU.EDU
Unsubscribe
```

Send the message and you'll be unsubscribed in a few Wambooli minutes.

- Occasionally, the address to which you send your unsubscribe message is different from the address you normally used for the mailing list. For the details, refer to the original message you were sent by the mailing list.
- You might receive a confirmation message telling you that you're officially unsubscribed. It might even request that you send back a return confirmation, just to be sure.
- The Liszt Web page contains specific instructions for unsubscribing to mailing lists. Refer there if you used that Web page to originally subscribe to the mailing list.
- Unsubscribe from a list if you find yourself skipping over a lot of the messages, or just generally un-eager to read them.

TIP: A lot of people unsubscribe when they go away on vacation. Typically, you'll first send a message to the list (only if you're a frequent contributor) telling everyone you'll be gone for a few weeks. Then you unsubscribe, leave town, and then re-subscribe when you return. That way, you won't have a gazillion messages in your mailbox when you get back from vacation.

- Expect to receive a few straggler messages from the mailing list after you unsubscribe. Don't let it freak you out; those messages were probably sent before you unsubscribed.

FYI: Original Oreo cookies were mound-shaped, not flat. (The word Oreo comes from the Greek word for "hill.")

PART FOUR

NEWS, INFORMATION AND FOLLY

22 Newsgroups, UseNet and AbUseNet

One of the Internet things people get excited about are the newsgroups. That's until they learn how improperly named the things are. They should really be called discussion groups or, more likely, *disgusting* groups. If you thought e-mail was impersonal, wait until you join in a discussion with several hundred anonymous people, most of whom have never interacted with anyone socially in their lives.

I shouldn't slam all the newsgroups. There are useful groups, and there are groups that dish out information like a second helping of Aunt Debra's green, fluffy Cool Whip dessert at Thanksgiving. Still, don't expect to find any "news" anywhere.

This chapter covers the broad base of newsgroups, in the following brief sections:

- **Some newsgroup questions and answers**
- **Using your news software**
- **Finding a newsgroup**
- **Subscribing to a newsgroup**
- **Closing your news window.**

Wambooli Newsgroup Q&A

Q: What is a newsgroup?

A: It's like a group discussion that anyone can participate in.

Q: You shouldn't end a sentence with a preposition.

A: Okay: It's like a group discussion in which anyone can participate.

Q: Do I have to participate?

A: No, you can just read the messages if you like. About 90 percent of the people who visit the newsgroups don't post (send messages). The official term for them is *lurkers*. There's nothing wrong with being a lurker. I lurk. You will, too.

Q: What is USENET?

A: It's the real name for what the newsgroups are.

Q: Where are the newsgroups? Is there a big newsgroup computer somewhere?

A: There is no main newsgroup computer, just as there is no main Internet computer. The postings sent to the newsgroups are sent to all the Internet computers around the globe that subscribe to newsgroups.

Q: How many newsgroups are there?

A: As this book went to press, the number was quickly approaching 15,000. This is why I told you back in Chapter 1 to find an Internet provider who offers a great majority of them. Some providers only give you access to 5,000 or so of the groups. (It's all really dependent on how much hard-disk storage space your Internet provider has, since storing the newsgroups takes up a lot of disk space.)

Q: These newsgroups sound like the forums on CompuServe or the BBSs on Prodigy.

A: In a way, they are exactly like that. However, keep in mind that most newsgroups are not moderated. There is no one filtering out inappropriate or obscene comments. While most of the participants behave themselves, there are a lot of teenage boys (of all ages) out there who like to ruin things.

Q: So anyone can send anything they want to a newsgroup?

A: Writing to a newsgroup is called *posting* and anyone can do it. Don't get me wrong: very few people are obnoxious on newsgroups. Most postings are informative and entertaining. As in real life, it takes only a small number of idiots to spoil things for the happy majority.

A few newsgroups are *moderated*. That means all the information posted does pass through someone in authority—the moderator. These groups are tamer and often more informative than unmoderated groups. Typically they'll have the word `moderated` in their name.

Q: Do I have to sign up or join a topic?
A: No. Though a newsgroup is like a mailing list (see Chapter 20), you don't have to sign up. You merely use your newsgroup-reading software to peek into various groups to see what's up.

You can keep a list of favorite newsgroups, which is like subscribing. Your software should be able to keep your favorites in a handy list so you don't have to search for them all the time. (Remember, there are some 14,000-odd newsgroups.)

So Many Newsgroups, So Little Time

Your Internet software should include a newsgroup reader. This is a special program designed to read messages stored in any of the thousands of newsgroups your Internet provider has to offer.

Start your newsgroup-reader software. This is a program used to view the newsgroups—or, as is the case with Netscape, it's part of your Web browser software.

► In Netscape, choose Window→Netscape News from the menu
It may take your news reader a few moments to gather up the list of newsgroups.

- A Busy thing in the news-reader window lets you know when all the newsgroups are present and accounted for.
- You might also see the text "Reading file" and "Document done" at the bottom of the browser window. Only when all that nonsense stops are all the newsgroups read and accounted for.

Eventually the Busy thing stops. At that point, the newsgroup-list part of the window (upper left) shows you a list of newsgroups you can peruse. This is covered in the next section.

- Figure 22-1 shows what the News window looks like. You will probably find fewer (or maybe more) newsgroups listed than are shown in the figure.

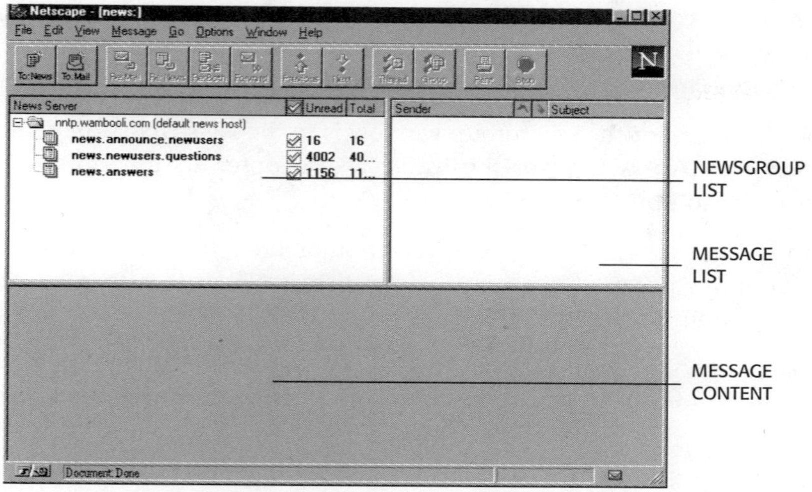

Figure 22-1. *Netscape's newsgroup-reading program.*

- If you don't see any newsgroups in the upper left part of the News window, double-click on the name of your Internet provider's server. In Figure 22-1 it's named `nntp.wambooli.com` (in the upper left part of the window).
- There are three parts to the group-reading window: the newsgroup list, message list, and content area.
- The newsgroup-list part of the window (upper left) displays the newsgroups. You can see only those newsgroups you subscribe to (your favorites), or you can force Netscape to show you all the newsgroups your Internet provider offers. You'll toy with this in just a few minutes.
- The message-list area (upper right) contains the messages available in a certain newsgroup. You must select a newsgroup from the left part of the window before any messages show up in the message-list area.

TIP: You can make the newsgroup-list area wider if you need to. Point your mouse at the bar that separates the upper left from the upper right part of the News window. The mouse pointer should change to a double-arrow pointy thing (see the margin). Drag your mouse to the right to make the newsgroup-list area wider.

- The message content area (bottom) displays individual messages. Like the message-list area, this part of the window will be empty until you start reading messages, which is discussed in Chapter 23.
- Notice how similar the newsgroup window is to the Netscape Mail window. It even works kind of the same. See Chapter 15 for more on Netscape's Mail program.
- If you haven't yet configured your newsgroup reader, the program may ask you a few personal questions before it starts. Refer to Appendix A for all the right answers.
- You can also use your browser to view newsgroups. See the section "Yes, You Can Use Your Web Browser to Find a Newsgroup" up ahead in this chapter.

Newsgroup Naming Nonsense

Like everything else on the Internet, newsgroups have funky names. In this case, they have short, curt words separated by periods. Fortunately, most of it can be deciphered by anyone who's ever worked the Jumble in the newspaper.

Most newsgroups will fall into the following categories:

`alt`	(the eclectic collection, bizarre things, alternative groups)
`comp`	(computer science topics)
`misc`	(random stuff)
`news`	(USENET topics)
`rec`	(recreation, hobbies, etc.)
`sci`	(scientific topics)
`soc`	(social issues)
`talk`	(debates)

Other categories exist, such as categories for specific countries; and your Internet provider may even have its own groups. Don't ask me what those are or what they represent, I haven't a clue.

The main categories are followed by a period and then by other descriptive words, each separated by a period. So information on adoption is found in the `alt.adoption` newsgroup; car racing topics are in `rec.autos.sport.nascar`; help for the computer game Doom can be found in `rec.games.computer.doom.help` and so on.

Searching High and Low for a Newsgroup

Out of the thousands of newsgroups, you'll probably want to check out a few, maybe subscribe to them. The hard part is finding the newsgroups. Netscape does just a horrid job of listing them in the News window, so there's no need to bother with that. Instead, you can use several easier methods of getting at the newsgroups, one of which is covered in each of the following sections.

Searching for a newsgroup in Yahoo

The best tool you have to find a newsgroup is Yahoo.

▶ Visit Yahoo

In your Web browser, type the following Web page address:

```
http://yahoo.com
```

Press the Enter key to venture off to the popular Yahoo Web catalog.

OR YOU CAN CHOOSE YAHOO FROM YOUR LIST OF BOOKMARKS.

You can use Yahoo's searching abilities to find a particular newsgroup. You just search for the word "USENET" plus the topic that interests you. For example, suppose you want to find a newsgroup about coin collecting.

▶ Type the following into Yahoo's search box

```
coins usenet
```

- If you were looking for any other topic, type that word first (instead of `coins` above) and then a space and then `usenet`.

▶ Click the Search button

Eventually, Yahoo displays any matching newsgroups that deal with your topic, such as coin collecting. In this case, the match would probably be the `rec.collecting.coins` newsgroup.

- If Yahoo comes up with a blank, consider searching for a similar topic. For example, "numismatics" or even "collectibles" instead of "coins."
- Yahoo may not find a match. If so, then there may not be a newsgroup on that topic. Refer to the following sections for information on the Wambooli USENET page, which you can also use to search for newsgroups.

► Click on the newsgroup link

Netscape opens its News window and adds the selected newsgroup to the bottom of the newsgroup list. Messages in that newsgroup then appear in the message list (upper right), ready for you to read.

- You might want to subscribe to the newsgroup you've just added. Refer to the section "Subscribing to the Newsgroups You Love" later in this chapter for the details.
- Refer to Chapter 23 for information on reading messages in a newsgroup.
- More information on using Yahoo to search for something can be found in Chapter 7.
- Even though the newsgroup exists, your Internet provider may not carry it—just as your cable service doesn't carry all the cable channels. If this happens, you'll see a "No such newsgroup" error in the Netscape News window.

TIP: If your Internet provider doesn't offer a newsgroup, you can (and should) write them, asking them to carry the newsgroup. In most cases, they'll be glad to comply.

Yes, You Can Use Your Web Browser to Find a Newsgroup

Just as you can use your Web browser to send mail, you can use it to read a newsgroup. All you need to know is the name of the newsgroup and then you can use its handy news URL to view the messages in that newsgroup.

► Switch to your Web browser window

You can use the Alt+Tab key combination to switch to your browser window if you were using it earlier. Otherwise, start your Web browser as you normally would.

- In Netscape, you can start a new browser window from the News window by pressing the Ctrl+N keyboard command.

A URL IS A COMMAND YOU TYPE INTO YOUR WEB BROWSER.

▶ Type in the news URL

If someone has given you the name of the newsgroup you want to visit, type it into the command box.

- Erase any text in the command box, then type in news, a colon, and then the name of the newsgroup. For example, type in the following command, but don't press the Enter key yet:

  ```
  news:alt.humor.best-of-usenet
  ```

- Hey! There are no slashes after the colon, as you would have in a Web page address.
- There is no period at the end of a URL command.
- There are never any spaces in a URL command, either.

▶ Press the Enter key

In Netscape, this command immediately opens (or switches you to) the News window, where the `alt.humor.best-of-usenet` newsgroup is dug up and its messages listed in the upper right part of the window.

- Some Web browsers display the newsgroups in the browser window itself. Older versions of Netscape do this. The newsgroup's messages are displayed as links. You click on the links to view the message contents. Or at least that's the way I remember it.
- You can now read the messages in that group, just as you would read any group in the News window. See Chapter 23.
- If your Internet provider doesn't subscribe to the group you specified, you'll see a "News Error! News host responded: No such group" error message displayed. Oh, well.

- Refer to Chapter 18, "Yes, the Web Browser Can Be Used to Send Mail," for more information on sending mail using your Web browser.
- The newsgroup `alt.humor.best-of-usenet` is a collection of silly (but real) messages from various newsgroups. This is an example of a moderated group, which you'll read more about in the next chapter.

Searching for a newsgroup on the Wambooli USENET page

The best way to search for a newsgroup, especially when you don't know its name, would be to have a whole list of them in front of you and then use some kind of Find command to look for what you want. Since I've always wanted a tool like this, I created one. It lives on the Wambooli USENET page.

► **Visit the Wambooli USENET page at the following address:**
`http://www.wambooli.com/usenet.htm`

Carefully type the above address into your Web browser. Press the Enter key to visit that page. Give it some time to appear; the sucker is very, very long.

Say you were planning a trip to Estonia for your next holiday. There's bound to be an Estonian newsgroup, eh?

► **Click the Find gizmo**
The Find dialog box is displayed.

► **Type `Estonia` into the Find What: text box**
You can type in upper or lower case; the Estonians, they don't mind.

► **Click the Find Next button**
In a few moments, your browser will have found any text containing the word "Estonia" in this list of newsgroups. In this case, there is a match on the `soc.culture.estonia` newsgroup.

- If the text you're searching for isn't found, then there probably isn't a newsgroup on that topic.
- Consider variations, such as "Greece" for "Greek" and so on. You can also use Yahoo, as described earlier in this chapter.

► **Click on any retrieved link to read messages in that newsgroup**
By clicking on the link in Netscape, you're taken to the News window, where that newsgroup's messages are displayed for you.

- If you get a "No such newsgroup" error, then your Internet provider may not carry that newsgroup.
- Sometimes you'll switch to the News window and the newsgroup won't show up. That usually means there are no messages in that newsgroup. Try another group.
- The Wambooli USENET page contains only about a third of the newsgroups available. The nice thing about it is that all the groups are listed in one place.
- Since the Wambooli USENET page is so long, consider saving it to disk. That way, you can have the list of newsgroups available on your hard drive at any time. See the section "The Joys of Saving a Web Page to Disk " in Chapter 8 for more information.

TIP: If you don't want to save the Wambooli USENET page to disk, then definitely bookmark it.

- If you're ready to read the messages in that group, refer to Chapter 23, "Reading the 'News'," for more details.
- You can switch back to the Wambooli USENET page by pressing the Alt+Tab key in Windows.

Subscribing to the Newsgroups You Love

Subscribing to a newsgroup works a lot like subscribing to a magazine. You can pick up a magazine at the store and read it. If you like the magazine, you can subscribe, and then get that magazine at your home or office every time it comes out. If you don't like the magazine (say it's all ads for cars and cigarettes), then you don't have to subscribe, but you can still always pick up another copy at the store if you like.

Newsgroups work like magazines. You can subscribe or just visit, depending on your mood. And for those you elect to subscribe to, there's really no true subscription form to fill out; nothing to pledge to; no sign-up as you would have with a mailing list. There aren't any fees involved, or weird rituals involving spanking or farm animals. Actually, subscribing to newsgroups is simply a way of letting your news-reading program know which newsgroups you love dearly, keeping them separate from the great hoard you could really care less about.

▶ Find a newsgroup you want to subscribe to--some group you feel you would want to read every so often

Refer to the previous few sections in this chapter for various techniques on finding newsgroups.

▶ In the upper left part of the News window, find the newsgroup's name

You'll see the newsgroup's long, confusing name listed; then a box; then two numbers.

▶ Click the mouse in the box after the newsgroup's name

This puts a check mark in the box, which means that this newsgroup is now one of your cherished. In Figure 22-1, you see the checkmark in all three newsgroups listed in the News window.

- Subscribe to as many newsgroups as you like.
- I would say, on average, most people subscribe to a handful of newsgroups. If you subscribe to anything over a dozen, then you probably won't have time to read them all.
- Even though you may not read them all the time, you may want to subscribe to newsgroups you read every so often. For example, you might want to subscribe to the `rec.travel.cruises` newsgroup and then drop in once a year before taking that annual cruise—but there's no need to read the messages there every week.
- To make sure the News window shows you only those groups to which you're subscribed, choose Options➜Show Active Newsgroups from the menu. In some versions of Netscape, the command to choose is Options➜View Subscribed. (They both do the same thing.)
- Unsubscribing to a newsgroup is done by clicking on the little box again, which removes the check mark. That removes that group from your subscribed list.
- You can resubscribe to an unsubscribed group at any time.
- If you're totally lost as to which group to subscribe to, refer to the Wambooli home page. There, I will list a "newsgroup of the month" that you can check out and possibly subscribe to.

I'm Done with the News

When you're done messing with newsgroups, you can close the news window. Choose File➜Close from the menu. This closes the News window, but does not quit Netscape. You can then go off and do other Internetty things as your heart desires.

- Don't choose the File➜Exit command unless you want to quit all of Netscape's programs.
- You can close the News window without disturbing anything that's going on in another Netscape window.
- You cannot open a second News window.

FYI: According to an August, 1976,* Ladies Home Journal *survey of boys and girls from the fifth grade through high school, their number-one hero was O.J. Simpson.

23 Reading the "News"

Newsgroups may not be the most popular place on the Internet, but they're certainly the busiest. People use e-mail for communications, the Web for research and entertainment and the newsgroups to absorb whatever remaining time they have in their lives.

Reading a newsgroup is a lot like reading your e-mail. Posting a message to a newsgroup works exactly like sending an e-mail message. The big difference is that the messages you read can be read by anyone, and what you send is sent to anyone who accesses that particular newsgroup. Yes, it's *very* public. It's also a very free place for people to express themselves.

This chapter covers the basics of reading and posting to newsgroups on the Internet. It does so in the following, brief sections:

- Reading messages in a newsgroup
- Reading a message thread
- Wambooli newsgroup terminology.

- **You will have much more success with this chapter if you've already read Chapter 22 on newsgroups in general, as well as Chapter 15 on receiving e-mail.**

Engrossing Yourself in Newsgroup Messages

If you understand how to read your e-mail, then reading messages in a newsgroup will be a super cinch. Everything works remarkably similar.

► Open your Netscape News window

Refer to Chapter 22 for more information on how this is done.

► Click on the newsgroup you want to read

Locate the newsgroup whose messages you want to read in the upper left, newsgroup-list part of the window. Click on that newsgroup once with your mouse.

► Watch as the messages appear

Any messages in that newsgroup appear in the upper right part of the News window. It takes a while for them to show up, especially if the group has several hundred messages in it. Please wait.

► Wait some more

Wait for the Busy thing to stop.

Think about Penelope, who had to wait 20 years for Odysseus to return from the Trojan war. And then, when he finally showed up, he disguised himself as a beggar who looked like Kirk Douglas.

► Start choosing messages to read

- To read a message, click on it with your mouse.
- The message's contents appear in the bottom half of the News window.
- New messages appear in bold type; messages you've already read appear in normal type.
- You'll definitely need to use the scroll bars when reading messages. Most newsgroups have dozens, if not hundreds, of new messages every day.

- Do not use the PageUp or PageDown keys on your keyboard to read the message's content. Those keys scroll another part of the News window, which probably isn't what you want.

You don't have to read every message; only bother with those on the subjects that interest you.

- Like the Mail window, there are Next and Previous gizmos for reading the next or previous message in a newsgroup.
- You can save newsgroup messages to disk. Just press the Ctrl+S key combination or choose File➔Save As from the menu. The newsgroup message is saved to disk in a format that Netscape's browser can read later. See Chapter 8, the section "Opening a Web page you find randomly stuck out there on the disk," for information on viewing a newsgroup message you've saved to disk.

- Printing a message is easier than saving. Just use the handy Print gizmo. Make sure your printer is on and stuffed with paper before you print a message.

Deleting old messages

Unlike e-mail messages, you do not delete newsgroup messages you've read. Instead, your browser automatically marks these messages as "read" in the

News window. (They turn from bold into normal text.) These messages won't appear again the next time you look at that newsgroup.

- To fool Netscape into thinking you've really read every message, you can use the catch-up gizmo: Click on the Group button to have Netscape mark all the messages in the newsgroup as read. That way, you can leave the group and come back later knowing all the messages will be new.
- On the flip side of the coin, don't think that because you didn't read a message that it will be there tomorrow. "High-volume" newsgroups generally don't keep old messages around very long. The older messages "fall off the cliff" to make room for new messages.

The joy of threads

For the most part, newsgroup messages tend to be comments to previous messages. For example, someone will post a message that essentially says, "Your mama." Then jillions of others will respond in kind, creating a message thread—like a conversation.

A better example might be a question someone asks. Like, someone in the `alt.colorblindness.support` group might ask, "Why is the sky gray?" That question will get a response and then the response will get a response. Netscape's News window keeps track of these message threads by organizing them in the upper right corner of the News window. (This is one reason the newsgroups take so long to display.)

THREADS ARE JUST A WAY TO ORGANIZE RELATED MESSAGES.

Figure 23-1 shows how a typical thread looks in the Netscape News window. The original message, written by Moses, was titled "Augusta." That message has a reply from Jeremiah. Then Methuselah has a reply to Jeremiah's reply. That's a thread.

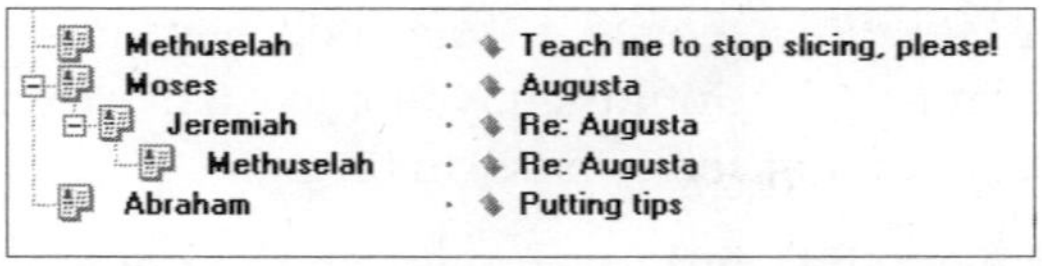

Figure 23-1. *A thread in the News window.*

- All replies to a message are indented one place to the right.
- A reply to a reply is indented one place further to the right.
- There is nothing extra you need to do to read a thread. Happily, Netscape organizes them all so you can read the messages in order. Just keep clicking that Next button.
- If the threads weren't there, the messages would appear in the list in the same order they were written, regardless of their topics. Following a series of messages that way would be like trying to read a book after all the pages fell out.

- If you want to skip a thread, click on the Thread catch-up gizmo. This tells Netscape to mark all the messages in that thread as read by you. Click the Next button to read the next new message.

TIP: If Netscape doesn't appear to organize your newsgroup messages by thread, then choose Options→Mail and News Preferences from the menu. In the Organization part of the dialog box, click your mouse by the Thread News Messages option. Click the OK button and Netscape does the rest.

That message is all numbers and monkey typing!

Some newsgroups don't have text messages, or at least text messages you can read. These are the *binary* newsgroups, which have messages that are really encoded files. Using special software called a *decoder*, you can take the monkey-typing text and translate it back into a real file. That way people can post sound files, programs and other binary information on a newsgroup just as you could post a text file.

- Getting and using a decoder is a major hassle. If this book ever has a sequel, I promise to discuss it at length. Until then, you can safely steer clear of the binary newsgroups and not really miss anything.
- Binary newsgroups typically have the word `binaries` in their name.
- Binary newsgroups hold information similar to the way incoming e-mail messages in Netscape hold attached files (see Chapter 17). The problem is that Netscape doesn't (at present) automatically translate the encoded, monkey-typing text back into a file for you.
- More information about posting messages to a newsgroup is covered in the next chapter.

Where did the message go?

Like credit cards and driver's licenses, some of the older messages in a newsgroup will expire. When they've done that and you click on the message in the upper right corner of the News window, you'll see an error message. For example:

`News Error!`

`News host responded:` **`Bad article number`**

`Perhaps the article has expired.`

Just keep clicking the Next button and eventually you'll find an article that hasn't expired.

Some Wambooli Newsgroup Jargon

Newsgroups have a lingo all their own. Strange words that are familiar to you—yet used in an unfamiliar way. I've collected some of this jargon and listed it below, along with an explanation of what it means and whether or not it's important.

Dev/Nul (or variations on that). When someone wants to ignore a message or someone posting a message, they'll often invite that person to send his message or himself to a place called dev/nul. This is a UNIX joke, something mainframe programmers and college computer geeks laugh about. Essentially, dev/nul is no place, like those slits in the medicine cabinet where you slide used razor blades. It's sort of the equivalent of telling someone to go to H-E-double toothpicks.

FAQ. This is an acronym for Frequently Asked Questions, which I would pronounce "fack." A lot of people new to a newsgroup tend to ask the same, basic questions over and over. To deal with this, the newsgroup regulars create a list of frequently asked questions—the FAQ. This list is posted to the newsgroup every so often, or it might be available on a Web page.

You'll encounter the term FAQ in one of two ways. First, you will see the FAQ list posted every so often as you visit a newsgroup. Read it. It will often answer a lot of basic questions you have. (FAQs are a wealth of knowledge.) Second, you may ask a basic question and someone may direct you to the FAQ. Don't be offended by this; unless the person is downright rude to you, they're really trying to do you a favor.

The Line Eater. In the olden days, some newsgroup-reading software would ignore the first line of any message, not displaying it at all. Whether the program did this out of spite or whether it did it because a grad student told a sophomore Pascal programmer to write the program, no one will ever know.

Because the program would ignore the first line of text in a newsgroup message, some users would put a blank line or a line with the words "line eater" at the start of their messages. Today's software doesn't have that problem, but you may still encounter some messages that start with the words "line eater" or something to that effect. Just ignore it.

ROT13. This is a simple way to scramble what could be an offensive message in a newsgroup, usually one of the humor or joke groups. ROT13 means "rotate 13." What happens is that every letter in the alphabet is temporarily replaced with another letter 13 characters away—like a simple decoder ring from a '50s kid TV show. So A becomes N, B becomes O and so on.

Here is a sample offensive message:

```
After 13 beers I just had to go.
```

Here is the same message, translated by ROT13:

```
Nsgre 13 orref V whfg unq gb tb.
```

No, it's not Dutch. It's just a message that has been "ROT 13'd" and now is not offensive to anyone (in any language). That is...unless you're reading a message that has been ROT13'd and you choose View➔Unscramble (ROT-13) from the Netscape menu. That translates the message back into original English, so you can read it and enjoy the potentially off-base message.

Spoiler. You'll often find spoilers in newsgroups that discuss movies or TV shows. The spoiler message reveals some plot element or other vital part of the show, something that would "spoil it" if you haven't yet seen the movie or TV show. For example:

```
Darth Vader is Luke Skywalker's father.
```

Since no one wants to blow it for anyone else, they will put the word *spoiler* in the message subject. That alerts potential readers—especially those who may not have yet seen the latest science-fiction alien-fest—not to read the message until after they've seen the show.

- Usually the greatest source of distress in any newsgroup is when someone posts a spoiler and doesn't label it as such. For example, in one of my favorite newsgroups, some joker posted a message with a subject line that announced one of the major characters would die in an upcoming episode. That's a Net no-no.

> **MODERATED NEWSGROUPS TYPICALLY HAVE THE WORD "MODERATED" IN THEIR NAME.**

- One way to avoid unexpected spoilers is to visit only moderated newsgroups. The moderator usually won't allow blatant spoilers unless they're labeled as such.
- Yes, there is someone who sits there and looks over all the messages. This person usually isn't paid; they typically volunteer their time.
- If you're going to post a spoiler—even a minor one—be sure you say so in the message's subject.

Spoiler space. When some people write a spoiler message, they also add about 25 blank lines at the start of their message. This "spoiler space" prevents some users from seeing the spoiler text if they should accidentally view the message. Instead, they'll just see the blank spoiler space.

Yeah, the object is to make the fact that the little girl's horse dies at the end of the movie a secret.

Oops!

FYI: According to the Victorian Era's* Lady Gough's Book of Etiquette *you should never shelve books by male authors next to books by female authors—unless the authors are married.

24 Posting Your Message to the World

Yes, you too can post a message to a newsgroup, contributing to the common good. This is a simple thing to do—especially if you're comfortable with sending e-mail. Unlike sending e-mail, though, posting a message to a newsgroup isn't a vital part of being on the Internet. Don't ever feel pressured into posting. Even in the face of severe taunting or temptation.

This chapter covers the topic of posting to a newsgroup in the following cheerful chunks:

- Posting a message to a newsgroup
- Sending a follow-up message
- Sending an e-mail reply
- Cross-posting
- Things not to post to a newsgroup.

- This chapter will run a lot smoother if you're already familiar with sending e-mail. Refer to Chapter 16 for the details.

I Think I Have Enough Guts to Actually Post a Message

There's nothing difficult about posting a message to a newsgroup. It's just as simple as sending e-mail...to everyone on earth. That can be intimidating. Even more so, since after you've read a few newsgroups, you realize that they aren't too forgiving or even nice out there in some newsgroups. Still, it's nothing to fear. If you feel like spouting off, do it. Here's how:

► **Visit the group you want to post a message to**

- Refer to Chapter 22 for more information on finding a specific newsgroup.
- If you just want to "test post" to see how it works, visit the `alt.test` newsgroup, which exists for this purpose.

► **Click on the To: News gizmo**

A window appears, looking very similar to the Mail Composition window Netscape uses (see Figure 24-1). The main difference is that the message is being sent to a newsgroup (`alt.computer.book.authors` in Figure 24-1) instead of a human being.

► **Type in a subject for your message**

The same rules apply for a subject here as they do when sending e-mail. Refer to Chapter 16 if you need to brush up.

► **Press the Tab key**

The cursor drops down into the message part of the Mail Composition window.

► **Type in your message**

- The same editing keys can be used here as when you compose an e-mail message.
- Use good writing skills!

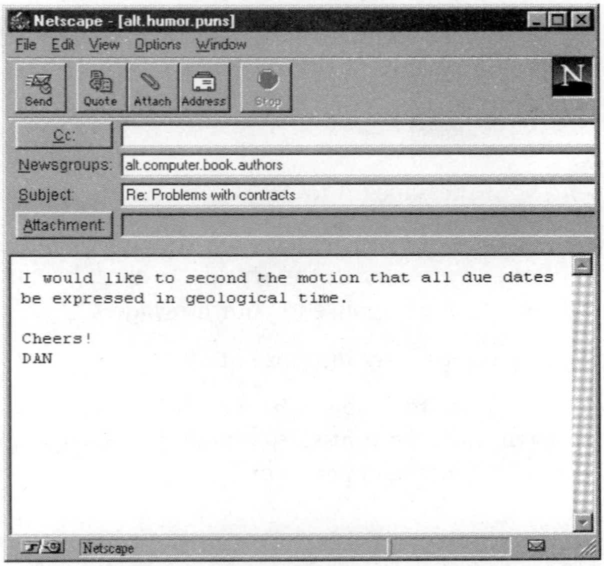

Figure 24-1. *Posting to a newsgroup.*

- E-mail etiquette also applies here. See "General E-Mail Etiquette" in Chapter 16.
- Keep in mind your message will be sent to hundreds of computers and read by potentially hundreds of thousands of people all over the world.
- Now everyone will know that you can't tell the difference between its and it's.
- Also keep in mind that anyone can respond to your message, either by posting another message to the newsgroup or by e-mail.
- If you have a signature file (see Chapter 18), it will be tacked on to the end of your newsgroup posting—just like in e-mail.

▶ Review your message

I just neglected to follow this simple rule and noticed a message in a newsgroup that contains several embarrassing typos and grammatical boo-boos.

- You can cancel your message by choosing File➜Close from the Mail Composition window. A dialog box appears, asking if you're sure you want to cancel. Click the Yes button. (This works just like it does in e-mail.)

▶ Send it

Click on the Send gizmo to send your message off to the world.

- It will take a few days—or maybe even longer—for your message to float around to every Internet computer in the world. So don't be surprised if it takes a few days to get a response to your message.
- Likewise, your message may not get any response at all.
- Also, for some reason, not all the messages you send will reach every Internet computer—not even all those that subscribe to the newsgroup you posted to. This is just weird, nothing personal.

FIRST-TIME POSTING ETIQUETTE

Fortunately, there is no first-time posting etiquette. Most people who post to a newsgroup simply read the messages and eventually get the urge to respond to one. Few of them say "This is my first post, so be gentle." In fact, in some newsgroups, that's a call for people to be rude to you.

Unlike talk radio, you don't need to identify yourself as a first-time poster. Just do it. Also, read the section on Poster Pests near the end of this chapter for some things you shouldn't do when you post.

Responding to a newsgroup message (a follow-up)

Just like with e-mail, you can send a reply as well as compose a new message for a newsgroup. For example, some nitwit may proclaim in the `rec.arts.startrek.tech` newsgroup that Warp factor 2 is really just twice the speed of light. Obviously, the moron doesn't know his warp coils from a phased particle accelerator. It's your duty to correct him.

With the message you want to respond to right there in the bottom half of the News screen, you do the following:

► Click on the Re: News gizmo

A Mail Composition window appears (see Figure 24-2). The newsgroup name is already filled in, as is the subject. Also, just like in e-mail, the entire original message is quoted and shown in the message part of the window.

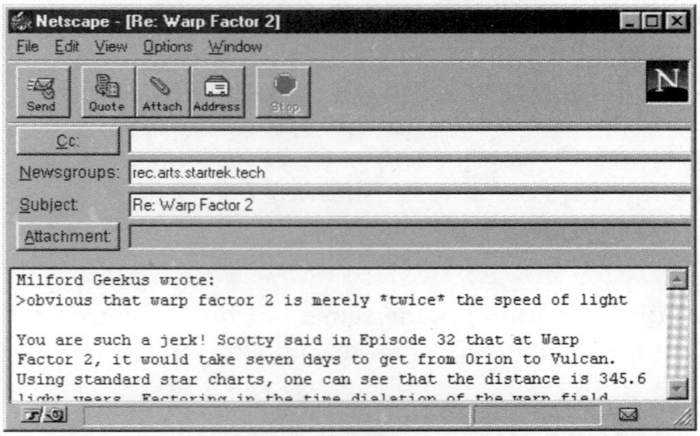

Figure 24-2. A reply to a newsgroup message.

► Compose your response

Again, this works exactly as it does in e-mail. The main difference is that your reply will be sent to a newsgroup and read by billions of humans and at least half of the heavenly host.

- Please, please pay special attention to the information in the section "All About Quoting E-Mail" from Chapter 16.
- The most important thing about quoting: Don't quote an entire message just for a one-line reply. People in newsgroups *hate* that. Only quote the relevant part of the message.
- Refer to the section "Don't be a Poster Pest" later in this chapter for information on "me too" posts, which are about the worst type of reply you'll ever read on the Internet.

► Review what you've written

This is always a good idea, especially in light of the many people who will read your wisdom.

▶ Send the message

Click on the Send gizmo and your reply will soon appear in the newsgroup for mankind to admire.

TIP: It might be a good idea to check the date of a specific message before you send a reply or follow-up. For example, the message you're replying to may be several weeks old. In that case, the newsgroup may have tired of it—or replies similar to yours may appear later in the list. Generally, I only reply to a message if it's just a few days old or less. That way I don't irk people by bringing up a dead subject.

- I know, all these little rules sound bothersome, but that's the way the newsgroups work. It's really quite different from opera.

Responding to someone with e-mail

If it is your whim to send a personal reply to someone who posted a message, then click on the Re: Mail gizmo. This automatically thrusts you into a mail composition window, with the poster's e-mail address already filled in and their newsgroup message quoted for your editing pleasure.

Refer to Chapter 16 for more information on sending the message. At this point you're essentially using e-mail and not the newsgroup reader.

Sending a message to several newsgroups at once (Cross-posting)

There might be a rare instance when you want to send a message to several newsgroups at once. For example, you might see Elvis filling up an '89 Caddy at the local Circle K and desire to inform all the folks in all the USENET Elvis groups.

▶ Gather up a list of the groups you want to post to

You can use Yahoo for this, or the Wambooli USENET page, or you can just select from your list of subscribed newsgroups.

For Elvis, there's really only one group worthy of an Elvis sighting and that's `alt.elvis.sighting` (I'm not making that one up). Still, you might also want to post your exciting message to the `alt.elvis.king` and `alt.fan.elvis-presley` groups just for good measure.

▶ Create a new newsgroup message

In the News window, click on the To: News gizmo. A Mail Composition window appears.

▶ Enter the names of your newsgroups in the Newsgroups text box

If there is any other text in the Newsgroups text box, delete it. Then type in the names of the newsgroups you want to post to, separating each pair by a comma. For example:

```
alt.elvis.sighting, alt.elvis.king, alt.fan.elvis-presley
```

- It doesn't matter if there is a space after the comma or not.

TIP: If you can't see the Newsgroups text box, choose View→Newsgroups from the Mail Composition window's menu.

▶ Continue composing the message as you normally would

Refer to the section "I Think I Have Enough Guts to Actually Post a Message" earlier in this chapter for more information on posting a message to a newsgroup.

- Some people cross-post because they know that not every Internet provider carries every newsgroup.
- A lot of cross-posting takes place in related groups. For example, there are several Star Trek groups and the people who frequent them usually cross-post to some or all of the groups.
- Obnoxious people tend to cross-post to *every* newsgroup.

Don't be a Poster Pest

There are good posters and bad posters. Bad posters are there to annoy people. You've probably seen their handiwork already. They post messages like "Star Trek isn't real, you twits!" to the various Star Trek groups, just to giggle and watch the fans get their foam rubber Vulcan ears all red and twisty.

There are terms for the USENET poster pests and the bad types of posting they do. I've defined a few of them below. Don't ever catch yourself doing any of this.

Flame. A flame is a heated response, and not necessarily a bad post. Typically, someone will get all flustered and uppity about something someone wrote and they will write a heated response (hence the term *flame*). Some posters even put `flame on` and `flame off` in their message, I suppose to let the reader know when they're mad and when they're sane. For example:

Here is my reply:

```
** FLAME ON **

You are obviously an uneducated mono-neuron who
spawned from a toxic waste spill and cattle manure.
How you manage to use a keyboard without firing a
single synapse is beyond all of mankind. May you
suffer the boils of 1,000 sinners.

** FLAME OFF

Have a nice day!
```

Flames are possible since posting to a newsgroup, like e-mail, is impersonal. Some of the people who write flames are in real life the calmest, most well-adjusted folks you'll ever meet. There's something about the computer that just doesn't bring out the gentleness in human nature...

"Me too!" This is a general term I give to people who should have responded to a message with e-mail. Instead, they posted a personal reply to the newsgroup. Or maybe someone writes a long diatribe and then the Poster Pest quotes the entire thing and writes down at the bottom "I agree."

Me-too postings happen a lot on the "dirty picture" newsgroups. Someone will say they have a naked picture of some actress or actor and it will be followed by zillions of replies along the lines of "Send me one, too!" This type of message should be sent via e-mail and not posted to the newsgroup where everyone on the Planet Earth can read it and be annoyed by it.

SPAM. A spam is a multiple posting of an irritating message, usually of a religious, political, commercial, or "make-money opportunity" nature. This is usually done by some bonehead in a marketing department who doesn't understand the nature of the Internet and of newsgroups in particular.

"Hey, Judy! Why not post an ad for our new back massager to the Internet! There's millions of potential customers out there with back trouble!"

No, thank you. It's a dumb idea.

Spamming a newsgroup with an advertisement usually gets the person who posted the message into some trouble. People on the newsgroups will instantly send them hate mail. Those who don't send hate mail are usually annoyed by the commercial interruption and will probably not think fondly of the product (or whatever) in the future.

Don't be ignorantly innocent about the Internet. Don't spam. (On the other hand, solicited mail is accepted. Many people sign up for mailing lists for just this purpose. In that case, the advertisement is not considered a spam.)

Trolling. A troll is a provocative post, something designed to annoy people in the worst way. These usually include racial or sexist slurs directed toward otherwise innocent or well-intentioned newsgroups. The idea is that the poster will upset the regular readers of the newsgroup, often to the point of shutting the group down.

Some newsgroup readers will spot a troll and post a follow-up message, identifying the troll for everyone else. They'll usually explain that the best course to take is not to respond to the troll at all. Since attention is what the troller really wants, ignoring him will make him go away.

* If you really, really want to know how to be more obnoxious on a newsgroup, you can visit the following Web page:

`http://www.indirect.com/user/steiners/usenet.html`

This page isn't really designed to teach you how to be more obnoxious. It's a joke! Instead, use it as a reference for what *not* to do when you post to a newsgroup.

FYI: The name SPAM (for the food) comes from the SP for spice and the AM from ham.

Appendix A

Some Items Your Internet Provider Should Provide You With

Contrary to being trivia, each one of the bits in the following table (A-1) plays some vital role in getting your computer connected to the Internet. Your Internet software may ask for this during its setup operation, so it's necessary to get all the information now, as well as keep it in one place.

Bit o' Trivia	What your Internet provider told you	What it means
Connection	SLIP or PPP	The method by which your computer contacts the Internet provider. SLIP is the old method, PPP is the new one. What they stand for isn't important. Your software may not even ask for one.
Login name		The name you'll use to "log in" to the Internet provider.
Password		Your password (you don't have to write it down here if you are concerned about others seeing this).
Other instructions		Write down whether or not you need to start a "TTY window" where you must choose an option from a text menu or type a command to start using the Internet. If so, write the instructions here.
E-mail name		The name you use for electronic mail, which may or may not be the same as your connection name.
E-mail password		You don't have to write this down, just don't forget it.
Access phone number		Dial this number to connect.
DNS Server #1		A series of four sets of numbers, each separated by a period. This may also be referred to as the "Name Server" or "Domain Name Server."
DNS Server name		(Optional) The network name for the DNS Server.
DNS Server #2		An optional second DNS Server number.
DNS Server name #2		(Optional) The network name for DNS Server #2 .
Domain name		The Internet provider's computer name, such as `MICROSOFT.COM` or `WHITEHOUSE.GOV`.
POP3 Mail server		The name of your provider's POP3 mail server (if available).
POP3 Mail server number		(Optional) The number for the POP3 mail server.
SMTP Mail server		The name of your provider's SMTP mail server (if available).

Bit o' Trivia	What your Internet provider told you	What it means
SMTP Mail server number		(Optional) The number for the SMTP mail server.
NNTP (News) server		The name for your provider's NNTP server.
NNTP server number		(Optional) The number for the NNTP news server.
Gateway		A series of numbers you may need when installing the Internet on Windows 95.

Table A-1. *Net trivia your Internet provider should provide.*

The following table (A-2) contains additional information that may be required by some installation programs. If you're using Netscape, then you probably won't need any of this information. Still, it's a good idea to ask your Internet provider about it anyway.

Bit o' Trivia	What your Internet provider told you	What it means
Your IP address	DYNAMIC or ____.____.____.____	If your provider gives you the same address every time you call, write it here. Otherwise, you have a "dynamic" address.
Net mask		Usually 255.255.255.0, though your provider may have some other number chain to type in.
Web home page		The name of your Internet provider's home page. Or you can use `http://www.wambooli.com/`
File manager		The address name or number of the Internet provider's network file manager (optional).
Gopher server		The address name or number of the Internet provider's gopher server (also optional).
Other trivia		

Table A-2. *Random bits of information and Net trivia your Internet provider should provide.*

Network Gobbledygook and Whatnot

Most of the network information your Internet provider gives you may involve network names or numbers. For example, a network name may be:

```
network.org
```

The number may look something like this:

```
84.244.96.2
```

These are both ways the Internet identifies computers. In fact, both items describe the same thing—a computer's address or location on the Internet. The names, such as `network.org` (pronounced "network-dot-org"), are merely shortcuts for humans who don't like the numbers, `84.244.96.2`. It helps to think of the numbers as phone numbers for computers on the Net. Carefully copy down the information either way.

In addition to the Internet setup information, you should also know a few things about your modem. It may help to fill in—or have your computer guru fill in for you—the information in Table A-3.

Bit o' Trivia	What your computer guru told you
Communications (modem) port	COM1 COM2 COM3 COM4
Speed (or Baud rate)	__________ BPS
Phone line	TONE PULSE
Call Waiting	NO / YES: Number to dial to disable call waiting: ______________________
Number to dial for "outside line"	
Number to dial for long distance	

Table A-3. *Modem information you may need for your Net connection.*

APPENDIX B

General Info on the Online Services' Browsers

The major online services, America Online, CompuServe and Prodigy, all understand the Web hype. When private Internet providers came on the scene, the Big Boys realized Internet access was a service they could offer, so they did. In many respects, the Web browsers you get on the major online services are on the same par as Netscape. (Well, the first version of Netscape, anyway). And not only that, but you still get all the other goodies (news, stock quotes, etc.) that the service regularly offers. The only drawbacks are the connect speed, which is low, and the cost per hour, which is high.

Okay. I'm not here to debate the merits of sacrificing your monthly pizza money to pay the Prodigy bill. If you live in the sticks, or if you already subscribe to an online service and want to check out the Web, you can do it quite easily. The following sections elaborate how it all works.

A COUPLA WARNINGS

Warning #1: If you have not yet used the Web browser on your national online system, you might have to upgrade your software. This is done automatically for America Online and Prodigy; the files are magically sent to your computer when you first try to access their browser. For CompuServe, you'll need the WinCIM program, at least version 2.0.1. This can be ordered free from the CompuServe store. The disk will take a fortnight or so to show up in your mailbox.

Warning #2: The online services change their setup and screens at least twice a year. The information you see in this book is general and shouldn't change much. If it does, you can read about any major differences between this book and the online services' Web browsing ways on the Wambooli update page: `http://www.wambooli.com/updates.htm`

Getting at Prodigy's Web Browser

There are a number of ways to attack Prodigy's Web browser. The first appears when you sign on. The main sign-on dialog box (Figure B-1) contains options for you to connect to a Web site as your first Prodigy duty.

▶ **Click the mouse on the Web Browser line in the Select destination: box**

Do this after typing in your prodigy User ID and Password.

▶ **Click on the Connect button and you're ready to go**

If you're already using Prodigy, you can visit a Web site using the Jump command:

▶ **Type Ctrl+J in Prodigy to display the Go To dialog box**

The Go To dialog box is shown in Figure B-2.

▶ **Click the mouse on the Web URL radio button**

▶ **Type the Web address into the Jump text box**

Look for where it says `http://` and type the address in that box.

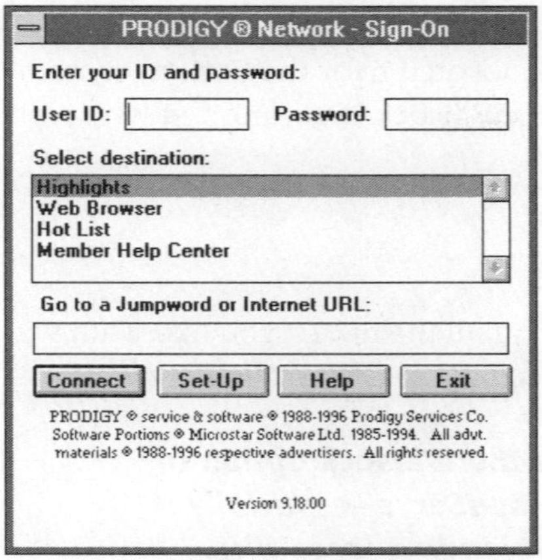

Figure B-1. *The Prodigy Sign-On dialog box.*

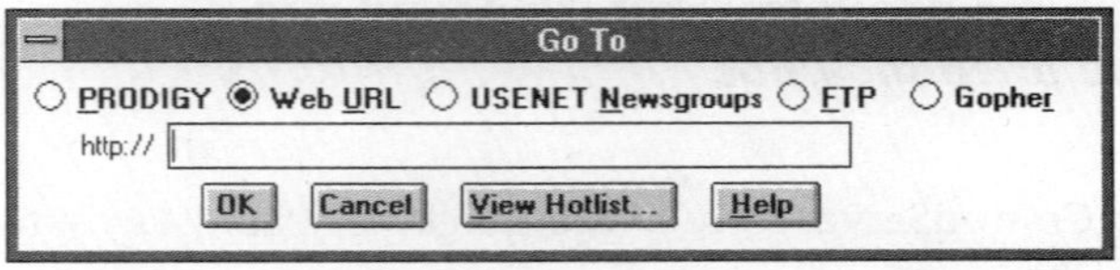

Figure B-2. *The Prodigy Jump dialog box, which also gets you at the Web.*

▶ **Click OK**

Prodigy fires up its Web browser to take you to that site.

Getting at CompuServe's Web Browser

Before you even dial CompuServe, you must make sure you activate the Winsock setting. This is what makes access to the Internet possible (at least with the current version of WinCIM).

▶ **Start WinCIM**

WinCIM is the CompuServe Information Manager for Windows. It must be at least version 2.0.1 or the Internet thing just doesn't work.

▶ **Choose Special→Session Settings from the menu**

The Setup Session Settings dialog box appears.

▶ Activate Winsock

Click your mouse in the box by Use Winsock, located near the bottom center of the dialog box. When the box has an X in it, Winsock is on and ready to work for you.

▶ Click OK

The Setup Session Settings dialog box closes.

- CompuServe's Winsock option can be on all the time if you like. That way you can use the Internet any time you dial up CompuServe. Even so...

TIP: My advice is to switch the Winsock option off when you're just using CompuServe—especially if you're uploading and downloading large files. Winsock is kind of unstable and may cause CompuServe to hang up on you. CompuServe may disagree with me about this, but I've found it to be true more often than not.

You're now ready to dial up CompuServe. Here is the quick, Internetty way to do this:

▶ Click on the big Internet button in the main Explore Services window

Clicking the button forces WinCIM to dial up CompuServe. (If you haven't done this before, you'll notice a little "dialer" icon appear when you connect with CompuServe. That's Winsock in action.)

The main Internet window appears.

▶ Click on the Enter a Web Site button

This displays a dialog box where you can enter a Web page address (the `http://www` thing), or just click the OK button to visit CompuServe's main home page.

After a few twists and turns, you'll see the CompuServe Web browser (which is a version of Mosaic) appear on your screen.

-  Once you're on CompuServe, you can instantly visit any Web site you want by using the Go command. Click on the Go button on the main toolbar or press Ctrl+G on the keyboard. The Go dialog box appears. Type in the Web page address and click the OK button. CompuServe will instantly jump to attention, firing up the Web browser and connecting you lickety-split.

Getting at America Online's Web Browser

After signing on to America Online (AOL), the quick way to get to the Web browser is to use the Keyword command:

▶ **Press Ctrl+K**

The Keyword dialog box appears.

▶ **Type the keyword `Web`**

Press Enter and the Web browser appears. Now you're ready to surf.

- When you're using AOL's Web browser, you're connected to the Web just like anyone else. All the instructions that apply to other Web browsers also apply to AOL's.
- Remember to maximize AOL's browser so that it fills the entire screen. That way, you can enjoy more of the Web without having to futz with the scroll bars.

Closing your online service's browser

To close your online service's Web browser, just close the browser's window.

- Closing any window in Windows is done by choosing the File➜Close command from the menu.
- Remember that when you close an online service's Web browser window, you aren't quitting the online service. That way you can go out and check your stock quotes, download a game or barge into a chat room without having to re-dial the modem. These are the conveniences for which our ancestors struggled.

Appendix C

Domain Name Nonsense

The domain name is usually the last part of a Web-page or e-mail address. It's typically three letters long and describes what organization you use to access the Internet. Here's the run-down since you cared enough to turn to this out-of-the-way appendix to find this information:

Domain thing	Meaning to those who care
`com`	*Commercial organizations (also "companies," though that's technically incorrect)*
`edu`	*Educational institutions, primarily universities*
`gov`	*Government organizations*
`mil`	*Military organizations in the U.S. (Army, Navy, Air Force, etc.)*
`net`	*Another suffix, not specifically* `com` *but not anything else either*
`org`	*Organizations, primarily nonprofit, though that's not a hard and fast rule*

Figure D-1. *Domain names and their meanings.*

Other Nonsense You Might See

There may be a second suffix, after the domain name, that tells you that the address is in a foreign country and which country that is. For example:

```
thequeen@buckingham.palace.org.uk
```

The above (fictitious) e-mail address describes someone at some location which is an `org` (organization) in the `uk` (United Kingdom). Other suffixes from other popular places are listed below. This is not a complete list.

Code	Country
aq	*Antarctica*
ar	*Argentina*
au	*Australia*
at	*Austria*
be	*Belgium*
br	*Brazil*
bg	*Bulgaria*
ca	*Canada*
cl	*Chile*
cn	*China*
co	*Colombia*
cr	*Costa Rica*
dk	*Denmark*
ec	*Ecuador*
eg	*Egypt*
ee	*Estonia*
et	*Ethiopia*
fi	*Finland*
fr	*France*
de	*Germany*
gr	*Greece*
hk	*Hong Kong*
hu	*Hungary*
is	*Iceland*
in	*India*
ie	*Ireland*

Code	Country
il	*Israel*
it	*Italy*
jp	*Japan*
ke	*Kenya*
kr	*Korea*
lv	*Latvia*
lt	*Lithuania*
lu	*Luxembourg*
my	*Malaysia*
mx	*Mexico*
nl	*Netherlands*
nz	*New Zealand*
no	*Norway*
ph	*Philippines*
pl	*Poland*
pt	*Portugal*
ru	*Russia*
sa	*Saudi Arabia*
sn	*Senegal*
sg	*Singapore*
si	*Slovenia*
za	*South Africa*
es	*Spain*
se	*Sweden*
ch	*Switzerland*
tw	*Taiwan*
th	*Thailand*
tn	*Tunisia*
tr	*Turkey*
ua	*Ukraine*
uk	*United Kingdom*
us	*United States*
uy	*Uruguay*
uz	*Uzbekistan*
va	*Vatican City*
zw	*Zimbabwe*

Figure D-2. *Some country codes.*

Glossary

Address

The location of something on the Internet. When you talk about an address on the Internet, you're talking about an electronic address, like a home page location or someone's e-mail address. Most addresses look like a fruit salad of strange keyboard characters plus some barely recognizable text. A typical e-mail address would be:

```
president@whitehouse.gov
```

A typical Web page address would be:

```
http://www.wambooli.com
```

Address Book

A program for storing e-mail addresses and names. This allows you to easily select a person from the list and have the program automatically insert their e-mail address into any message you're writing.

Applet

This is a little Java program your Web browser can run on the Internet. Since most Java programs are tiny little things, they are applets instead of applications.

Archie

An old method of searching through the vast sum of information on the Internet. You can still access some Archie servers through the Web, though using a tool like Yahoo yields far better results.

BPS

An acronym for Bits Per Second, the rate at which information travels through a modem and over the phone lines. To get a rough idea of how fast that is, just take the BPS speed number and lop off the last two zeros, such as 280 for a 28,000 BPS modem. That tells you roughly how many words the modem can transmit every second. So if a 28,000 BPS modem were a human, it could read 280 words per second. A slower, 2400 BPS modem only transmits 24 words per second.

Busy thing

A graphical image your browser displays when it's busy. This indicates that the browser is waiting for information. When you see it, you wait too. Clicking your browser's Stop button will stop the Busy thing, but that also stops information from coming into your computer (until you click the Reload button).

Netscape's Mail and News windows also have Busy things, which tell you when the program is talking with your Internet provider, getting new information, or just wasting time to annoy you.

Cyber

A prefix used to refer to something that's on the Internet or something that happens electronically. Cyberspace is a nickname for the Internet. Cyberfun would be fun you have on the Internet. Cybersex refers to the confusion caused when a 42-year-old man logs onto an AOL chat forum and pretends to be 19-year-old Linda from Pasadena.

Domain

The last part of a computer's name or your e-mail address. It's used to identify what type of organization you belong to when you access the Internet. Domain names ending in `mil` are military; `gov` is used by government organizations; `com` by commercial companies, and so on. Refer to Appendix C.

Download

To transfer information or a file from another computer into your computer. I suppose the term came about because, in the olden days, the big computers were all on top of hills and all the menial laborers like you or I lived in the valley.

So when you needed to get information from the big computer, it came *down* the hill and was downloaded into your PC. I also suppose I'm making that up, but it's how I remember the term. Also see *upload.*

E-mail

Electronic mail, also called email. It's a term that describes both the program used to create e-mail and the messages themselves.

Emoticon

See *smilies.*

Forms

Fill-in-the-blanks parts of Web pages.

Frames

A Web page divided into two or more areas is said to be riddled with frames. Not every Web browser can display frames—which drives some Web users nuts. Frames are nifty if used properly, but most of the time people just junk up their Web pages with frames and it makes everything hard to see.

You can move the frames around if you like. Use your mouse to "grab" a frame border and drag it one way or the other to make the frame larger or smaller.

FTP

An acronym for File Transfer Protocol, an ancient UNIX program that allowed files to be sent between two UNIX computers using a network or the phone lines. In modern parlance, FTP refers to a way you can access files on a UNIX computer using your Web browser. It also refers to separate programs that can be used to send files between your computer and other computers on the Internet. Basically, FTP is sending files back and forth.

Gopher

Gopher is a collection of information, found on the Internet, which can be Web pages, file archives, whatever—but it's all in one spot. You can use your Web browser to view information stored on a gopher server. For example, a lot of collections of stuff—such as TV show trivia, song lyrics, and other collected information—can be found on gopher servers. They appear in your Web browser window just like any other list of information, complete with links and such.

Home page

The first Web page you see when you first start your Web browser. Your home page can be any page on the Web, from a page you design yourself to your Internet provider's home page to some other page you select. The home page is also displayed when you click your browser's Home gizmo.

Host

When you use a modem to call up another computer, that other computer is called the *host*. This is what your Internet provider's computer is whenever you use the Internet. I suppose your computer would then be the *guest*, but that's not how it works.

HotJava

The name of a Web browser developed by Sun Microsystems.

HTML

Acronym for HyperText Mark-up Language, the instructions embedded in a Web page document that tell your Web browser how to display the text, how things are formatted, where graphics go, which Web page to go to for a link, and other information.

HTTP

Acronym for HyperText Transfer Protocol, the secret codes by which your Web browser reads Web pages on the Internet. HTTP is actually a command you give the Web browser to go out and hunt down a certain Web page. The HTTP is followed by the address of that Web page somewhere on the Internet.

HTMTLP

An acronym I just made up.

Internet

A large network of computers that send, receive and store information.

Internet provider

A company that offers access to the Internet for regular Joes like you and me. They sell accounts on their computer, which you can access using your own computer and special Internet software. This service is provided for a monthly or hourly fee.

ISP

Acronym for Internet Service Provider, what this books calls an Internet Provider. The key word here is Service, which is what they should provide you with. Odds are you probably have an Internet Provider and not an Internet Service Provider.

Java

A programming language used to create applets, or little programs that live on the Web. Your Web browser can run these programs, which appear on your screen just as if they were programs running on your computer.

Many of the Internet pundits feel that Java will revolutionize the Web, allowing you to run real programs—like word processors, spreadsheets and databases—on the Web instead of right on your computer. Presently the Java applets merely amuse.

JavaScript

A simple type of programming language (related to Java) that can easily be included on a Web page. JavaScript is more responsible for some of the zany things you see on the Web than Java itself. For more information, refer to one of the many JavaScript pages on the web; use Yahoo to search for "JavaScript."

K, KB

Abbreviations for *kilobyte,* discussed next.

Kilobyte

A measure of 1,000 characters of information. This is approximately equal to one-half page of information on your computer screen. For graphics, a postage-stamp-sized image might be about 4 kilobytes in size. Most Web graphics are anywhere from 36 to 120 kilobytes in size.

The reason kilobytes are important is that they let you know how long it will take for you to view or download a file from the Web. A hefty file of 700 kilobytes will take a good chunk of time to send from one computer to another—usually over 5 minutes on a fast, 28.8K modem.

Krakatoa

East of Java.

Link

A reference to a Web page, which takes you to that Web page if you click on it with your mouse. The Web is all about information and links to related information. The links appear on a Web page as underlined text, which you can click your mouse on. That takes you to another page on the Web (or some other Internet resource) that offers additional or related information. Links can appear on a Web page as both text and graphics.

Lurker

Someone who visits a newsgroup or mailing list but does not participate or post messages. This is perfectly okay; the majority of people who use the Internet do not post or send messages to mailing lists. They lurk.

M, MB

Abbreviations for *megabyte*. See *megabyte*.

Mail

Another term for e-mail or electronic mail. It can also refer to the program used to read and compose e-mail. See *e-mail*.

Mailbox

A storage location for electronic mail on your Internet provider's computer—just like a real mailbox, though this one is specifically for e-mail. The term mailbox isn't used much after you set up the Internet and start sending and receiving e-mail. It's only part of the service your Internet provider should offer, that being the ability for you to have an e-mail account on their computer.

Megabyte

A measure of one million bytes. This is a large size value. Some files on the Internet are one megabyte or larger in size. If you want to download or view such files or images, it will take a considerable amount of time.

Modem

A device that takes digital information from your computer and translates it into sounds that can be sent over the phone lines. It can also take the sounds and translate them back into digital information that the computer understands. The word modem is actually a contraction of the words modulator-demodulator, which are the techy terms for translating digital information into sounds and back again.

Multipart

A message that's posted to a newsgroup in several pieces. This is usually shown by part numbers in the message subject: Part (1/3), then (2/3) and finally (3/3). You'll find these mostly on binary newsgroups.

Newbie

Someone who is new to the Internet or, more specifically, to USENET. It's a derogatory term, often used against someone when they innocently break some un-written Internet rule. Many bold people, however, gladly admit that they're newbies and ask others for help. Mostly newbies are just people new to some aspect of computing, such as the Internet. But there are some old geezers on the Internet (which means they're in their 40s but act like they know it all) who refer to anyone who's been connected to the Internet since 1978 as a "newbie."

Newsgroup

A public forum for folks on the Internet to exchange information and ideas. Each newsgroup is targeted to a specific topic, and people contribute information or comment on what others have said—like a public e-mail forum. Sometimes this can get out of hand, but most of the time you'll find a lot of good information in the various newsgroups. Newsgroups can be read using your Web browser. In Netscape, a separate News window appears to let you view the information in the groups.

PPP

Acronym for Point-to-Point Protocol, a way of accessing the Internet from your PC. When you use PPP, your computer is actually connected to the Internet just like any other computer on the Internet. This is the preferred way to connect, though many Internet providers also offer the older SLIP method. See *SLIP*.

Quote

To list the contents of a previous message in your reply. Quotes are typically marked by greater-than signs in the first column:

```
Mark Twain wrote:
> It is curious that physical courage should be so
> common in the world, and moral courage so rare.
```

Search Engine

A Web page that catalogs thousands of other Web pages and contains the smarts to let you search through all that information. Yahoo is a popular search engine on the Web.

Server

A computer you access, one that contains information. Usually used in a phrase, such as "the server is down," which means no one gets any information.

A server is also a larger platter, usually with a domed lid, used to serve food. It is not a generic term for a waiter or waitress; a human "server" is a servant.

Shareware

Essentially free software, though the author would like you to voluntarily contribute money for his efforts. For example, some warm-hearted soul may write some nifty Internet program and then hand it out free to whomever wants it. If you like the program and use it a lot, you're expected to send the author some money for it. It's all voluntary and makes everyone feel good when you do it.

Signature

Similar to the signature at the bottom of a letter or document, this is a bit of text automatically tacked on to any e-mail or USENET message you create. Typically it's a salutation, your name, maybe your Web address, a quote and other interesting information. You can set up Netscape so that it automatically adds your unique signature to every e-mail or USENET message you send.

SLIP

Acronym for Serial Line Internet Protocol, a method of accessing an Internet provider from your PC. This is the second most popular method, after PPP; many Internet providers offer both, depending on what your software can handle. See *PPP*.

Smilies

Text characters inserted into a message to denote a light tone or other emotion. The most common smiley is the happy face— :-) —where the two colons are eyes, the hyphen a nose and the right parenthesis a smile. There are many, many (too many) variations, and there are even books written on the art of smilies, proving once again that some people just have way too much time on their hands.

UNIX

An operating system used primarily on larger computers. The Internet was developed on this type of computer, so a lot of the Internet things you do, and a lot of the terms, come from UNIX. It isn't the prettiest operating system in the world, but it's pretty powerful.

Upload

To send a file from your computer to another computer. See *download* for a cheerful description.

USENET

An umbrella term for Internet newsgroups. Pronounce it as *YOOZ-net.*

Wambooli

Can be used to describe something great and nifty, or as a nonsense word to inject when you don't understand something.

Web

A shortcut term for the World Wide Web.

Web server

A computer, or a program on a computer, that dishes out Web pages to people on the Internet. When you type in a Web address, the `http` part of the address actually notifies a computer's Web server to send you a Web page.

A Web server is not the same thing as having your own Web page. If you do have a Web page, then it's the Web-server software on your Internet provider's computer that allows other people to view your Web page.

World Wide Web

The best way for viewing information on the Internet. The World Wide Web is composed of various pages, each of which can contain text, graphics, and links or references to other pages on the World Wide Web. This makes the Web full of information, educational facts, references and just plain goofy stuff.

WWW

An abbreviation for the World Wide Web.

WWWW

World Wide Web with the Waiting.

INDEX

F

G

O

P

Q

R

S

W

More from Peachpit Press

25 Steps to Safe Computing

Don Sellers

With planning, many computer-related health problems can be avoided. *25 Steps to Safe Computing* tells you how to reduce your risk with well-illustrated, easy-to-follow advice. It contains ergonomic tips on setting up work areas, as well as chapters on backache, headache, tendinitis, radiation, pregnancy, kid's concerns, and much more. *$5.95 (72 pages)*

America Online 3 for Windows 95: Visual QuickStart Guide

Maria Langer

With almost 6 million members, America Online is the world's largest online service provider. America Online 3 for Windows: Visual QuickStart Guide provides an easy, step-by-step guide for beginners to getting up and running with AOL and for intermediate users to gain more in depth understanding of the service. The book helps readers go from installing the newest version of the software to exchanging e-mail, using newsgroups and the Web browser, and participating in forums and live chats. Key America Online areas, such as Entertainment, NewsStand, Computers and Software, Marketplace, and Kids Only, are described and illustrated, and appendices offer lists of shortcut keys, forums, and companies. *$17.95 (288 pages)*

A Blip in the continuum, Windows Edition

Robin Williams and John Tollett

In this full-color book, author Robin Williams and illustrator John Tollett celebrate the new wave of type design known as "grunge" typography. The book consists of famous and not-so-famous quotes about type and design set in a range of grunge fonts, using rule-breaking layouts. The illustrations, created in Fractal Design Painter, complement the text. Includes a companion disk with 21 of the best freeware and shareware grunge fonts, several of which were newly created for this book. *$22.95 (96 pages w/ disk))*

CHAT

Nan McCarthy

CHAT is a fast-moving, compelling story of online romance that will appeal to all cyber-junkies and anyone looking for an entertaining story. Bev, a tough-minded book editor, cautiously begins corresponding with Maximilian, a flamboyant copywriter who approaches her after seeing her messages in an online writers forum. Their relationship gradually becomes more intense and their e-mails less inhibited as the story unfolds entirely through their messages to one another. *$7.95 (136 pages)*

Clip Art Crazy, Windows Edition

Chuck Green

Here's everything you need to incorporate sophisticated clip art into your desktop-created projects. *Clip Art Crazy* offers tips for finding and choosing clip art, along with a vast array of simple designs showing how to incorporate clip art into your documents and presentations. The CD-ROM includes almost 500 reproducible samples, culled from the archives of leading clip art design firms. *$34.95 (208 pages w/ CD-ROM)*

Home Sweet Home Page and the Kitchen Sink

Robin Williams with Dave Mark

This exciting new book/CD-ROM combo provides all the tools you need to get online and create Web pages. The *Home Sweet Home Page* book takes a friendly, non-technical approach to planning and designing interactive Web pages with easy-to-follow instructions and delightful illustrations. The CD-ROM provides everything else you need to finish creating your pages, including connection software for AOL, CompuServe, and AT&T. *$24.95 (208 pages w/ CD-ROM)*

Internet Explorer 3 for Windows 95/NT: Visual QuickStart Guide

Steven Schwartz

This book is for anyone who wants or needs to browse the World Wide Web. This hands-on guide takes a straightforward, visual approach that enables even those with little past browsing experience to get up and running quickly. New Microsoft Internet Explorer users will find the step-by-step instructions easy to follow and fun, and readers with some Microsoft Internet Explorer experience will benefit from the explanations of important new features with particular emphasis on using new plug-ins such as ActiveX and JavaScript. *$16.95 (208 pages)*

Jargon: an informal dictionary of computer terms

Robin Williams

Finally! A book that explains over 1,200 computer terms in a way that readers can understand. This book is a straight-forward guide that not only defines computer-related terms but also explains how and why they are used. It covers both the Macintosh and PC worlds. No need to ask embarrassing questions: Just look it up in Jargon! *$22.00 (688 pages)*

The Little PC Book, 2nd Edition: A Gentle Introduction to Personal Computers

Lawrence J. Magid with Kay Yarborough Nelson

Wouldn't you love having a knowledgeable, witty, endlessly patient pal to coach you through buying and using a PC? Well, you do. Popular columnist and broadcaster Larry Magid's expertise is yours in *The Little PC Book,* described by *The Wall Street Journal* as "the class of the field." This edition includes the latest on Windows 95, the Internet, CD-ROMs, and more. Includes a handy Windows 95 Cookbook section. *$18.95 (384 pages)*

The Little Windows 95 Book

Kay Yarborough Nelson

Your guide to Windows 95. This easy, informative, and entertaining volume spotlights the essentials so you can get to work quickly. Short, fully-illustrated chapters explore the Windows interface in detail, offering tips and tricks the manual doesn't. Each chapter includes a handy summary chart of keyboard shortcuts and quick tips. *$12.95 (144 pages)*

Netscape 3 for Windows: Visual QuickStart Guide

Elizabeth Castro

This book is the perfect introduction to the latest version of Netscape, the most widely used browser of the World Wide Web. You'll learn how to transfer files, read and send e-mail, use the address book, and post to newsgroups. Additionally, the book covers Netscape Gold, with helpful information on how to format your own Web page.
$16.95 (288 pages)

The PC Bible, Second Edition

Eric Knorr

The PC universe is expanding, and the second edition of *The PC Bible* has grown along with it. Sixteen industry experts collaborated on this definitive guide to PCs, now updated to include Windows 95 and Internet access. Beginning and advanced users will benefit from this book's clear, entertaining coverage of fonts, word processing, spreadsheets, graphics, desktop publishing, databases, communications, utilities, multimedia, games, and more. Winner of a 1994 Computer Press Award. *$29.95 (1000 pages)*

PageMill 2 for Windows: Visual QuickStart Guide

Maria Langer

PageMill 2 for Windows: Visual QuickStart Guide is a richly illustrated, step-by-step guide to using all the features of PageMill. As with all books in Peachpit's highly successful Visual QuickStart series (with more than a million copies in print), information is presented in a graphic, visual fashion, with hundreds of screenshots accompanied by clear instructions and loads of helpful tips.
$15.95 (184 pages)

What's on the Internet, 3rd Edition

Eric Gagnon

This new edition is bigger and better than ever, with entirely updated reviews and a greatly expanded business section. *What's on the Internet* provides an informative, fun, and useful way to find out what online discussion and information groups exist on the Internet and how to connect with them. There are mini-reviews of 2,300 of the most popular newsgroups, a bonanza of Frequently Asked Question (FAQ) files, a 5,500-word subject index, and a list of more than 8,000 Internet newsgroups. *$19.95 (440 pages)*

The Windows 95 Bible

Fred Davis

Here's absolutely everything you need to know about Windows 95, from installation and interface design to telecommunications and multimedia. This fun-to-read, easy-to-use reference is packed with detailed illustrations, plus insider tips and tricks. Reviewing the previous edition, *The New York Times* wrote, "Toss out the other Windows books. This one is the best." (Finalist, Computer Press Awards).
$29.95 (680 pages)

Windows 95: Visual QuickStart Guide

Steve Sagman

Windows 95, the long-awaited upgrade of Microsoft's operating system, offers an improved interface, faster performance, and numerous enhancements. This fast-paced, easy-to-read reference guide uses the same approach that's made other books in the Visual QuickStart series so popular: illustrations dominate, with text playing a supporting role. *Windows 95: Visual QuickStart Guide* provides a thorough tour of Windows 95, from introducing the basics, to managing your computer, to communicating online with Windows 95. *$14.95 (192 pages)*

Order Form

USA 800-283-9444 • 510-548-4393 • FAX 510-548-5991
CANADA 800-387-8028 • 416-447-1779 • FAX 800-456-0536 OR 416-443-0948
http://www.peachpit.com

Qty	Title	Price	Total
	SUBTOTAL		
	ADD APPLICABLE SALES TAX*		
	SHIPPING		
	TOTAL		

Shipping is by UPS ground: $4 for first item, $1 each add'l.

*We are required to pay sales tax in all states with the exceptions of AK, DE, MT, NH, and OR. Please include appropriate sales tax if you live in any state not mentioned above.

Customer Information

NAME

COMPANY

STREET ADDRESS

CITY STATE ZIP

PHONE ( ) FAX ( )
[REQUIRED FOR CREDIT CARD ORDERS]

Payment Method

❑ CHECK ENCLOSED ❑ VISA ❑ MASTERCARD ❑ AMEX

CREDIT CARD # EXP. DATE

Tell Us What You Think

PLEASE TELL US WHAT YOU THOUGHT OF THIS BOOK: TITLE:

WHAT OTHER BOOKS WOULD YOU LIKE US TO PUBLISH?

PEACHPIT PRESS • 2414 Sixth Street • Berkeley, CA 94710